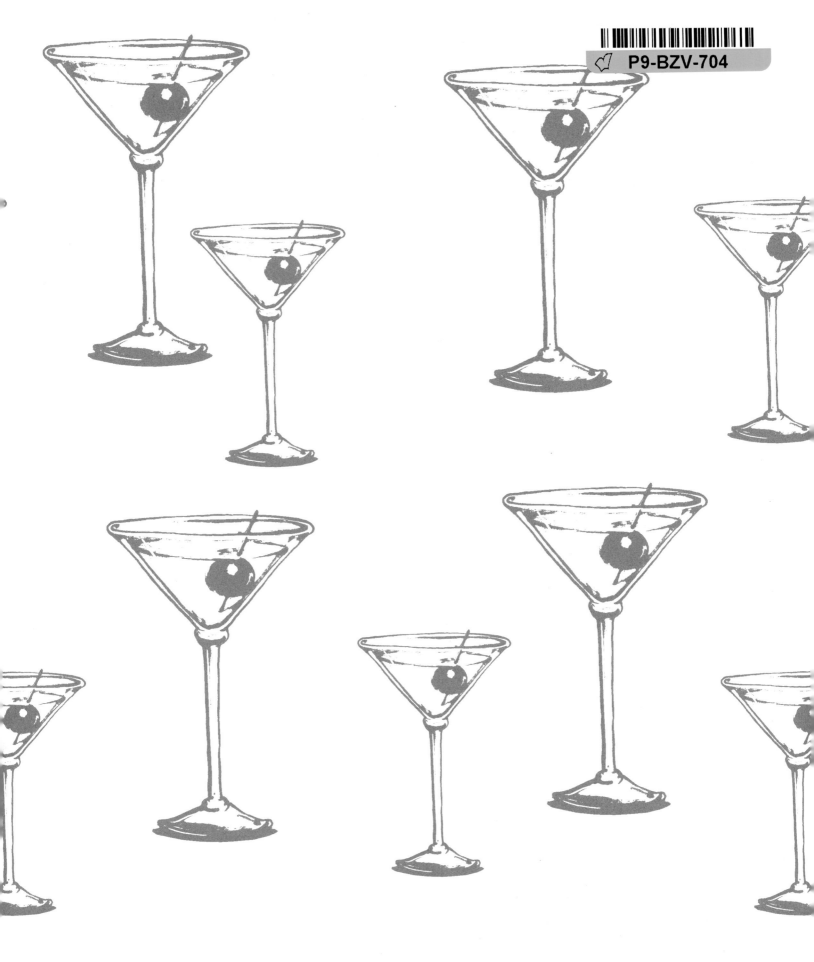

InStyle
parties

InStyle

parties

the complete guide to easy, elegant entertaining

From the editors of *In Style*

Written by Jennifer Tung

Illustrations by Tracy Dockray

Produced by Melcher Media for In Style Books
and Time Inc. Home Entertainment

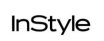 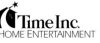

In Style

Managing Editor: Charla Lawhon
Executive Editors: Maria Baugh, Martha McCully
Assistant Managing Editor: Patrick Moffitt
Features Editor: Honor Brodie
Senior Entertainment Editor: James Patrick Herman
Senior Design Editor: Jacqueline Goewey
Assistant Editor: Anna Nordberg
Editorial Assistant: Kate Auletta
Imaging Manager: Steve Cadicamo
Imaging Specialist: Rey Delgado
Production Associate: Bijal Saraiya

Editorial Director, Books: Mary Peacock
Vice President, Development: Amy Ford Keohane

President: Stephanie George
Publisher: Lynette Harrison Brubaker
General Manager: Maria Tucci Beckett
Director of Public Affairs: Sheri Lapidus
Associate Director of Public Affairs: Paul Reader

Time Inc. Home Entertainment

Publisher: Richard Fraiman
Executive Director, Marketing Services: Carol Pittard
Director, Retail & Special Sales: Tom Mifsud
Marketing Director, Branded Businesses: Swati Rao
Director, New Product Development: Peter Harper
Assistant Financial Director: Steven Sandonato
Prepress Manager: Emily Rabin
Product Manager: Victoria Alfonso
Associate Book Production Manager: Suzanne Janso
Associate Prepress Manager: Anne-Michelle Gallero

Melcher Media

This book was produced by Melcher Media, Inc.
124 West 13th Street
New York, NY 10011
www.melcher.com

Publisher: Charles Melcher
Associate Publisher: Bonnie Eldon
Editor in Chief: Duncan Bock

Project Editor: Lia Ronnen
Editorial Assistant: Lauren Nathan

Design by Subtitle
Wine Editor: Fred Seidman
Party Resource Editor: Francine Maroukian

Front cover photograph © 2005 Maura McEvoy
Copyright © 2005 by Time Inc. Home Entertainment
Photography © 2005 by those specifically listed on
page 192
Illustrations © 2005 Tracy Dockray

Cover credits

Photograph by Maura McEvoy
Clothing Stylist: Bobette Cohn
Food and Prop Stylist: Roscoe Betsill
Hair and Makeup: Danielle Vignievick
Model: Rebecca Meyer
Dress by Halston

Published by *In Style* Books

Time Inc. Home Entertainment
1271 Avenue of the Americas
New York, NY 10020

First printing September 2005
ISBN: 1-932994-11-4

Library of Congress Catalog Control Number:
2005928565

In Style Books is a trademark of Time Inc.

table of contents

introduction

Entertaining well isn't a talent bestowed on the lucky, obsessive-compulsive few. It's a state of mind. Here's the secret: Giving a party, whether dinner for 8 or drinks for 50, doesn't have to be intimidating, stressful or exhausting. With the right attitude and some savvy planning, it can be fun, exhilarating and, once you get the hang of it, even easy. Whatever the occasion, from intimate supper to full-blown bash, a party is an invitation to connect with friends and have fun—and that applies to hosts and guests alike. Entertaining should be, simply put, entertaining.

Some organization helps, of course. That's where savvy planning, and this book, come in. The first section, The Basics, provides everything you need to know about creating a welcoming environment and smoothly carrying a party through from beginning to end—with plenty of stylish shortcuts on the way. The section covers invitations, which set the tone for a special occasion, and the decorations and music, which bring a party vividly to life. It also offers the smartest ways to plan a menu, shop, stock a bar, set a table, serve cocktails and feed a crowd.

Once you've read the fundamentals, dive into the next section of the book: 16 of the most popular Party Guides published in *In Style* magazine. These festivities, dreamed up by top celebrity party planners on both coasts, include dinner parties, cocktail soirées, cookouts and special occasions like birthdays, showers and even Oscar night and Super Bowl bashes. What, besides star power, do they have in common? Playful themes, fresh, simple recipes, sexy drinks, lively décor, handy timetables, and a stylish, non-stuffy approach. Follow them closely, mix up elements from different guides to suit your unique vision, or simply use them as inspiration.

For more ideas, check out the Resource Guide at the end of the book, a list of food and décor sources from across the country (all tested by the editors at *In Style* for excellent quality, flavor and consistency). Whatever you might need to make your life easier and your party more special—from classic dinner plates affordable enough to buy in bulk to the tastiest mail-order hors d'oeuvres and the best tamales from Texas—is at your disposal. All it takes to get the party started is a phone call or click of the mouse.

Above all, remember this: The goal of successful entertaining isn't to impress people with your hard work and perfectionism. It's the conversation, the laughter, and the impromptu samba dancing they'll remember long after the party's over.

—Charla Lawhon, Managing Editor, *In Style*

the basics

Entertaining is a refreshingly democratic undertaking. It doesn't matter if you barely know how to boil water or consider yourself a talented chef, live in a 500-square-foot studio or a mansion, or keep yourself on a strict budget or an unlimited one. With a festive spirit and creative ideas, you're capable of anything. Whether you're a first-time hostess or an accomplished party-giver with limited time, make your life easier by not tackling every detail on your own. Instead, revel in what you don't have to do. There's no need to spend a fortune, clean your entire house, or cook every course (or any course, for that matter). There's no need to run all over town shopping or to hire a catering team, florist or DJ. What you do need is a concrete primer on the key elements of entertaining. This section will cover essentials such as invitations, bar and kitchen equipment, food and beverage lists, and stylish table settings. It will clarify the nitty-gritty etiquette matters and ensure that you always have the right amounts of ice, liquor, coat hangers and serving dishes on hand. And it will spell out how to create a festive atmosphere in your home with color, lighting and music. Finally, don't forget to wear some-thing stunning, shower guests with your charms, and have a blast. With all the basics in place you'll be totally prepared and in the mood to party when your guests arrive.

Scarlett Johansson waves her plane-ticket–inspired invitation to John Travolta's 50th birthday bash in Los Cabos, Mexico.

the invitations

You can spend days, even weeks, envisioning a wonderful party: who's there, what you'll serve, where the festivities will unfold. But it isn't official until you invite the guests. You can do this in a variety of ways, ranging from a quick phone call to a beautifully printed or engraved card. Whatever the format, all invitations serve the same purpose: They set the tone for a celebration and provide guests with all the information they need. On a lighter note, they get everyone (host included) excited for a good time.

pick the right invite

To figure out the best way to invite guests, think about the kind of party you want to give and choose invitations with the same feel and level of formality. If it's a very casual occasion, like a dinner party with close friends or impromptu drinks to toast a friend's promotion, a phone call is perfectly appropriate. If you want to tell a large number of people about a last-minute gathering in your home (weekend barbecue, group viewing of a TV show finale), invite them by e-mail. For more organized or formal events (a large dinner party, cocktail party, birthday or holiday open house) written invitations are in order. The easiest method is to send traditional fill-in-the-blank invitations. You may think of them as unimaginative, but that's an old stigma.

These days, plenty of stationery companies offer chic, well-designed styles customized for all kinds of occasions. Another even more classic choice is to write the information on a high-quality note card—a personalized card is ideal. Custom-printed invitations, which you order at a stationery or department store, or online, up the style quotient and are exciting to receive. These are most commonly used to celebrate a milestone birthday, anniversary, engagement or shower. Engraved or letterpress invitations signify an extremely fancy party and a posh setting and are typically reserved for weddings. Of course, all those guidelines are just that: guidelines. You can bend the rules however you'd like, as long as the invitation clearly tells guests what to expect.

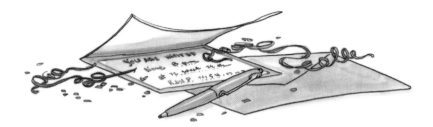

when and where

Beyond making a striking first impression, the role of the party invitation is to convey facts. Here's what to include:

The reason for the party (and what to expect to eat and drink): Be as specific as possible. If the occasion is a friend's birthday, write something such as "Please join us for cake and champagne to celebrate Lucy's 30th." (Make sure the birthday girl doesn't mind sharing her age.) If it's a cocktail party, you might say "You're invited for drinks and hors d'oeuvres." That way, people won't expect dinner.

The date and time: For most parties, especially dinners, a starting time is sufficient. If you want guests to leave at a certain time, include an ending time. This is most appropriate for early cocktail parties (from 6:30 P.M. to 8:30 P.M., for example), showers, brunches and kids' parties. To avoid a crush at an open house, invite guests in staggered blocks: one set of invitations can say "3:00 P.M. to 6:00 P.M.," the next can say "4:00 P.M. to 7:00 P.M.," and so on.

The location: If you're inviting people who have never been to your home, include a map and/or directions.

An RSVP line: Include a phone number and/or e-mail address so people can tell you whether or not they will attend. (The phrase "Regrets only" is too open-ended.) If you don't hear from someone and the party is a few days away, follow up with a phone call.

Any other relevant information: If it's a surprise, say so on the invitation. If it's a wedding or baby shower, include registry information. Unless it's a costume party, a black-tie affair or you want everyone to wear, say, white, don't dictate a dress code. Terms like "festive" and, worse yet, "creative" only cause confusion. The invitation itself (the wording, style, typeface and quality of paper) should tell people what to wear.

perfect timing

There's something luxurious about looking forward to a great party. For that reason, coupled with the fact that everyone is overbooked these days, send invitations well in advance. Compile your guest list at least six weeks before the party date. To encourage plenty of lively interaction, invite friends from different areas of your life, some who have met and some who haven't, and blend couples with single people. Mixing guests of different ages, and even generations, can also enrich the group dynamic. For a small cocktail or dinner party, mail invitations so that guests receive them about two weeks in advance. For a more formal occasion or a big bash, send invitations four weeks in advance. If your party is scheduled during the busy holiday season or on a major holiday (a Fourth of July barbecue, for instance), call or e-mail guests a week or two before mailing the invitations and ask them to save the date.

Jennifer Garner hosts a fund-raiser at a private estate in Beverly Hills.

Janel Moloney enjoys the outdoor cocktail hour at an environmental benefit hosted by West Wing star Bradley Whitford and his wife Jane Kaczmarek.

the bar

It's as predictable as margaritas on Cinco de Mayo: Upon arrival, guests always head straight to the bar. There's a reason for this—the mere act of holding a glass, even if it's filled with club soda, puts people at ease. Here's what you need to know to be ready for any occasion.

the basics

Certain essentials (flat and sparkling water, regular and diet sodas, lemons and limes) belong in every home bar. Beyond that, the style and size of your party determine what you pour. The most basic options are wine and beer, which makes sense at casual gatherings and big parties, like open houses, where you want to keep things as streamlined as possible. For more variety, set up a modified bar, which includes wine, beer and a handful of standard liquors and mixers. And if you're hosting a true cocktail party or formal affair, set up a full bar, which is stocked to make just about every mixed drink under the sun.

There's some room for variation: You can add champagne or sparkling wine to any kind of bar, and you can choose not to serve red wine or dark-colored cocktails if you have light furniture or carpeting. To instantly upgrade a wine and beer bar or make a classic cocktail party feel extra special, try this party trick: Pass out a signature drink. If you mix a killer mojito or you're famous for your bone-dry martinis, serve them in large quantities. Otherwise, choose a cocktail that suits the mood and food of the occasion: kir royales before a French meal, mint juleps at a Kentucky Derby brunch.

Quantities: These figures are easy to work with: A 750 ml bottle of wine pours 4–6 glasses and a 750 ml bottle of spirits makes about 16 drinks. But for a more accurate breakdown, talk to a salesperson at a good liquor store. He or she can fine-tune quantities, factoring in the number of guests, the length of the party, and any specific preferences you may have (for example, if you have a large contingent of bourbon or beer drinkers coming).

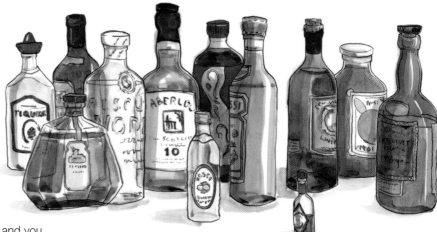

glass types

There's a specific kind of glass for every cocktail, and you can rent the whole gamut if you'd like. But since it's impossible to predict what people will want, it's much simpler to stock up on a few general styles (in equal numbers) that are appropriate for a variety of drinks. These glasses will keep you covered for a party of any size.

All-purpose, 11-oz. stemware glass: This is suitable for red and white wine, sparkling water, sangria and champagne (but only in a pinch; if you love bubbly, invest in flutes). Look for one that isn't too narrow or too round. (If you would like to keep things really simple, these are fine to use for mixed drinks and sodas too.)

8- to 10-oz. highball glass: This is ideal for water, soda, beer and most mixed drinks.

Old-fashioned: Also known as a lowball, whiskey or rocks glass, this short tumbler is appropriate for any drink served on the rocks.

Classic 4- to 6-oz. cocktail, or martini, glass: It's a bit disorienting to drink a martini or cosmopolitan from anything else, so invest in a set of six or eight. You'll feel glamorous every time you use them.

what to stock

For a cocktail party of 50, for example, assuming guests enjoy a variety of drinks, you'll be in good shape with this shopping list:

2 liters of **vodka**
1 small bottle (375 ml) of **dry vermouth** for martinis
1 liter each of **rum, scotch (blended), bourbon, tequila, triple sec** and **gin**
1 bottle of **Rose's lime juice**
1 bottle of **Worcestershire sauce**
1 bottle of **Tabasco sauce**
2 gallons each of **orange** and **cranberry juice**
1 gallon each of **grapefruit** and **tomato juice**
6 liters each of **tonic water, seltzer, cola, diet cola,** and **club soda**
10 bottles each of **red** and **white wine**
2 cases of **beer**

Garnishes: For a basic or modified bar, stock up on lemons and limes (a dozen of each). A full bar calls for green olives, cocktail onions, maraschino cherries (a couple of jars of each), orange slices and lemon twists. You may also need coarse salt for margaritas and celery stalks for Bloody Marys.

Ice: Make sure you have two pounds of ice cubes per guest, plus lots of crushed ice to keep beer and white wine cool. Rather than making it in your freezer (a huge hassle) or buying bags at the grocery store (the ice tends to meld into huge chunks), have commercial ice cubes, which stay separated, delivered the day of your party.

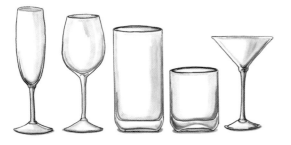

barware

Proper accessories complete a well-stocked bar. These tools of the trade will have you mixing in style.

Corkscrew: The most practical and essential bar gadget is a "waiter's tool," which folds up like a pocketknife and combines a blade to cut the foil on wine bottles, a corkscrew and a bottle opener.

Ice scoop: A metal ice scoop is a wise purchase. Regular spoons are too shallow or small, and tongs are frustrating.

Shaker: The key to cold, well-mixed cocktails (and most have built-in strainers). For a big party, keep two on hand.

Long-handle spoon: This does double duty: It stirs mixed drinks and mashes ingredients like mint leaves and lime wedges.

Small chopping board and knife: For cutting and peeling lemons and limes.

Shot glass or jigger: Crucial for pouring accurate quantities. A shot glass holds 1½ oz. of liquid. A jigger holds 1½ oz. on the larger side and 1 oz. on the smaller end.

Napkins: Provide three paper cocktail napkins per guest; nine or 10 if you're serving hors d'oeuvres.

Pitchers: Use simple, attractive glass or plastic ones to hold mixers such as sodas and juices.

Glassware: Allow three glasses per guest for a two-hour party. (For a dinner party, plan on two glasses plus the wine-glasses set on the table.)

shop and save

When buying and storing drinks, keep these practical tips in mind:

Buy in advance: Soda stays bubbly for at least a month, beer has a shelf life of three to six months and alcohol lasts months, even years. Store all in a cool, dry place like a garage or basement.

Buy in bulk: You'll save money and always have extra bottles around for last-minute entertaining.

Don't buy liquor in big bottles: There's something tacky about making guests hoist a half-gallon jug of booze to make a cocktail. Even though it costs a little more, buy liquor in one-liter bottles (eventually you can buy big bottles and replenish the small ones for parties). They look nicer and are easier to handle.

Ask about the return policy: Usually you can take back bottles that haven't been opened or chilled, but rules vary from store to store.

Have it delivered: This will save you a huge chunk of time. Schedule delivery for the evening before or the morning of the party.

Chill with care: White wine and all mixers should be chilled when you serve them. It takes at least two hours for a bottle of wine to chill in the refrigerator. A short cut: Fill an ice bucket (or big bowl) two-thirds full with a mixture of half ice and half water, and submerge the bottle for 25 minutes. Never put wine in the freezer (it alters the flavor and still takes longer than the bucket method), and never put chilled beer and other carbonated drinks back in room-temperature storage: The fluctuations in temperature make bubbly drinks go flat.

cocktails

Now that the logistics of the home bar are in place, you can shift your attention to something sexier: tasty drinks. With dozens of Web sites devoted to cocktail recipes, it's a cinch to concoct anything from an appletini to a zombie. Master these five classic recipes, and you'll be ready to make anything.

Martini: Fill a shaker ¾ full with ice and pour in a splash of very dry vermouth. Shake well. Gently pour the vermouth (through the strainer, leaving the ice in the shaker) down the drain. Pour 2 oz. vodka or gin into the shaker. Shake well; pour into an ice-cold (chilled in the freezer) martini glass. Garnish with a few olives, a twist of lemon peel or, to make a Gibson, cocktail onions.

Cosmopolitan: Combine 1½ oz. vodka, 1 cup ice, and a ¼ oz. each of lime juice, cranberry juice and triple sec in a cocktail shaker. Shake well and strain into an ice-cold martini glass. Garnish with a lime wedge.

Champagne cocktail: Put 1 sugar cube and 2 dashes bitters (a bitter-tasting aromatic flavoring made of herbs and roots) into a chilled champagne flute. Fill the glass with champagne. A twist of lemon peel is optional.

Margarita: Rub the rim of a cocktail glass with a wedge of lime and dip the rim in a saucer of coarse salt. Put 1½ oz. tequila, ½ oz. triple sec, 1 oz. lime juice and a few handfuls of ice in a shaker (there should be enough ice that the liquid fills the shaker). Shake well and strain into the glass. Garnish with a wheel of lime.

Bloody Mary: Pour 3 oz. tomato juice, 1½ oz. vodka, ½ tsp Worcestershire sauce, 2–3 drops Tabasco sauce and a dash of lemon juice in a shaker. Add salt and pepper to taste. A pinch of celery salt or a few celery seeds and ½ tsp horseradish are optional. Shake well and strain into a highball glass over ice cubes. Garnish with a wedge of lime or celery stalk, or both.

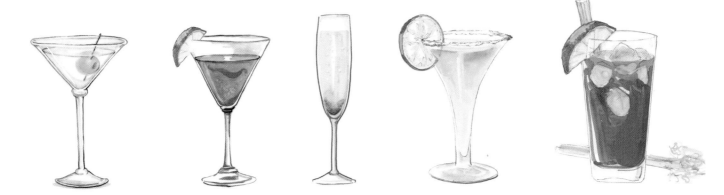

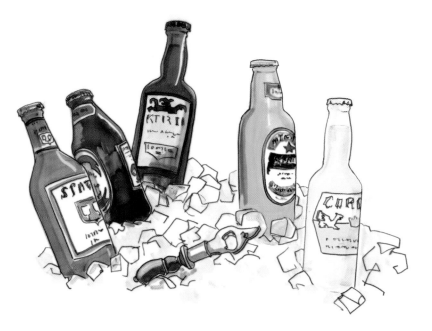

beer

High-quality brews go hand in hand with a big celebration or a festive, casual meal, and thanks to a surge in micro-breweries and beer pubs in this country in the past decade, choices abound. There are two types of beer: lagers, which are pale, dry, light and refreshing, and ales, which are robust, loaded with fruity and spicy flavors, and higher in alcohol content than lagers. To make the best selections for your next party, look at these descriptions of the different types and their optimal food matches.

lagers

Type: pilsner
What it tastes like: This amber-colored beer is dry, crisp and flowery, with some bitterness.
What to serve it with: Fried and spicy foods, as well as any kind of fish

Type: pale lager
What it tastes like: Mild and fizzy, with no bitterness or aftertaste
What to serve it with: Hors d'oeuvres and spicy Latin or Asian dishes

Type: dark lager
What it tastes like: Flavored with roasted barley or malt, it tastes rich, malty and sweet.
What to serve it with: Roast chicken or sausage dishes

ales

Type: pale ale
What it tastes like: Dry and slightly bitter, with traces of fruit
What to serve it with: Roast beef, prime rib or steak

Type: brown ale
What it tastes like: This full-bodied, copper-colored ale is sweet and malty. Some brown ales have hints of fruit.
What to serve it with: Flavorful red meats, wild game or sausage

Type: porter
What it tastes like: Made from roasted barley or barley malt, porters taste much like bittersweet chocolate.
What to serve it with: Hearty soups and stews or meats with rich, brown sauces

Type: stout
What it tastes like: Stout is the darkest, densest ale. It ranges from sweet and dry to extremely bitter (burnt-tasting) and has intense malt and caramel flavors.
What to serve it with: Shellfish, hearty stews or wild game

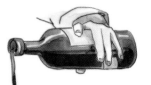

wine

Wine is a rich, boundless topic. If you want a complete education or dream of being a sommelier, there are hundreds of books and courses to choose from, and millions of bottles to taste. For entertaining purposes, it isn't necessary to get bogged down in technical terms and flowery adjectives or to spend a lot of money. All you need are some facts about the basic kinds of wines and the foods they complement. For extra guidance, pick up a copy of *Wine for Dummies,* by Ed McCarthy and Mary Ewing-Mulligan; *Wine With Food,* by Joanna Simon; or *The Wine Lover's Cookbook,* by Sid Goldstein; and cultivate a relationship with a local wine merchant. He or she will get to know your tastes and give you specific tips and suggestions. If you try something you love, or discover an amazing food-wine combination, write it down for future reference. Overwhelmed? Not to worry. Just refer to this breakdown of the major wine grapes when planning what to serve at a luncheon or dinner party.

whites

Grape: chardonnay
What it tastes like: Ranging in style from crisp and mineral-y with citrus notes to full-bodied and opulent with flavors of butterscotch, vanilla, hazelnut and toasty oak
What to serve it with: Oysters, poached salmon, grilled tuna, seafood risotto, seared scallops, fish in a light butter or wine sauce or roast chicken
Best sources: California (Napa Valley, Sonoma and Central Coast), France (Burgundy)

Grape: gewürztraminer
What it tastes like: Spicy and floral, extravagantly aromatic with a pronounced flavor of lychee
What to serve it with: Bold spicy dishes, such as Thai curries, Szechuan and Hunan cuisine or Asian fusion dishes
Best sources: France (Alsace), Washington State

Grape: pinot grigio (known in Alsace as pinot gris)
What it tastes like: Fruity and light with hints of apple, peach, or pear, pinot grigio has a subtle taste, which makes it very easy to drink.
What to serve it with: Shellfish, grilled fish, roasted chicken or pork tenderloin. It's also great with omelets or frittatas.
Best sources: Italy (Alto Adige and Provincia di Pavia), France (Alsace)

Grape: riesling
What it tastes like: Crisp and refreshing, with a floral perfume and notes of tart apple and citrus. Riesling can be dry *(trocken)* or have various levels of sweetness from *kabinett* and several levels on up to *trockenbeernauslese,* one of the great dessert wines of the world.
What to serve it with: Hors d'oeuvres, white asparagus, smoked salmon and fish, especially trout, in a sauce. It's a particularly good match with Asian and fusion food. And it's a classic warm-weather wine.
Best sources: Germany (Mosel-Saar-Ruwer, Rheingau, Rheinhessen and Pfalz), France (Alsace), Austria (Wachau, Kamptal and Kremstal)

Grape: sauvignon blanc
What it tastes like: Grassy, fruity and herbal, with, in the best examples, a lovely mineral character
What to serve it with: Raw shellfish, steamed mussels and clams or grilled fish. The classic great match is with a chalky fresh goat cheese.
Best sources: France (Sancerre and Pouilly Fumé from the Loire Valley), New Zealand (Marlborough), South Africa (Stellenbosch)

reds

Grape: cabernet sauvignon
What it tastes like: Can be concentrated and lush, with layers of flavors such as black currant, blackberry, cassis, tobacco, cedar, sometimes eucalyptus and even chocolate or licorice. Tannins give the wines great aging potential.

What to serve it with: Steaks and chops, roast beef, leg of lamb or burgers.
Best sources: France (Bordeaux), California (Napa Valley), Western Australia (Margaret River), Italy (Tuscany)

Grape: merlot Predominantly used as one of the components of Bordeaux blends, merlot also makes a great wine on its own, reaching its zenith in Château Petrus in Pomerol, one of the few Bordeaux that is 100% merlot.
What it tastes like: Soft, fruity and intense, with rich plum and dark berry flavors and a velvety texture
What to serve it with: Merlot is delicious with roast leg of lamb, baby lamb chops, roasted duck or squab.
Best sources: France (Bordeaux), Italy (Tuscany and Umbria), California (Napa Valley)

Grape: nebbiolo
What it tastes like: A black grape, indigenous to Piedmont, which makes incredibly long-lived wines with a beautiful ruby color and marvelous aromas of dark plums, rose petals, lavender and espresso. The greatest nebbiolo wines are Barbaresco and Barolo; those labeled nebbiolo are less expensive and good for everyday drinking.
What to serve it with: Braised meats or roasted game.
Best sources: Italy (Piedmont—Barbaresco and Barolo)

Grape: pinot noir
What it tastes like: Marvelous silky texture, restrained fruit and a seductive earthiness. Probably the most nuanced of all the red varietals. At its best, it's magic. But there is a wide range in quality and price.
What to serve it with: Boeuf bourguignon and other beef stews, prime rib and côte de boeuf, roasted veal and lamb or seafood such as salmon. Pinot noir is one of the more versatile reds, beautiful with a wide range of foods, but too delicate for strong or spicy flavors.
Best sources: France (Burgundy), California (Russian River Valley, Carneros and Central Coast), Oregon (Willamette Valley)

Grape: syrah (known in Australia as Shiraz)
What it tastes like: Full-bodied with a firm acidity, flavors of wild herbs, black pepper, and dark cherries and plums, woven with intoxicating hints of Asian spices
What to serve it with: Roasted and grilled beef and sausages, lamb and game, especially feathered game, even organ meats such as kidney and liver. Syrah is one of the main components used in blends that make up the majority of Rhône wines, the most famous being Côte Rotie, Hermitage, Crose-Hermitage, Cornas, Gigondas and Châteauneuf-du-Pape.
Best sources: France (Rhône Valley), Southern Australia (Barossa Valley, Clare Valley and McLaren Vale), California (Central Coast)

Grape: sangiovese
What it tastes like: Distinguished dry red with overtones of dried cherries, tobacco and spice
What to serve it with: Cured meats such as salami and prosciutto, aged sheep's milk cheese, roast pork and grilled chops or pastas with meat ragus
Best sources: Italy (Tuscany for Chianti Classico and Brunello di Montalcino and many Super Tuscans)

Grape: tempranillo
What it tastes like: Made well, tempranillo can be lush and seamless. It has a sweet tone to the fruit and a dry finish. It tastes of red fruit, smoky wood and wild herbs. Sometimes it has a perfume of cedar.
What to serve it with: Cured sausages, serrano ham, roasted suckling pig, roasted baby lamb or grilled meats
Best sources: Spain (Rioja and Ribera del Duero)

Grape: zinfandel (known in Italy as primitivo)
What it tastes like: They range in style from restrained and elegant to full-bodied, superextracted fruit bombs. Dark ruby-purple in color, the wines taste of cherries, dried plums and spice.
What to serve it with: Barbecued or smoked meats, ribs, burgers, cheeses or wild boar
Best sources: California (Napa Valley and Sonoma)

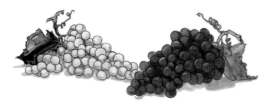

which wines, exactly?

The following list of wine producers includes picks for best all-around value in taste, cost (between $8 and $25 per bottle) and general availability. Armed with this list, you'll never wander aimlessly around the wine store.

white

Chardonnay
Au Bon Climat (Central Coast, California)
Brocard (Burgundy, France)
Louis Jadot (Burgundy, France)
Mt. Eden (Santa Cruz Mountains, California)
Verget (Burgundy, France)

Gewürztraminer
Hugel (Alsace, France)
Trimbach (Alsace, France)

Pinot grigio
Aloise Lageder (Alto Adige, Italy)
Livio Felluga (Friuli, Italy)
Venica (Friuli, Italy)

Riesling
Gunderloch (Reinhessen, Germany)
Hugel (Alsace, France)
J.J. Prüm (Mosel-Saar-Ruwer, Germany)

Sauvignon blanc
Babcock (Central Coast, California)
H. Bourgois (Sancerre, France)
L. Crochet (Sancerre, France)
Neil Ellis (Stellenbosch, South Africa)
Villa Maria (Marlborough, New Zealand)

red

Cabernet sauvignon
Chateau Montelena (Napa Valley, California)

Hess (Napa Valley, California)
Marquis Phillips (McLaren-Vale, Australia)
Penfolds (Barossa Valley, Australia))

Merlot
Falesco Vitiano (Umbria, Italy)
Havens (Napa Valley, California)
Newton (Napa Valley, California)

Nebbiolo
Produttori del Barbaresco (Piedmont, Italy)
Icardi Nebbiolo (Piedmont, Italy)

Pinot noir
Castle Rock (Sonoma County, California)
Chalone (Chalone, California)
Louis Jadot (Burgundy, France)
O'Reilly's (Oregon)
Saintsbury (Napa Valley, California)

Sangiovese
Castello della Paneretta Chianti (Tuscany, Italy)
Felsina Chianti Classico (Tuscany, Italy)
Marchese Antinori Chianti Classico (Tuscany, Italy)

Syrah and syrah blends
Guigal (Côtes du Rhône, France)
Jaboulet (Rhône Valley, France)
Ojai Vineyards (Central Coast, California)
Qupe (Central Coast, California)
Vieille Ferme (Rhône Valley, France)

Tempranillo
Emilio Moro (Ribera del Duero, Spain)
Muga (Rioja, Spain)
Pesquera (Ribera del Duero, Spain)

Zinfandel
Ravenswood (Sonoma County, California)
Ridge (Sonoma County, California)
Rosenblum (Sonoma County, California)

special occasion wines

For a special occasion, these wines will have you digging deeper into your pockets ($25 and up) but the wines are unique.

white

Chardonnay
Louis Jadot Corton-Charlemagne (Burgundy, France)
Louis Latour Corton-Charlemagne (Burgundy, France)
Neyers (Napa Valley, California)
Ramey (Napa Valley, California)

Riesling
F.X. Pichler (Wachau, Austria)
Franz Hirtzberger (Wachau, Austria)

red

Cabernet sauvignon
Cos D'Estournel (Bordeaux, France)
Joseph Phelps Insignia (Napa Valley, California)
Pichon-Lalande (Bordeaux, France)
Ridge Monte Bello (Santa Cruz Mountains, California)

Nebbiolo
Angelo Gaja Barbaresco (Piedmont, Italy)
Bruno Giacosa Barbaresco (Piedmont, Italy)
Domenico Clerico Barolo (Piedmont, Italy)
Enrico Scavino Barolo (Piedmont, Italy)

Pinot noir
Groffier premier or grand crus (Burgundy, France)
Dujac premier or grand crus (Burgundy, France)

Shiraz
Clarendon Hills (Barossa Valley, Australia)
Torbreck Descendant (Barossa Valley, Australia)

Syrah
Guigal (Côte Rotie, France)
Jamet (Côte Rotie, France)

Syrah and Rhône varietal blends
Beaucastel (Rhône Valley, France)
Pegau (Rhône Valley, France)

Tempranillo
Torre Muga (Rioja, Spain)
Ramirez Ganuza (Rioja, Spain)

champagne

People tend to refer to all sparkling wines as champagne, but only bubbly made from grapes grown in the Champagne region of France qualify for that name. In other regions, sparkling wine, which is white or pink and gets its fizziness from carbon dioxide, goes by other names. In Spain it's called cava; in Italy it's known as spumante and in Germany it's sekt. In other countries that produce high-quality bubbly, such as the U.S., Australia, New Zealand and South Africa, the name sparkling wine suffices. There are many excellent sparkling wines on the market, but Champagne is considered the gold standard because it's made using a centuries-old technique and aged for years (versus months in most other places). The cool climate and chalky soil of Champagne also produce highly acidic grapes, which are perfect for sparkling wine. Which ones to buy? Dom Pérignon, Taittinger Comtes de Champagne and Krug Grande Cuvée are highly recommended for a special occasion. Good options for under $25 are California sparkling wines from Schramsberg, Roederer Estate and Domaine Carneros.

Courtney Thorne-Smith enlists dinner guest Kimberly Williams-Paisley's help in the kitchen before a feast in her Los Angeles home.

the food

Food plays a starring role in every party, whether it's a bowl of mixed nuts with cocktails or a Thanksgiving feast. Whether you're serving simple hors d'oeuvres or an elaborate meal, or supplementing a store-bought entrée with a few homemade sides, a few common strategies will ensure delicious results every time. If the thought of cooking for large groups gives you pause, fear not. With a few pointers on failsafe techniques, savvy timing and the glory of prepared foods and takeout, even the first-time cook can stay cool in the kitchen.

plan your menu

Every party meal begins with a flash of inspiration—an inkling of what you're in the mood to eat and to share with friends. These general rules of cooking will keep you covered no matter what you crave.

Use readily found fresh ingredients. These will make your life easier and the food taste better (nobody wants to eat pale, mealy tomatoes in December).

Decide how your guests will eat. Your next consideration is whether guests will eat at a table, or serve themselves from a buffet and either sit or stand around in a larger space.

For a buffet, consider the logistics. It's impossible to use a knife and fork while standing, so serve things like rice, cut up vegetables, and bite-size pasta versus linguine. Avoid anything with bones. At a seated buffet, it's fine to serve roasted meat (which can be cooked and sliced in advance), but much harder to cook and replenish individual lamb chops.

Be realistic. Unless you find cooking exciting or relaxing, don't feel pressured to wow guests with your culinary skills. The point of entertaining is to surround yourself with good friends and good things to eat. People are always thrilled to be invited to someone's home for a wonderful meal. They certainly don't—or shouldn't—care whether you peeled every shrimp or baked each cookie yourself.

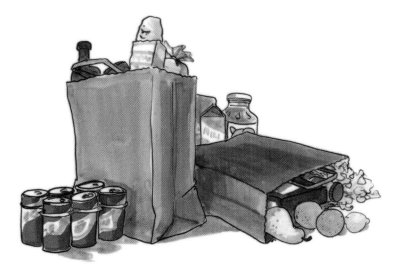

Outsource. Buy frozen hors d'oeuvres such as mini quiches, pigs in blankets and mushroom phyllo triangles, or order spring rolls or Chinese dumplings from a nearby restaurant. Desserts are also simple to buy, as are regional specialties like North Carolina pulled pork and New Mexican tamales, which you can order a week or more in advance and flaunt as the centerpiece of your party.

Don't cook fish. This doesn't apply to seafood pastas, bouillabaisse and paella. And if you're a master with seafood, or fish is a huge part of your diet, ignore this point. Otherwise, take note: Fish is typically fried, seared or roasted, which must be done right before you serve it and requires meticulous timing.

preparation

In theory, flash-fried oysters sound like an exciting and impressive appetizer, but in reality, they could cause more trouble than they're worth. When cooking for large groups, don't make any dish that requires great precision or last-minute maneuvers and don't make too many different dishes. You'll spend much of the evening in the kitchen while your guests live it up in the other room (larger quantities of fewer dishes is a better idea). Every Party Guide in this book includes a specific timetable, but here are some general planning tips.

Shop early. Stock up on dry goods (paper towels, garbage bags, tableware, soda, alcohol, olive oil, condiments) as far in advance as possible. Buy groceries and ice one or two days in advance.

Get a head start in the kitchen. The day or evening before an event, prepare as much of the food as possible. Wash and dry lettuce for a salad, snap off the ends of green beans, make dipping sauce, bake dessert. Stews, casseroles, soups and vegetable purées can also be prepared in advance. If you're really organized, make them a week before and freeze them.

Choose Bolognese sauce over Alfredo. Tomato-based sauces can simmer for hours, but cream sauces are cooked at the last minute and involve tricky blends (and constant stirring) of cream, butter, eggs and cheese.

Embrace your oven. Braised meats like lamb shanks cook for several hours so you can start them early in the day. When they're done, all you have to do is remove the meat from the liquid, reduce the liquid into a flavorful sauce, and serve. Roast chicken and beef can "rest" for half an hour or more so you can time them correctly before things get last-minute hectic in the kitchen.

Save simple tasks for last. It's unrealistic to think that you can have every detail in place when the doorbell rings. Certain steps, like dressing and tossing the salad, warming bread in the oven, slicing meat and transferring food to serving platters, are perfectly appropriate once guests have arrived because they're contained, tidy and easy to do while gabbing with friends.

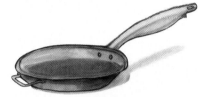

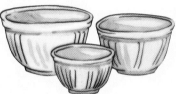

kitchen gear

If you already have a well-stocked kitchen, turn the page.
If you don't have two pot lids to rub together, this checklist of
essential equipment will get you cooking.

Pots and pans
8- and 10" high-quality nonstick skillets
3-cup saucepan with lid
2- and 3-quart saucepans with lids
3-quart sauté pan with lid
6- or 8-quart stockpot (shorter and squatter are more versatile)
7-quart Dutch oven that can go from the oven to the table
Roasting pan

Knives and chopping boards
All-purpose 6" chef's knife
4" paring knife
Serrated bread knife
Kitchen scissors
Small, medium and large plastic cutting boards

Spoons, spatulas and other tools
2 long-handle wooden spoons, 1 solid and 1 slotted
Nonmetal spatula (for nonstick pans)
Long cooking fork
2 pairs of tongs, in varying lengths, with spring locks
2 whisks: a small flat whisk for emulsifying sauces and
   dressings and a medium-size balloon whisk for whipping
   cream and beating eggs

Baking equipment
Set of mixing bowls
Rolling pin
Extra-large nonstick mat for rolling pastry
2 metal baking pans: an 8" x 10" or 9" x 13" rectangle
   and an 8" or 9" square
1 or 2 metal muffin/cupcake pans
1 or 2 metal or Pyrex pie pans
8" or 9" square or round cake pans
Set of rectangular Pyrex baking dishes in different sizes
Cookie sheet (those with small edges are more versatile):
   12" x 14" or 14" x 16" rectangle
Cooling rack

Miscellaneous
Large measuring cup for liquids and a set of flat-bottom
   measuring cups for dry ingredients
A set of measuring spoons on a ring
Large colander
Can opener
Vegetable peeler
Salad spinner
Cheese grater/fruit zester
Instant-read meat thermometer
Ice cream scoop
Timer

Appliances
Food processor
Handheld or standing mixer
Immersion blender

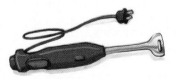

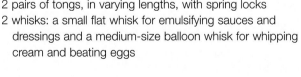

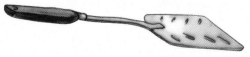

the cheese plate

A light spread can feel incomplete without cheese. It's perishable, of course, so you can't buy it in bulk and put it in a cupboard. But when stored properly—in the vegetable bin in the refrigerator, individually wrapped in wax paper or foil—cheese (which is essentially fermented milk solids, or curds) continues to age naturally and stays good for a few days (soft varieties) to a few weeks (hard ones). Buy it periodically; if you don't eat it with crackers, you can always grate it for omelets or macaroni and cheese. When entertaining, try to serve three to five kinds of cheese; any more and the flavors will meld or compete. The following descriptions of different types of cheese will help you narrow your selection. And if you go to a gourmet or cheese shop, ask a salesperson for guidance—and samples. Take cheese out of the refrigerator half an hour before you serve it to let its flavors unfold.

Type: fresh and fresh-ripened
What they are: Mild, slightly tart fresh cheeses are uncooked and unripened, and range in texture from thick and creamy to moist and curdy. Fresh-ripened cheeses are briefly ripened, slightly pungent, white in color and have no rinds.
Classic examples: A few fresh cheeses are Italian mascarpone, ricotta and soft mozzarella. Fresh-ripened cheeses include Boucheron and Montrachet.

Type: soft-ripened; aka bloomy rind
What it is: These rich, creamy cheeses have a high butterfat content and semisoft consistency. Molds are applied to their surfaces, causing them to ripen from the outside in (the moldy exteriors are edible).
Classic examples: Brie, Camembert, and double and triple creams like St. André

Type: washed rind
What it is: These are the "stinky" cheeses. During the ripening process, they're brushed, rubbed or submerged in a brine of salt water and wine, beer or brandy, which promotes a moldy exterior and a pungent scent and flavor.
Classic examples: Pont l'Eveque, Münster and Liverot

Type: semi-hard
What it is: These mild cheeses, which are made from uncooked curds (milk solids) are ideal for snacking or dessert. Some of them, like Bel Paese, Havarti, Mozzarella, Provolone and Gouda, melt smoothly, which makes them great for cooking.
Classic examples: Morbier, Saint Nectaire, Tomme de Savoie

Type: hard
What it is: The curds that make up these hard, tangy cheeses are heated until they solidify and then pressed with weights into a firm consistency. Hard cheeses grow more pungent and crumbly with age.
Classic examples: Gruyère, Appenzeller, English-style Cheddar, Emmenthal, Jarlsberg, Manchego

Type: blue-veined
What it is: After being sprayed or injected with mold spores and aged in caves or cellars, bluish-green veins marble the interiors of these intensely flavored and pungent cheeses.
Classic examples: Gorgonzola, Roquefort and Stilton

the party-ready pantry

When friends drop by unexpectedly, it's important (and gracious) to offer them a drink and something to eat, regardless of what time they show up. The key to mastering such moments is to stock your pantry with a variety of high-quality dried, canned and jarred goods that can be combined in many delicious ways or, if you have a bit of notice and can dash to the store, easily enhanced with fresh produce or meat to make a quick supper. The following items are available at most high-end grocery stores and gourmet shops, or from specialty food Web sites. (See Resources for specifics.) Keep them on your shelves and restock when necessary, and you can invite people over at the drop of a hat.

snacks

Beautiful presentation makes all the difference. Arrange snacks on an attractive cutting board, in a tapas tray with separate compartments, and in a few small, pretty bowls. Don't forget to include any fresh veggies you may have like radishes, cherry tomatoes or baby carrots. You may also want to buy a long, narrow dish to hold olives, and a beautiful cheese knife. Here's what to keep in the kitchen:

Smoked or spiced nuts
Oil-cured black and green olives: To eat as is or as tapenade to spread on crackers or sliced French bread. (It's nice to keep jarred olives in the fridge too.) An opened jar lasts six months.
Crackers: Plain and flavored with herbs or pepper to serve with cheese, tapenade, pâté, salami or other spreads. Crackers stay crisp and fresh for three to five days once the vacuum-packed seal is opened; toss any leftovers after that.
Sliced baguettes: Freeze them in resealable freezer bags. To serve, defrost and toast.

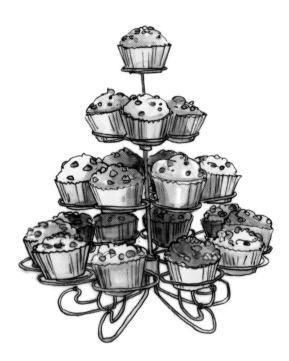

Cheese straws: They stay fresh as long as crackers do.
Dried fruits: Serve with cheese and nuts.
Charcuterie: Cured salami can be stored in the refrigerator for up to three months.
Cheeses: See opposite page.
Mustards: A strong, grainy one; a smooth Dijon; and something seasoned with jalapeño or honey to serve with salami or sliced ham on crackers or bread.
Wasabi peas or frozen edamame

desserts

Around tea time and after dinner, people tend to crave something sweet. Keep a few of these goodies on hand, and be prepared to offer guests coffee and tea or an after-dinner drink too.

Biscotti
Scottish shortbread
Cookies
Pound cake: Keep in the freezer.
Chocolate hazelnut spread: Spread on pound cake.
Brandied cherries: Serve on pound cake or with ice cream.
Ice cream, gelato
Chocolates and chocolate-covered preserved fruit
Toffee or brittle

Faith Ford and her husband, Campion Murphy, preside over a beautifully set dining table at a party celebrating the publication of Ford's Southern cookbook, *Cooking with Faith*.

the table

At a luncheon or dinner party, the dining table is the center of the action, the place where guests and hosts convene for the main event. In other words, it better look darn good. That's not to say your table should be swathed in taffeta or anchored with an ice sculpture. It just needs to be pretty, inviting, not too busy and a clear reflection of your personal style. The goal is to express your taste and make the tabletop work with the mood of the occasion. A general hint: Don't strive for perfection. Mix styles, colors and materials until you strike the right balance between festive and functional.

tableware

Stock up on these multipurpose basics and, if you have room to store them, aim to have 12 to 16 place settings, which will accommodate most dinner parties.

dishes

Plates: A dinner plate measures nine to 10½-inches in diameter and works well as a main plate. A salad plate is eight inches in diameter and is suitable for salad, dessert or cheese. A bread-and-butter plate is six inches or smaller in diameter.

Bowls: Shallow soup bowls, which measure six to 10-inches in diameter, are ideal for soup, pasta, stew and chili.

flatware

A basic place setting: This consists of a dinner knife (you can substitute a steak knife if necessary), an all-purpose "place" spoon (smaller than a tablespoon and larger than a teaspoon) and a standard dinner fork, which is seven inches long.

Other key pieces: Salad forks, dessert utensils—forks and spoons (or dessert knives)—and bread-and-butter knives. If you serve fish often, you may want to invest in fish forks and knives too.

serving pieces

Dishes: You'll probably need one large oval platter to serve a roast; one or two small oval platters to serve chops or other pieces of meat; one or two deep bowls to serve soft foods, such as mashed potatoes or creamed spinach; one or two shallow bowls to hold firm vegetables, fruit or rolls; and one salad bowl. A very big, shallow bowl is also nice for serving unstructured entrées such as pasta, paella or pot roast.

Utensils: Essentially, you need spoons with both shallow and deep "bowls," spoons with holes in them to serve foods with juices that you want to drain, flat pieces (including pie servers for dessert) to pick up solid items, and a large fork to pierce dense foods. One or two of each is all you need.

Other serving items: Round out your tableware with pitchers for water, decanters for wine, salt and pepper shakers, sauce and gravy boats, and trays for carrying multiple dishes to the table.

glassware

What you need: Each place setting requires at least two glasses: one water goblet, which holds at least six ounces of liquid when mostly filled, and one red or white wineglass, depending on what you're serving with the meal. (If you plan to serve both red and white, place both kinds of glasses on the table.)

Glass shapes: White wineglasses are slightly narrower and straighter than red wineglasses in order to concentrate the flavor of white wine and slowly release its delicate bouquet. Red wineglasses are bigger and rounder to accommodate the more robust aroma and flavors of reds. To simplify matters, you can buy a large quantity of all-purpose, or Paris glasses, which work for both reds and whites.

folding napkins

Keep things clean and modern by folding napkins into one of the following simple shapes. If you want to add a subtle adornment, tie a length of ribbon or colored twine around a folded or rolled napkin; you can slip a single flower or sprig of herbs underneath it.

Cylinder: Start with a small rectangle or square. Fold it lengthwise into thirds and place it folded-side down on the center of the plate.

Rectangle: Fold the napkin into a small rectangle and place it to the left of the forks.

Triangle: Start with a rectangle. Fold it over once or twice to make a square. Fold the square in half diagonally to form a triangle. Place it next to the forks, with the folded side closer to the plate.

Square: Start with a rectangle. Fold the napkin over once or twice, depending on how big it is, then make a square that fits well on the center of the plate. Put it on the plate with the open side facing right.

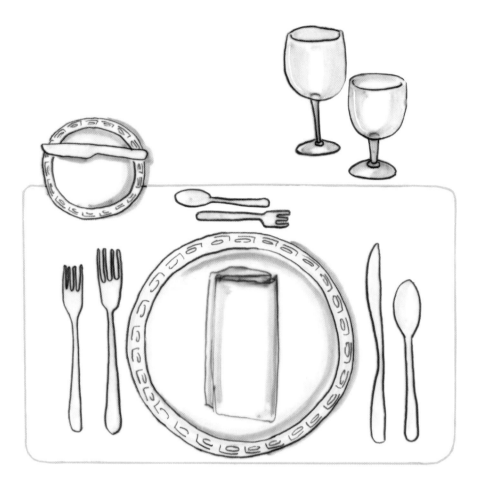

linens

When choosing tablecloths, runners, place mats and napkins, it's important to factor in the look of your dishes, glasses and flatware, plus the décor (especially the color scheme) of your dining area. Start with a neutral tablecloth (white, ecru or biscuit), then branch out with more vivid or patterned ones; the same applies to runners. Similarly, buy several sets of place mats and napkins in different hues and patterns, then combine sets in different ways to create different moods. Think about textures too: Smooth weaves go well with porcelain and china; coarser cloths better suit pottery and stoneware.

setting the table

Setting the table for a party shouldn't be intimidating. Though etiquette books offer a variety of ways to do it properly, depending on the level of formality of the meal and the food being served, there's one foolproof technique:

Put down a plate. To the left of the plate, place forks (typically just salad and entrée forks) in the order in which guests will use them, with the first one farthest out. To the right, place knives and spoons, with knives closest to the plate and blades facing in. Again, order them so that you work your way inward as the meal progresses. Lay dessert utensils (fork and spoon, or fork and knife) horizontally across the top of the plate, spoon on top with its handle to the right. For fork and knife, the fork is on top, handle to the left. You can also bring these out when you serve dessert. Arrange glasses on the upper right side of the place setting at a diagonal angle. Napkins go either on the plate or to the left of the forks.

For peace of mind: Set the table in the morning, or even the night before a party. No one wants to deal with so many small components at the last minute. If you're serving a buffet, arrange the chafing dishes or platters and serving utensils early too, and for large buffets with many dishes, label each, using a Post-It, with the food you plan to put in it.

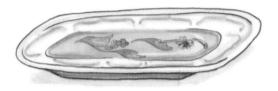

serving styles

Once you've cooked and laid out your finest china, it's time to get the food from the kitchen to the table. Here are the four most standard serving methods:

Family-style
What it is: Food is brought out in large serving dishes and placed on the table. Guests pass them around and serve themselves.
When it works: At a casual or semiformal dinner, or when you have enough room on the table for the large bowls and platters
Getting seconds: Food is passed around again as needed.
Helpful tips: To save yourself from last-minute scrambling, fill water glasses, set out plates of salad (or any other first course), and light candles before guests sit down.

Plated
What it is: Food is arranged on individual plates in the kitchen and brought out to guests.
When it works: At a slightly formal dinner or when there's not enough room on your dining table for serving dishes
Getting seconds: The host refills plates, or passes around serving platters, then returns them to the kitchen.
Helpful tips: Put bread, condiments and beverages on the table. Guests can help themselves to those things.

Seated buffet
What it is: Food is laid out on a large table. Guests serve themselves and sit down to eat at a fully set table
When it works: When you have a large number of guests and enough tables and chairs to accommodate them. Seated buffets often take place at weddings and other large, formal parties, but are nice for smaller casual gatherings too.
Getting seconds: Guests help themselves.
Helpful tips: Set up a buffet table near the kitchen and place it a few feet away from the wall if possible so guests can walk all the way around it. Use medium-size serving dishes and replenish food often—it will be fresher and look more attractive—and leave enough space between dishes for people to put down their plates if necessary. Stack plates on one or two ends of the table.

Standing buffet
What it is: Guests serve themselves from a buffet—place sets of silverware folded or rolled into napkins next to the stacks of plates—then stand or sit wherever they want, including sofas, stairs and cushions on the floor.
When it works: When you invite a big group of people for an informal meal. This works well at open houses too.
Getting seconds: Guests help themselves.

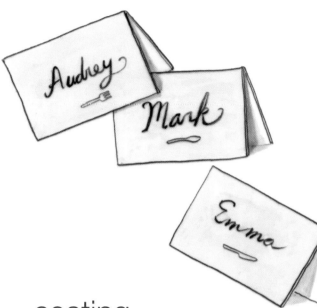

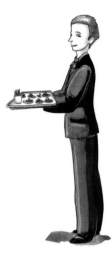

seating

There are all kinds of rules and regulations floating around about how to seat guests at a dinner party. Never put couples together! Boy, girl, boy, girl! While those do make sense in certain instances, they're really more of a starting point. The overall idea when seating people is to ensure fun, spirited conversation throughout the meal.

Evenly distribute your liveliest, most outgoing guests and mix old friends with new ones (don't group your closest chums together at one end of the table—they're likely to ignore everyone else). Alternating genders and dividing couples can lend an innocently flirty energy to a party, but neither is mandatory.

Once you decide where you want guests to sit, put out place cards so you don't have to act like an air-traffic controller at mealtime. Place cards make a party—and your guests—feel extra special. Formal, calligraphed cards are fine for black-tie dinners, but when entertaining in your home, take a lighter approach. Write names on colorful card stock, or stencil initials on strips of paper and wrap them around napkins. Use gold or silver paint pen to write names on large leaves or baby pumpkins.

extra help

When a guest list exceeds 15 or 20, depending on your space situation and anxiety level, it could be time to seek professional help. Renting equipment and hiring a bartender and a waiter (or two), may cost money, but it's guaranteed to save time, energy and your sanity.

Rentals

Renting plates, glassware and flatware makes sense when entertaining a crowd, especially if guests will be spread out among several rooms; they're more likely to abandon several wineglasses in one night and to drop and break things. Party rental companies (that's how they're listed in the phone book) can determine the quantities you need based on your head count; be sure to arrange the details a few weeks in advance. They deliver everything the day of the party, and all you have to do is return things to their original crates for pick-up the next morning. You can also rent larger items such as coat-racks, tubs for wine and beer, and industrial-size trash cans for the kitchen. Prices vary across the country, but full supplies for a party of 25, including delivery and pickup, typically cost several hundred dollars.

Hired help

A small hired staff will also ease your load considerably. A bartender keeps the drinks flowing during cocktail hour and can help serve food and clear plates at dinner. A waiter can set up the bar, heat and pass hors d'oeuvres, serve a meal, man a buffet, and clear and clean dishes. If you're unsure of how many waiters you'll need, call a catering company and describe your party. If you end up with more than one, assign them specific jobs. For example, one takes coats while the other heats the spinach pastry puffs; or one washes dishes while the other serves coffee and dessert. You can hire professionals from a catering company or enlist a few college kids in the neighborhood. Either way, plan to pay $20 to $30 per person per hour, for four to five hours, and don't forget to tip 15 to 20 percent in cash at the end of the night.

Beyoncé and Tommy Hilfiger soak up the fresh, tropical atmosphere at Hilfiger's Mustique home before a party celebrating their collaborative fragrance, True Star.

the décor

The way you decorate your home for a party depends entirely on the size and mood of the shindig you're throwing and the amount of effort you're willing to make. Embellishments can range from simple and understated to outrageous and over the top. Regardless of the final look of your space, there are four general elements you'll need to think about: furniture placement, lighting, music and flowers.

preparation

Clear the way. Remove all clutter from your party space and stash it in a designated room. That means stacks of magazines and mail, remote controls, laptops, big plants, kids toys, video games with long, tangled cords—anything that can get in the way of guests.

Beautify the bathroom. Cleanliness is important, but so is easy access. Remove all personal belongings from the sink and counters (toothbrushes, contact lens cases, shaving cream) and store them in the linen closet. Place an elegant bottle of liquid soap near the sink and a basket filled with dense, high-quality paper or cloth napkins nearby for drying hands. Place an extra roll of toilet paper in a visible spot, and light a candle or two so guests don't have to turn on a glaring, mood-killing overhead light.

Protect furniture and rugs. For big parties, spray Scotchgard onto fabric upholstery and roll up valuable rugs. Always place coasters on surfaces that stain easily, such as wooden coffee tables and end tables.

Designate a convenient place for coats. If you're inviting more than 10 guests, it may be easiest to rent a coatrack and place it in your foyer. Otherwise, you can make room in a coat closet near the front door (be sure you have enough hangers) or pile coats on a bed. Just make sure to take everyone's coats the second they walk in the door.

Make plans for pets and children. Unless the event is very casual, keep pets away from the party area, and hire a babysitter to feed and entertain young children in a separate room.

furniture

When setting up a room for a cocktail party or open house, imagine a chic hotel lounge: Clusters of comfortable sofas and chairs are sprinkled around, perfectly placed so different groups of people can have different conversations. Try to achieve the same vibe in your home.

Rearrange furniture. Create a few areas for people to gather, and make sure there's plenty of space for others to walk between them without tripping over a handbag or an extended leg.

Spread out surface areas. Evenly distribute coffee and side tables so that everyone can grab food and set down a drink easily. Scatter large throw pillows for extra seating.

Use common sense. As mentioned in previous sections, the location of bars and buffets should encourage traffic flow and discourage congestion. If you need more chairs and tables than you own, borrow them from a friend or rent them from a party supply company.

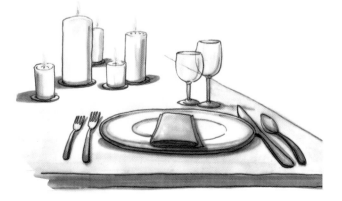

lighting

In theater, props mean nothing without effective lighting. The same applies to party spaces. That doesn't mean you should be installing strobes or stringing white Christmas lights around your banister. It means that lighting is a crucial aspect in creating a sexy, inviting atmosphere. Here, some illuminating tips:

Rearrange lamps. You want your party space to be enveloped in an even glow. Make sure that bar and buffet areas have a little extra light so guests can serve themselves without spilling or breaking anything.

Buy inexpensive dimmers. Found at hardware stores, you can attach them to your lamps and light fixtures. Your space should be dark enough to feel special and intimate but light enough to see other people's faces—and the food.

Install yellow or pink light bulbs. These colors cast warm, flattering light. Invest in a couple of uplights, which are shaped like canisters and sit on the floor. The best spots for them are behind the bar or buffet.

Place unscented votive candles in loose clusters on all surface areas: tables, buffets, mantels and windowsills. A few subtly scented candles keyed to the party's theme or season can be lovely—just place them away from food, fabric, plants and books. White votives are classic and versatile, so buy them in bulk. Candles of varying heights can also create a warm, romantic ambience.

Keep surrounding rooms dark. This will enhance the jewel-box feel of the party area. If you don't want the other rooms to be pitch-dark, switch to low-wattage bulbs.

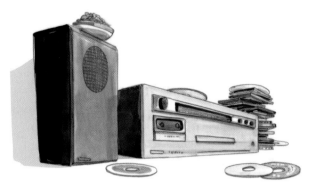

music

If you've ever seen a crowd evacuate a dance floor when "The Chicken Dance" starts playing, you understand the power of music at any kind of party, be it an elegant supper or your cousin's wedding. It can truly make or break the mood, so spend some time planning what to play. The simplest approach is to shuffle party-worthy CDs in your stereo. But there are lots of other options. Some pointers:

Start the process a few weeks in advance. Whenever you send out invitations is a good beginning point. Jot down artists or songs as you think of them. A few days before the event, make a few mix CDs or create a party playlist for your digital music player. Once you have several hours' worth of tunes, you're set for the evening.

Customize the soundtrack to your party. A dinner might begin with light jazz and segue into Latin music. Brunch goes down smoothly with classical, folk and bluegrass. A cocktail party could evolve from reggae and light funk to hip-hop and, if guests really start dancing, disco. Getting together with a bunch of old friends? Bust out the greatest hits of the '70s, '80s or '90s—whichever decade applies. And a luau wouldn't be complete without some Don Ho and the Beach Boys.

Think outside the CD box. Interesting, energetic music can be found everywhere. Check out the soundtrack, international music and compilation sections at the CD store. Raid friends' collections. If you have an iPod, surf iTunes for celebrity playlists and other eclectic mixes.

When compiling a mix, blend different genres and genders. Rock, rap, jazz, country, soul and even Broadway show tunes can coexist, as long as the songs flow smoothly into one another. The secret is to keep the feeling consistent—nothing should sound jarring. For specific music ideas, check out the song list provided for each party in this book.

flowers

At home, the simplest floral arrangements are often the most beautiful and charming. There's no need to spend hundreds of dollars or fuss over the shade of every single petal. Simply go to a flower shop or market and pick out the prettiest, freshest-looking blooms. Then arrange them using these basic tips:

Keep things streamlined. A dizzying combination of shapes and colors is both busy and inelegant. Stick with monochromatic flowers or a few shades in a similar palette. Shapes and textures should complement each other, not fight for attention.

Use chic vases. The vessel should never upstage the flowers. Plain glass cylinders and bowls and silver mint julep cups are timeless, but other materials, like ceramic, wood and tinted glass, can be just as sleek if they suit your party setting.

Spend less without sacrificing style. If your budget is limited, buy a few large blooms and float them in low, clear bowls of water. If you're limited to grocery store bouquets, give them a quick makeover: Buy a few bunches and remove all greenery and baby's breath. Trim stems down to five or six inches. Group similar colors together in small vessels.

Don't limit yourself to flowers. Fresh herbs, lush tropical greenery, branches of berries, boughs of holly, pinecones and fruit all make lovely centerpieces.

Place flowers in all the right spots. Put arrangements where people will see them: in the entryway and on the bar, coffee table and buffet, and anywhere else guests will congregate. It's also nice to place a small arrangement, or even a few buds in a small glass, in the bathroom. Centerpieces belong, obviously, in the center of the dining table. You can place a large arrangement in the middle of the table or put several small ones in a line down the center. Make sure they don't block people's vision or take up too much surface area.

Isabella Rossellini enjoys a meal in the
garden of her Long Island home.

the hostess

With the help of the Basics, you've planned and prepped without breaking a sweat. You've cooked, decorated and dimmed the lights. The champagne's chilled, the stereo's cued, and guests are due in less than an hour. There's only one more detail to take care of: slipping into a festive outfit and a celebratory mood. Here's how to make the most of playing host.

dress the part

After all the time and effort you've put into your party, you deserve to be the bright, shiny center of attention. Revel in the spotlight. Wear an outfit that's striking and glamorous, something with a wash of sparkle, an eye-popping color, or a dramatically dipping back. Make sure it's comfortable and flattering, and not too structured or confining. Have fun with accessories. Tuck a flower into your hair or slip on a pair of bejeweled Moroccan slippers. Bring out your most ornate chandelier earrings or a stack of gold bangles. Most important, give yourself plenty of time to get dressed, put on makeup, and do your hair. (If you can squeeze in a manicure and pedicure a day or two before, go for it.) The less rushed you are, the more pulled together you will feel for the rest of the evening.

take care of your guests

This almost goes without saying, but there are a few key things a gracious hostess can do to put her guests at ease. The first is to stay near the front door while people are arriving, so nobody walks in and feels stranded. Next, get a drink into guests' hands pronto, by leading them straight to the bar or handing them a pre-made signature cocktail. Introduce disparate guests by mentioning a person, place or interest they have in common, and rescue wallflowers by drawing them into a lively group. Try to spend the majority of a meal at the table, with friends. You'll be poised to restart stilted conversations, help guests get better acquainted, and, of course, bask in the fruits of your labor and the bliss of being surrounded by people you truly enjoy.

the parties

When planning a party from scratch, brain-storming for creative, original ideas (no pressure!) can add undue stress. This section of the book eliminates that worry entirely. Think of the 16 Party Guides ahead as bashes in a package: prestrategized, pretested and guaranteed to please a crowd. Each one is loaded with specific information on creating an inviting environment and working a theme, however subtle, into every aspect of a gathering. And, of course, each guide provides recipes or suggestions for all the food and drinks (including affordable wine selections under $20), so you can make or buy every tasty bite (and sip) on these pages. Although the kinds of parties run the gamut from dinners to baby showers to barbecues, each guide is broken down into the same easy-to-follow format. Setting the Scene covers invitations, décor, music and any other mood-setting details. Countdown spells out exactly what to do when starting a few days, or even weeks, before the party. And Even Easier offers a slew of time-saving, 11th-hour tips, just in case you decide on Saturday morning to throw a Sunday brunch. So jump right in. And remember to use these guides however they best suit you. Recreate a fabulous party wholesale, from invitations to party favors, or pick and choose the most appealing parts, just as you would at a buffet. Either way, the outcome will be delicious.

Rebecca Gayheart engages in lively conversation at a dinner thrown by Cynthia Rowley and Ilene Rosenzweig.

dinner parties

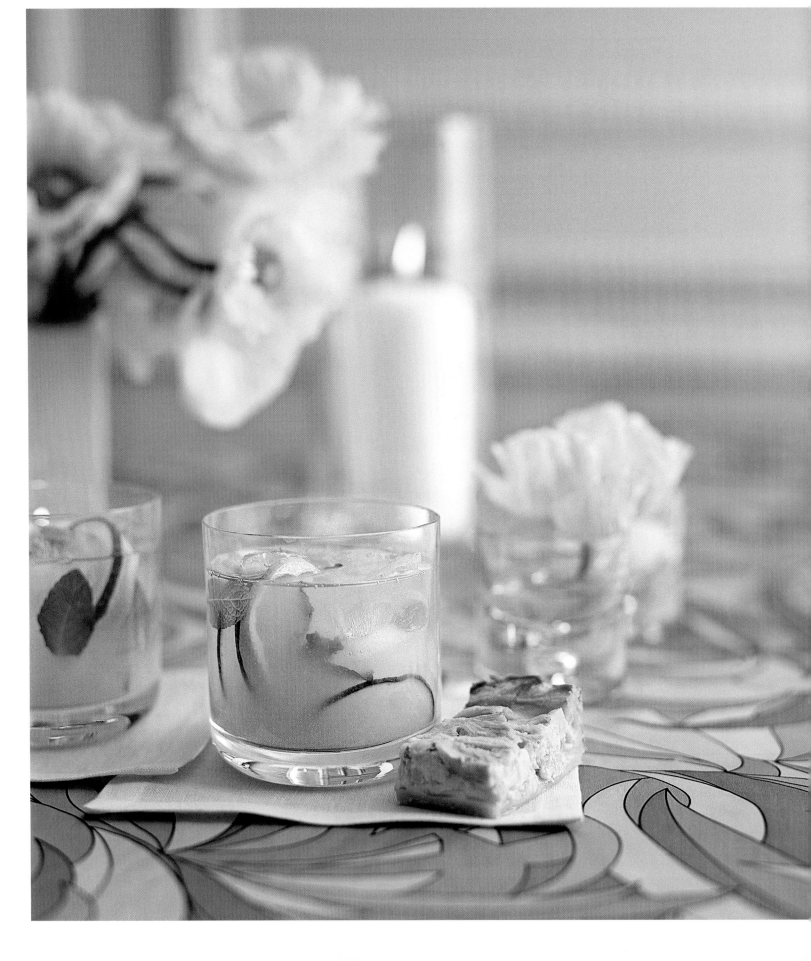

spring dinner

Spring is a time of renewal and optimism. Welcome the lightest, brightest season of the year with a relaxed but elegant dinner party for eight designed by Los Angeles party planner Mindy Weiss, who has orchestrated wedding celebrations for Adam Sandler, Tori Spelling, Gwen Stefani and Jessica Simpson, among others. Choose an easy menu that celebrates the bounty of the season's produce, decorate your table with fresh blooms, and serve fizzy citrus cocktails. Follow Weiss's advice on creating a festive yet intimate atmosphere, and before long everybody will catch the fever.

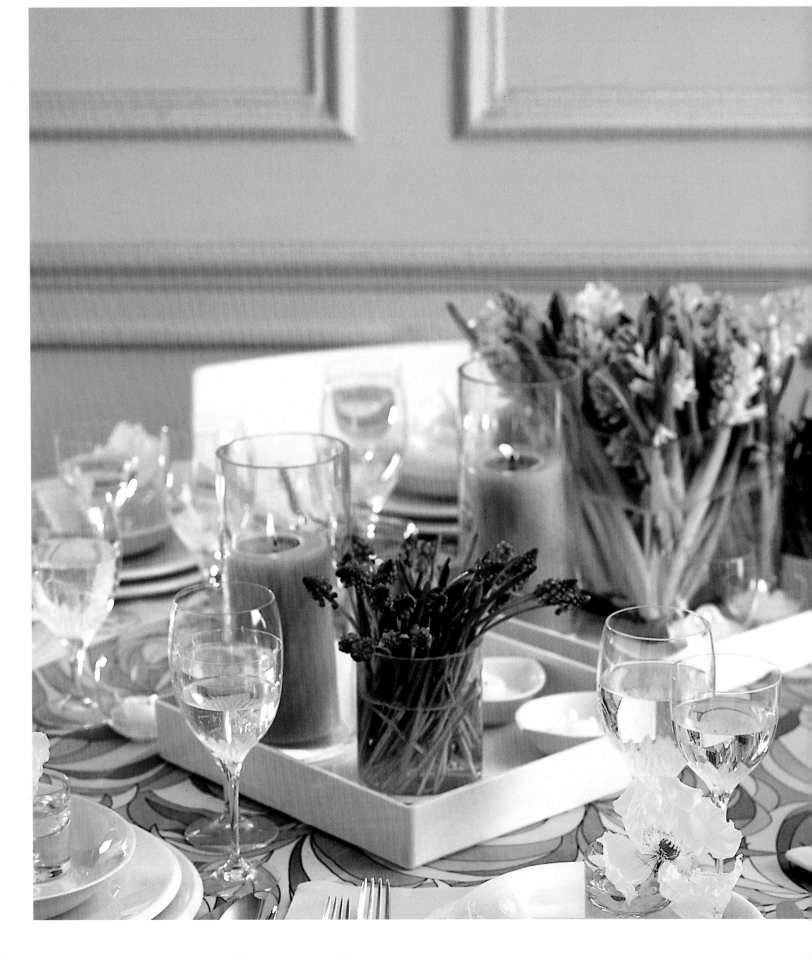

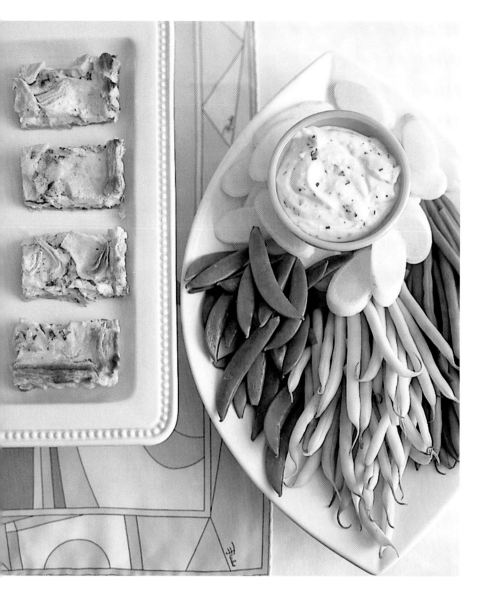

the menu

Signature drink: Spring fling
Hors d'oeuvres: Crudités with Caesar dip, goat-cheese tart with artichoke hearts and tarragon
Main course: Sweet pea soup, lime-cilantro chicken, celery-root potatoes, sautéed spring vegetables
Dessert: Cheesecake with chopped pistachios and lemon zest

setting the scene

The invitation: Set the mood by sending a handwritten note on paper in a light shade of spring green, or write the party details on cards with a simple floral motif.
The décor: Design an elegant, lively look with a palette of warm greens, yellows and bright white, with hints of blue. Cover a table with a white tablecloth and a swath of colorful Pucci-style fabric (as shown above), which you can easily find at a fabric store (a scarf works too). Top the runner with square trays filled with low vases of spring blooms (such as hyacinths, sweet peas and muscari), moss green pillar candles in hurricanes and white votives. At each seat, lean a place card against a shot glass holding a single flower.
The music: Opt for mellow but sophisticated pop from singer-songwriters with a jazzy flair: Diana Krall's *Love Scenes,* Norah Jones's *Feels Like Home* and Sondre Lerche's *Faces Down.* Or download an eclectic mix of songs that is bound to put spring in the steps of your guests: Ella Fitzgerald's "Blue Skies," Frank Sinatra's "Spring Is Here," James Taylor's "First of May," Donna Summer's "Spring Affair"—and include a few seasonal classical selections such as Stravinsky's "The Rite of Spring" and Vivaldi's Allegro from "Spring."

countdown

Three weeks: Send invitations.
One week: Buy music and wine; order flowers at your local florist.
Two days: Buy groceries and bar items.
Day before: Pick up flowers. Buy cheesecake. Make soup; refrigerate.
Morning of: Chill wine. Arrange flowers.
Five hours: Set up table and bar. Prepare crudités and Caesar dip; refrigerate.
Four hours: Make tart; keep at room temperature.
Three hours: Marinate chicken. Make a pitcher or two of cocktails, minus the club soda (add right before serving).
Two hours: Shell and cook fava beans (or, for a simpler recipe, defrost frozen baby lima beans) for sautéed vegetables; reserve. Prep the rest of the spring vegetables.
One hour: Make celery-root potatoes.
20 minutes: Set out hors d'oeuvres and cocktails in the living room. Light candles. Start music.
Right before dinner: Broil chicken. Warm soup and mashed vegetables. Sauté spring vegetables. Later, top cheesecake with chopped pistachios and lemon zest; serve with coffee.

even easier

Don't splurge on pricey cut flowers. Go for a simple but charming "lawn" centerpiece. Buy a flat of wheatgrass ($15–$20; at florists) and place white tea lights in clear glass votive holders in the grass.
Instead of making the Caesar dressing, add a few drops of fresh lemon juice to a good-quality bottled Caesar dressing (try Newman's Own) and sprinkle it with chopped fresh parsley.
Rather than spending too much time on the goat-cheese tart, buy ready-to-heat appetizers such as mini spinach quiches, Swiss cheese–and–bacon cups, and leek-potato puffs (see Resources).

picking spring vegetables

To choose and store the freshest, tastiest spring produce, watch out for these details and follow these tips:

Artichokes: The freshest are heavy and firm and squeak when you press the bulb, with leaves curving inward on top of each other, like scales, rather than sticking out. The cut at the stem should be clean, with no dark coloration. Store artichokes for up to five days in the refrigerator crisper. Canned and frozen artichoke hearts (not the jarred version in oil) are good substitutes.
Asparagus: Check the top of the asparagus stalk for firmness. It should be tight, not mushy, limp or wet, and the bottoms shouldn't be wilting or shriveling. Store for up to three or four days in the crisper.
Fava beans: These double-shell beans are tough to substitute because they're so unique, but if you must, use fresh or frozen lima beans. Store fresh beans up to four days in the crisper.
Leeks: Use them instead of onions in soups and vegetable dishes. Store for up to four days in the refrigerator.
Peas: Taste for freshness; they won't be as sweet if they're old. Pods should be fresh, bright green and without wrinkles. Store uncooked fresh pods for no more than two to three days in the crisper. Frozen peas are always a good substitute.

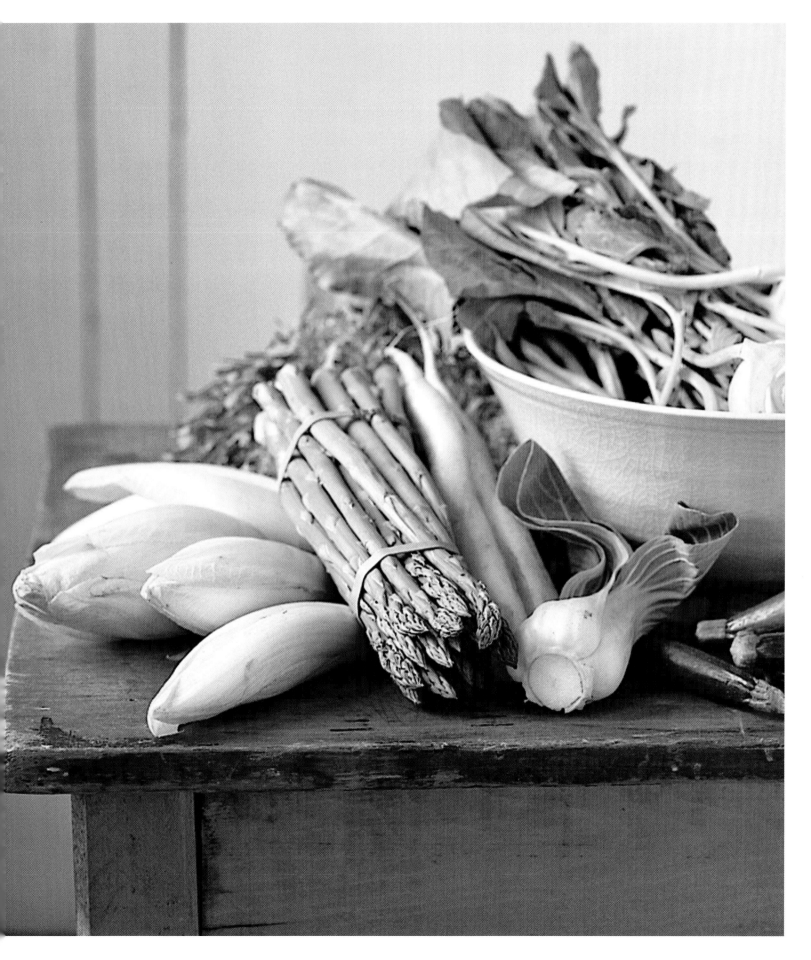

what to pour

Spring fling (serves 8): In large pitcher, mix 1⅓ cups sugar, 1 cup fresh mint leaves, and 2 lemons and 1 cucumber sliced into thin rounds. Add 2 cups each vodka and fresh lemon juice from about 10–12 lemons; let stand for 30 min. Stir to dissolve sugar. Chill for 30 min. Add 2 cups club soda; serve over ice in rocks glasses, garnished with lemon and cucumber slices and mint leaves.

Wine picks: Pour a crisp sauvignon blanc from California, such as Mason, Babcock or Duckhorn. Another great choice would be a Sancerre (which is a sauvignon blanc from the Loire Valley in France) from Henri Bourgois, Lucien Crochet or Jean Reverdy.

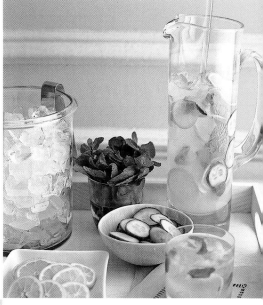

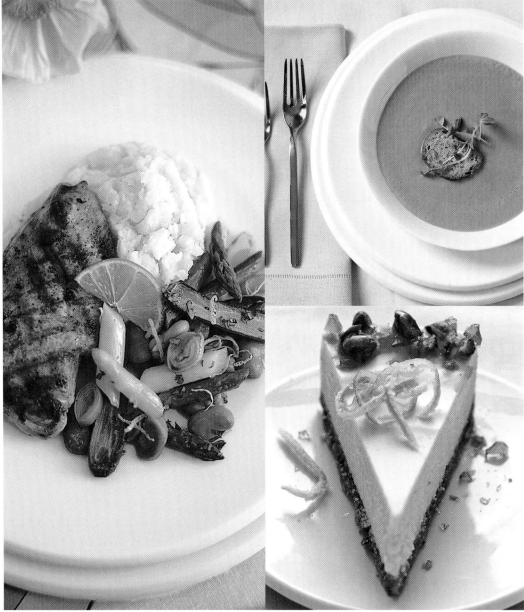

recipes

Caesar Dip
(Serves 8)
1 large garlic clove, coarsely chopped
1 cup mayonnaise
1 cup grated Parmesan cheese
½ cup packed flat-leaf parsley, chopped
2 tbsp fresh lemon juice
1 tsp anchovy paste
¼ tsp salt
¼ tsp pepper

For the crudités: 2 lb. total fresh vegetables, such as sugar snap peas; yellow and green string beans, trimmed and blanched; 1 large daikon radish, sliced on the bias; or 1 bunch red-and-white radishes, whole. For dip: sprinkle salt over garlic; mash to paste with fork. Combine with remaining ingredients. Arrange vegetables on platter with dip.

Goat-Cheese Tart with Artichoke Hearts and Tarragon
(Serves 8)
1 sheet frozen puff pastry, thawed
1 tbsp unsalted butter
1 small onion, chopped
8 fresh artichoke hearts, cooked, or 1 can (14 oz.) artichoke hearts, quartered
3 eggs
1 cup milk
1 tbsp chopped fresh tarragon
1 cylinder (3½ oz.) goat cheese, softened

On lightly floured board roll pastry sheet to fit into 8" x 11" tart pan with removable bottom. Chill 30 min. Heat oven to 375ºF. In saucepan melt butter. Sauté onion until soft, 5 min. Combine with artichokes. In bowl whisk together next 4 ingredients. Crumble goat cheese and stir into mixture. Spoon vegetables in pastry shell; pour egg mixture on top. Bake 30–35 min., or until filling has set. Serve at room temperature.

Sweet Pea Soup

(Serves 8)
5 tbsp unsalted butter
1½ cups thinly sliced leeks, white
   parts only
5 tbsp all-purpose flour
6 cups chicken broth
5 cups fresh or frozen peas
¾ cup heavy cream
Salt and pepper to taste
Pea shoots and croutons for garnish

Heat butter in Dutch oven over medium-high heat. Add leeks; sauté until soft, 4–5 min. Add flour, stirring until dissolved. Add broth; bring to boil, whisking constantly. Stir in peas; reduce heat and simmer, 10–15 min. Using an immersion blender, purée. Stir in cream; season with salt and pepper. Garnish with pea shoots and croutons.

Lime-Cilantro Chicken

(Serves 8)
5 cloves garlic, coarsely chopped
1 tbsp grated lime zest
¼ cup fresh lime juice
¼ cup fresh cilantro, chopped
1 tsp salt
½ tsp pepper
6 tbsp olive oil
8 boneless, skinless chicken breast
   halves (about 3 lb.)
Lime wedges for garnish

In food processor pulse first 6 ingredients. Add olive oil; process until blended. Pour into resealable plastic bag; add chicken and marinate in

refrigerator 3 hours. Preheat broiler. Place chicken on foil-lined baking sheet. Broil, turning once, 8–10 min., or until cooked through. To serve, garnish with lime wedges.

Celery-Root Potatoes

(Serves 8)
2 lb. baking potatoes, peeled
1 lb. celery root, peeled
4 tbsp unsalted butter
½ cup heavy cream
⅛ tsp ground nutmeg
Salt and pepper to taste

Cut potatoes and celery root into medium dice; cover with salted water in large pot. Bring to boil. Cook until tender, 20 min.; drain. In saucepan melt butter with cream. Return vegetables to large pot. Add cream mixture and nutmeg. Mash with potato masher; season with salt and pepper.

Sautéed Spring Vegetables

(Serves 8)
3 tbsp unsalted butter
1 large garlic clove, chopped
3 leeks, white part only, cleaned and
   thinly sliced
12 baby zucchini, halved lengthwise
1 lb. asparagus, trimmed, cut in 2"
   pieces
1½ lb. fresh fava beans, shelled and
   cooked (with skins removed), or 1½
   cups frozen baby lima beans, thawed
2 tbsp fresh lemon juice
2 tsp grated lemon zest
Salt and pepper to taste
Chopped parsley for garnish

In large skillet heat butter over medium heat. Add garlic and leeks; sauté 5 min. Add zucchini and asparagus; sauté 3 min. Add fava beans, lemon juice and lemon zest. Simmer 4 min., or until vegetables are tender. Season with salt and pepper. Garnish with chopped parsley.

Chopped Pistachios and Orange Zest

(Serves 8)

Place this recipe on top of a completely cooled homemade or store-bought cheesecake.

¾ cup candied oranges
¾ cup green pistachios,
   coarsely chopped
3 tbsp apricot preserve
12 candied orange peels

Place candied oranges around outer rim of cake surface. Brush with apricot preserve to glaze. Garnish with candied orange peel. Scatter pistachios evenly over candied orange. Refrigerate until ready to serve.

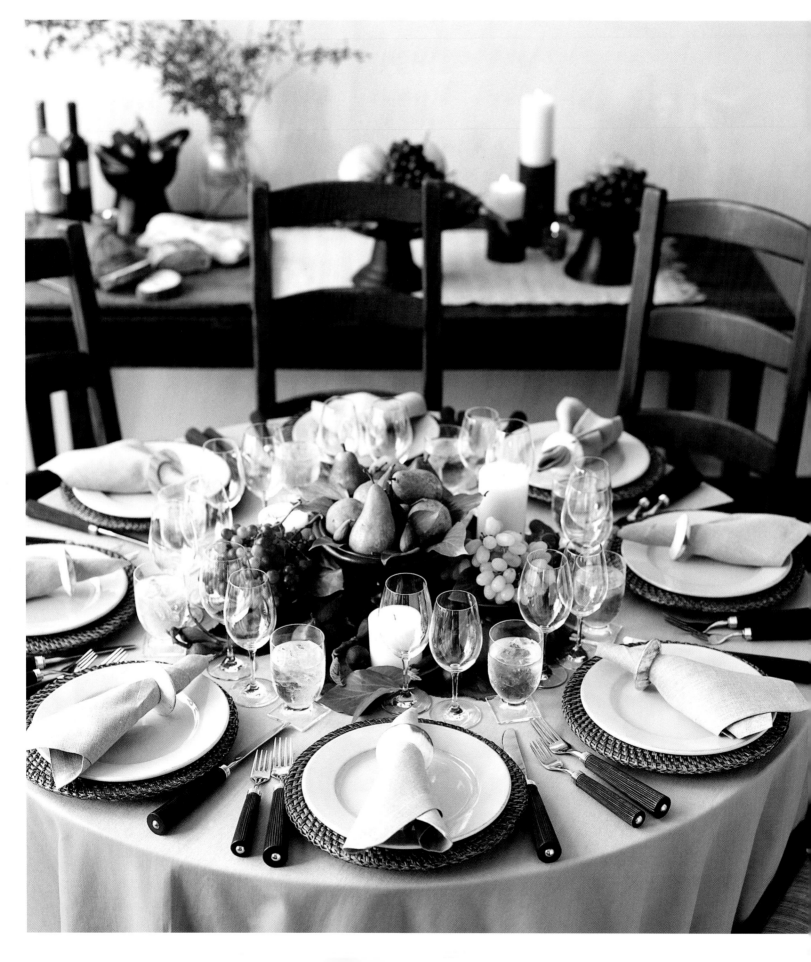

early autumn supper

The first crisp nights of fall call for cozy dinner parties with good friends. Napa Valley caterer Paula LeDuc (who catered the wedding of Christy Turlington and Ed Burns) ushers in the season with a sumptuous harvest dinner for eight. Charred eggplant caviar, assorted breads with olive oils, walnut-and-beet salad, and lamb loin with rosemary and garlic are just a few of the items on the menu that take a cue from rustic Italian cuisine. Influenced by both Italy and Napa Valley, the full flavors of the meal are heightened with an appropriate—and delicious—wine pairing for each course.

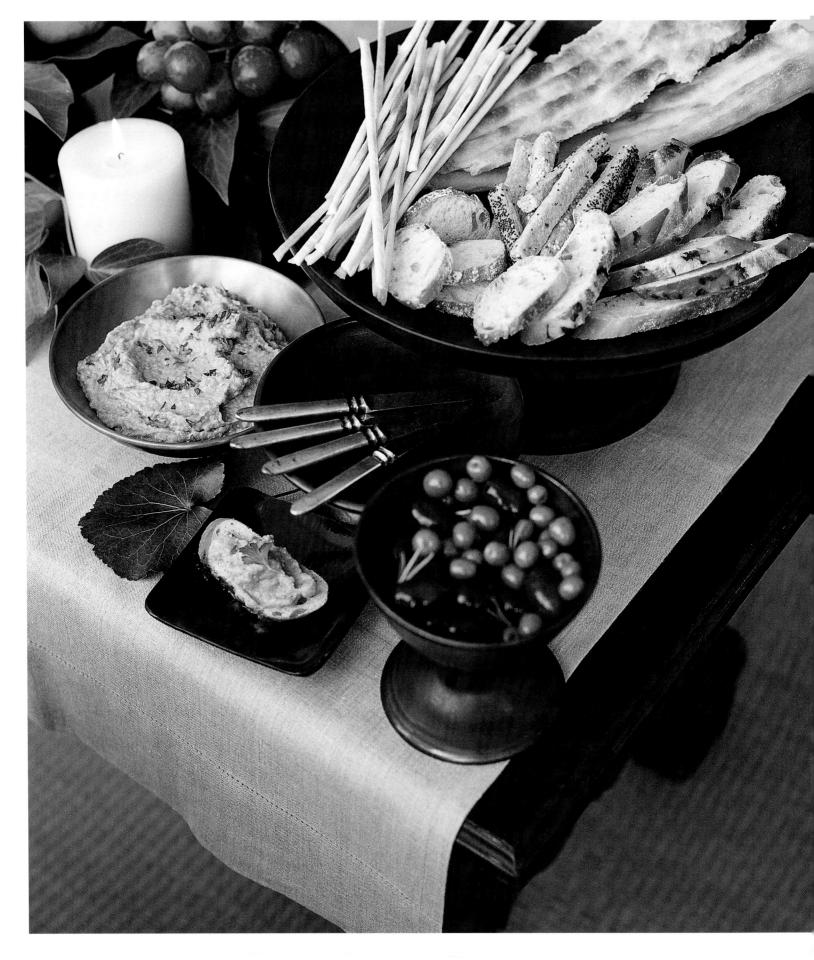

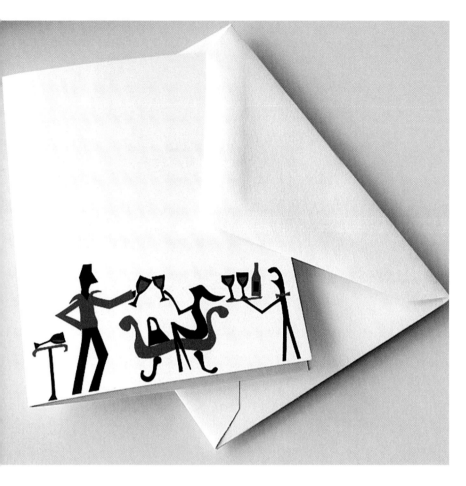

the menu

Signature drink: Early autumn cocktail
Hors d'oeuvres: Charred eggplant caviar served with assorted breads, olives and olive oils
Salad: Roasted beet salad with watercress and orange segments
Main course: Rosemary-and-garlic-infused lamb loin with cabernet sauce, marinated tomatoes, creamed corn and sautéed zucchini
Dessert: Peach sorbet with pistachio-ginger twists served in ice bowls

setting the scene

The invitation: Establish the mood of the meal with whimsical notecards featuring a wine bottle or wineglass motif (above).
The décor: To seat eight guests comfortably, use a large round table. As a nod to the change in season, create a palette of rich yellows, browns, oranges and deep, leafy greens accented with warm wood tones and grapelike purples. Cover the table to the floor with an ivory or sage cloth. Place yellow or green plates on rattan or wicker chargers and set each place with wineglasses and red and white glasses.

The centerpiece: Instead of flowers, anchor the table with a centerpiece of green, gold and purple fruits. Begin by covering the center with a bed of green leaves. On top of the leaves, place varying sizes and heights of cream-colored pillar candles. Add small wooden containers or pedestal dishes and fill each with one type of seasonal fruit: green or purple grapes, green or gold pears, purple plums, green or purple figs.

The music: Jazz songbirds hit the perfect note for an early autumn supper. Mix the greatest hits and classic love songs from these legends in the CD changer: Billie Holiday, Ella Fitzgerald, Sarah Vaughan and Lena Horne. Or download an appropriate mix of autumn-themed tracks that are as different and colorful as, well, the tree leaves: Nat King Cole's "Autumn Leaves," Yo La Tengo's "Autumn Sweater," The The's "August and September," Frank Sinatra's "September of My Years," Earth, Wind & Fire's "September," Chet Baker's "September Song," Fiona Apple's "Pale September," Marianne Faithfull's "Flaming September," Van Morrison's "September Night," Dinah Washington's "September in the Rain," Bobby Darin's "Theme from *Come September*" and Miles Davis's "Fall."

countdown

Three weeks: Send invitations. Start saving milk cartons for ice bowls.

Two weeks: Buy candles, party favors and any needed table-top items.

One week: Make ice bowls. Unmold; wrap in plastic wrap and store in the freezer. Buy music and wine. Order leaves for centerpiece from a florist if necessary.

Two days: Buy groceries. Pick up leaves. Make eggplant caviar and twists.

Day before: Buy fresh bread. Prep beets, orange and walnuts for salad. Marinate lamb; make cabernet sauce. Set the table and arrange the centerpiece.

Morning of: Chill white and sparkling wines. Arrange flowers.

Four hours: Prepare creamed corn and zucchini; refrigerate.

One hour: Marinate tomatoes. Prepare grill if you're using it for lamb. Toast bread and set out eggplant caviar, olives and olive oils for dipping. Mix a pitcher of cocktails; chill. Arrange hors d'oeuvres on the coffee table.

20 minutes: Cook lamb and finish sauce. Start music. Light candles. Assemble salad plates.

As guests arrive: Reheat corn and zucchini.

Right before dinner: Slice lamb and warm sauce.

even easier

Pare down the centerpiece. Place a shallow wooden or glass bowl in the center of the table and fill it with one type of fruit; try a mound of green and purple grapes, or green pears with the leaves on if possible. Surround the bowl with cream-colored votive and pillar candles.

If eggplant caviar sounds too elaborate, buy baba ghanoush, a Mediterranean eggplant spread available in most grocery stores. Spark it up by mixing in fresh lemon juice, chopped parsley, finely chopped shallots, salt and freshly ground black pepper.

Rather than serving a variety of wines with the meal, choose one well-priced, versatile red, such as Allegrini Valpolicella from Italy. The wine's acidity and fruitiness will not overpower the salad, and it's hearty enough to complement the lamb.

Don't bother baking the dessert twists. Serve store- or bakery-bought almond biscotti or tiny assorted cookies with the sorbet instead.

Instead of making the ice bowls, serve dessert in frozen glass bowls. Just rinse them under cold water and put them in the freezer.

perfect wine pairing

When serving wine with a meal, it's best to progress from sparkling and white wines to heavier reds. Match delicate flavors with lighter wines and hearty foods with rich, full-bodied wines. Or combine contrasting flavors such as a rich food with a crisp wine.

For this meal, try a sparkling white or rosé with the hors d'oeuvres; both have berry flavors that complement the smokiness of the charred eggplant. For the salad, a dry white wine like a sauvignon blanc or pinot gris will complement the sweetness of the beets and oranges. Pair the lamb with a red: Pinot noir is traditional with lamb, but a zinfandel or a syrah will complement the bold flavors in this recipe.

ice bowls in four easy steps

Dessert served in homemade ice bowls is a signature of LeDuc's, and it's guaranteed to end any meal with a splash. A tip: Make a couple of extras in case one breaks.

Cut 8 well-rinsed ½ gallon milk or juice cartons straight across, 5" up from the base. Then cut 8 1-quart cartons 3" up from the base.

Center the smaller cartons in the larger ones and pierce them with wooden skewers ½" from the top through both sides, keeping the top edges flush.

Add 4" of water (below skewers) in the space between the two cartons. If you'd like, add a few raspberry or mint leaves for a dash of color. Freeze for at least 48 hours.

To unmold: Remove bowls from freezer; leave out 15 min. Quickly run under cold water to release, then return to freezer. When serving dessert, plate the ice bowls over paper towels folded to bowl size to absorb melting water.

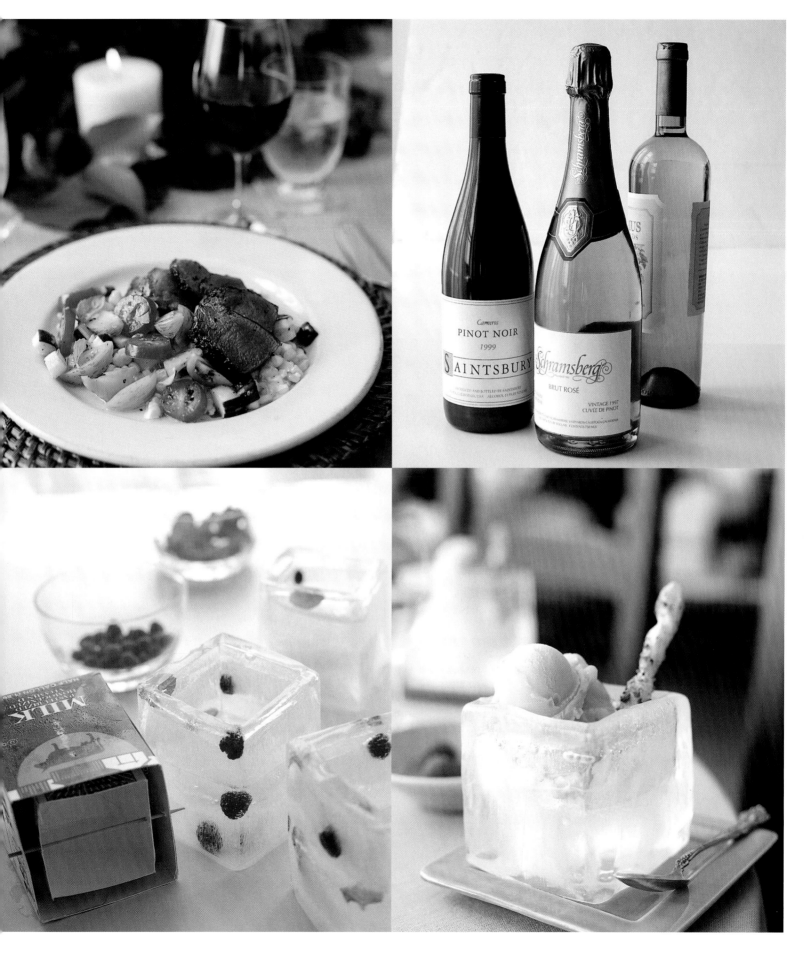

what to pour

Early autumn cocktail (serves 8): Combine 1½ cups vodka, 1 cup fresh lemon juice, ½ cup Galliano and ¼ cup honey liqueur. Shake; pour into ice-filled glasses. Garnish with flowering thyme sprigs.

Wine picks: With the eggplant hors d'oeuvre, serve a sparkling wine such as Schramsberg brut rosé or a Domaine Carneros brut from California. With the beet-and-orange salad, try a California sauvignon blanc from Mason or Voss, or a New Zealand sauvignon blanc from Villa Maria. With the lamb, pour a spicy California zinfandel from Ravenswood, Ridge or Rosenblum, or else a Gigondas (syrah) from Provence by Santa-Duc or Château de Saint Cosme. For those who prefer a lighter red, pour a Saintsbury pinot noir from California.

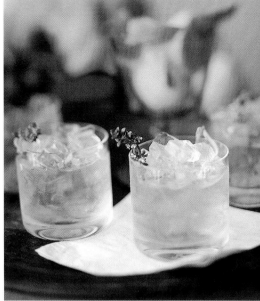

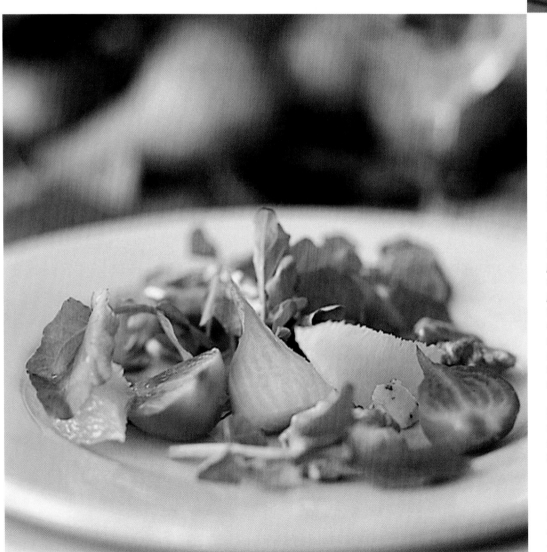

recipes

Charred Eggplant Caviar
(Makes 2½ cups)
3 small eggplants (about 1½ lb.)
2 large garlic cloves
⅓ cup olive oil
2 tbsp fresh lemon juice
¼ cup chopped, fresh flat-leaf parsley
Salt and pepper to taste
Flat-leaf parsley for garnish

Prepare a grill with medium-hot coals or heat oven to 400ºF. Pierce eggplant in several places. Place on grill or in oven and cook until tender throughout. Remove pulp from eggplant and place in bowl of food processor with garlic. With machine running pour in oil and lemon juice. Purée until smooth. Refrigerate, covered, until an hour before serving. Place in serving bowl; stir in parsley, salt and pepper. Garnish with parsley and serve with toasted bread for dipping.

Roasted Beet Salad with Watercress and Orange Segments
(Serves 8)
24 roasted baby golden and/or red beets, peeled then quartered
1 medium shallot, minced
½ cup olive oil, divided
2 tbsp red wine vinegar
Salt and pepper to taste
4 bunches watercress, cleaned

2 tbsp fresh lemon juice
1 orange, peeled and segmented
½ cup toasted walnuts
½ cup crumbled Stilton cheese

In large bowl toss beets and shallot with ¼ cup oil and the vinegar. Season with salt and pepper. Place watercress in another large bowl, and toss with remaining oil and lemon juice. Season. To serve, place greens on plates, spoon on beet mixture, and top with orange segments, walnuts and cheese.

Rosemary-and-Garlic-Infused Lamb Loin with Cabernet Sauce
(Serves 8)
2 loins of lamb (about 1½ lb. each), trimmed and tied
4 cloves garlic, thinly sliced
10 sprigs fresh thyme
6 sprigs fresh rosemary
2 tbsp olive oil, divided
Salt and pepper to taste
1 shallot, minced
1 cup cabernet sauvignon
1 cup lamb or beef stock
1 tbsp unsalted butter, softened
Rosemary or thyme sprigs for garnish

With sharp paring knife make small slits in lamb and insert garlic. Tuck thyme and rosemary sprigs under strings. Cover with plastic wrap and refrigerate overnight. Rub lamb with 1 tbsp oil and season with salt and pepper. Prepare charcoal grill with medium-hot coals or heat oven to 475°F. Grill or roast lamb 15–20 min., or until an instant-read thermometer registers from 125°F to 130°F (for rare) to 130°F to 135°F (for medium-rare) as it leaves the oven. Meat will continue to cook as it rests. Cover with foil and let stand while finishing sauce. For sauce: Heat remaining oil in skillet over medium-high heat. Add shallot and cook until it just starts to brown. Add cabernet sauvignon and stock. Boil until mixture is reduced to 1 cup, 18–20 min. Strain through fine-mesh sieve and stir in softened butter. Season to taste with salt and pepper. Discard string, rosemary

and thyme sprigs from lamb. Garnish with herb sprigs.

Marinated Tomatoes
(Serves 8)
1 medium shallot, minced
2 tbsp red wine vinegar
¼ cup olive oil
2 pt. red or yellow cherry, teardrop or grape tomatoes, halved
2 tbsp fresh basil, chopped
Salt and pepper to taste

In medium bowl combine shallot and vinegar; let stand 20 min. Stir in oil and tomatoes. Cover and let stand 20 min. Add basil, season with salt and pepper.

Creamed Corn
(Serves 8)
2 cups heavy cream
1 large shallot, minced
Kernels from 5 ears of corn
Salt and pepper to taste

In medium saucepan simmer cream and shallot until reduced to 1 cup. Stir in corn and cook 2–3 min., until heated through. Season with salt and pepper.

Sautéed Zucchini
(Serves 8)
2 tbsp olive oil
2 cloves garlic, minced
4 zucchini (about 1¾ lb.), chopped
1½ tsp fresh oregano
Salt and pepper to taste

Heat oil in large skillet over medium heat. Add garlic and cook until fragrant, about 30 seconds. Add zucchini and sauté until tender, about 10 min. Stir in oregano. Season with salt and pepper.

Pistachio-Ginger Twists
(Makes about 48)
1 pkg. frozen puff pastry sheets, thawed
1 egg yolk
⅔ cup sugar
½ cup finely chopped pistachio nuts
½ cup finely chopped crystallized ginger

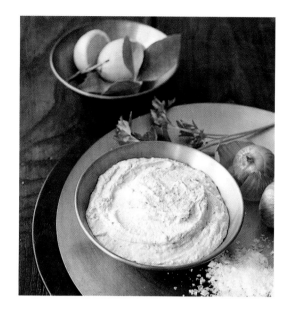

Place 1 sheet of dough on floured work surface, and roll out into 12" square. In bowl combine sugar, pistachios and ginger. In small bowl combine egg yolk with 1 tbsp water. Brush egg mixture over dough. Sprinkle half of filling over the bottom half of the dough. Fold top of dough over the filled bottom half, pressing gently to seal edges. Carefully slide onto baking sheet and refrigerate 30 min. Repeat with remaining sheet of dough. Heat oven to 350°F. Remove sheets from refrigerator. Roll each folded sheet into a 12" square, then cut into ½" strips. Hold each end and twist into corkscrew shape. Press ends onto parchment-lined baking sheet. Bake 18–20 min., or until golden and puffed. Let cool, then store in airtight container. Can be made up to three days ahead. Serve with ice cream.

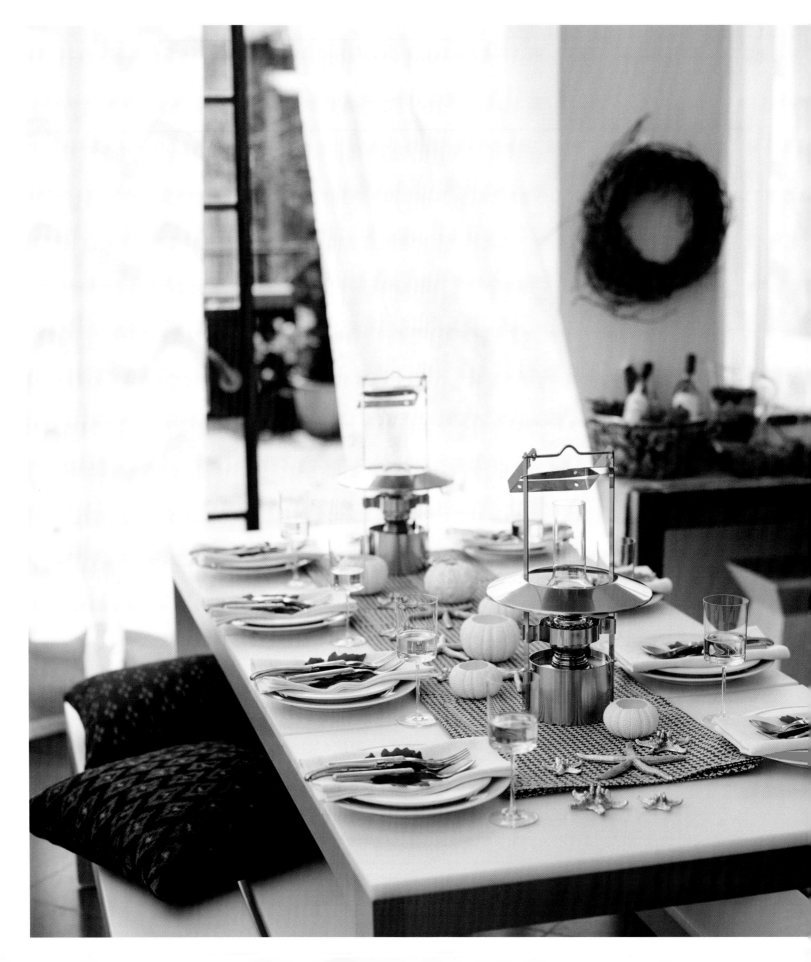

mediterranean dinner

Toast summer's twilight with a **relaxed dinner party for eight.** British hostess and cookbook author Nigella Lawson, who orchestrated this **Greek-inspired meal,** heeds traditional dining customs by forgoing any formal structure and serving **lots of light, tasty dishes** over three courses. Enhance the Greek ambience with **powdery white** and **deep blue décor,** and fresh, authentic ingredients; then sit back and enjoy a feast fit for the gods.

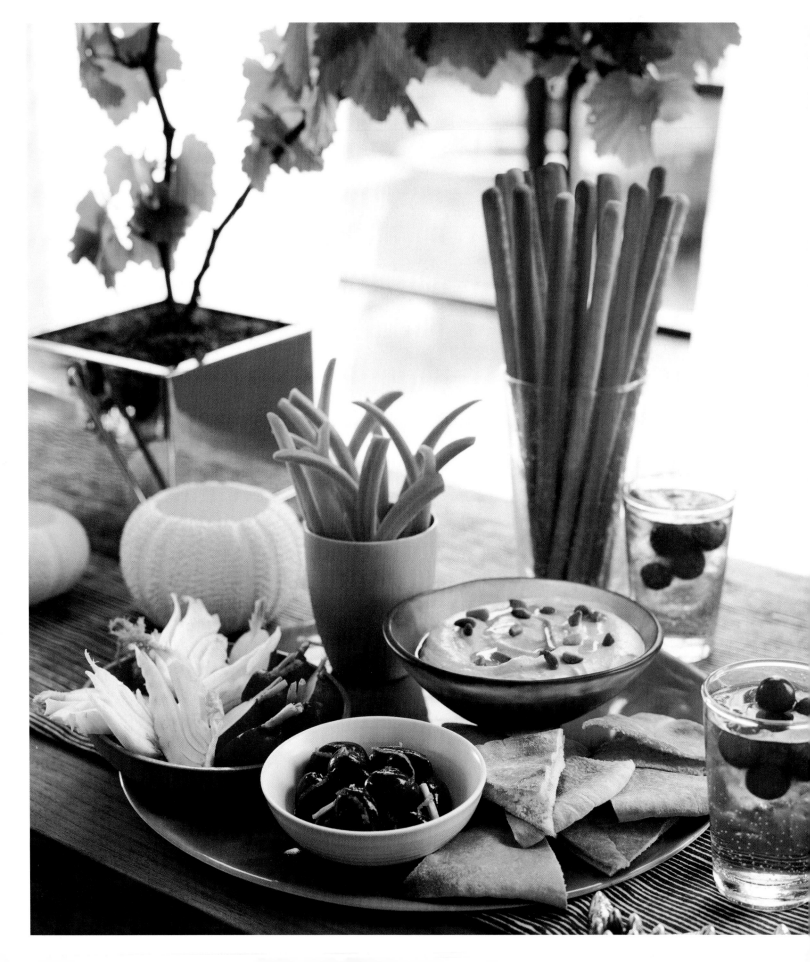

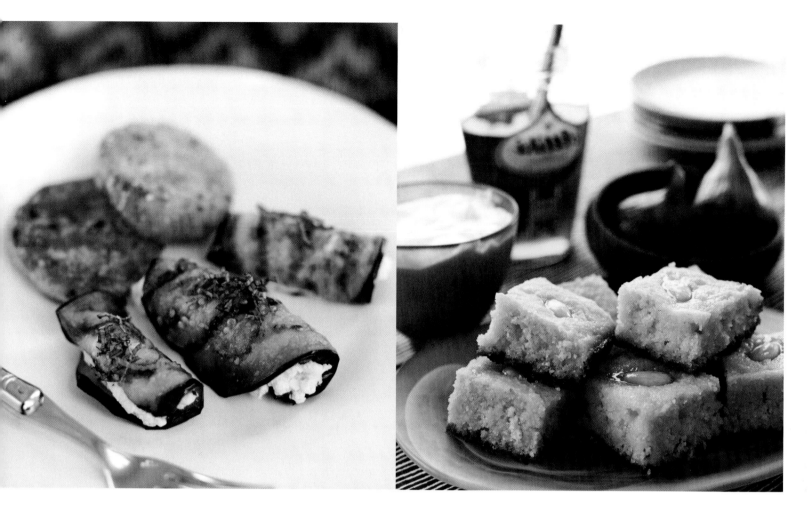

menu

Signature drink: Grapevine
Bar snacks: Marinated olives, pistachios, toasted almonds
Appetizers: Hummus with toasted pine nuts and crudités; grilled eggplant with feta, mint and chili; mini dill-potato pancakes
Main course: Ultimate Greek salad, bay-scented roast chicken with retsina and dried figs, Greekish lamb pasta
Dessert: Sticky semolina cake and fresh figs with yogurt and honey

setting the scene

The décor: Place a chilled pitcher of grapevine cocktails, tumblers and snacks on the bar, and arrange grapevines (order them from your local florist) and/or clusters of red grapes around them as accents. Drape the dinner table with a white tablecloth (or, for a more casual vibe, thick white butcher paper), a blue-and-white-checked or striped runner, and big white cloth napkins. Add hurricane lamps, pitchers of ice water, and clear or white votive candleholders.

The menu: During cocktail hour, offer bowls of pistachios, toasted almonds and marinated olives. Begin dinner with light Mediterranean bites like grilled eggplant and classic hummus served with fresh radishes, fennel spears, carrots, breadsticks and pita slices. Switch to clean plates for the main course of chicken, pasta and salad. Finish with cake and figs.

The music: Fittingly, the most popular Mediterranean-style music can best be described as breezy—play any number of popular Ibiza-style chill-out compilation CDs of cool electronica to set a contemporary Mediterranean mood, or for a more authentic (albeit campy) vibe, play bouzouki music and Greek divas such as Nina Mouskouri and Melina Mecouri. For a retro jet-set glamorous touch, Brigitte Bardot's musical endeavors in *Best of Bardot* will evoke the height of Saint-Tropez chic.

countdown

Three weeks: Send invitations.
Two weeks: Order flowers, grapevines and music.
One week: Order specialty foods and ingredients (see Resources).
Two days: Buy bar items and all groceries except for fresh meat and poultry. Toast almonds.
Day before: Buy fresh meat and poultry. Chill wine, white grape juice and vodka. Make hummus; refrigerate without adding olive oil and pine nuts. Marinate chicken.
Morning of: Make pasta sauce and semolina cake. Bake potatoes. Prep, but don't cook, potato pancakes. Arrange flowers.
Four hours: Set up the table and bar. Grill and assemble eggplant appetizers; refrigerate.
Two hours: Sauté potato pancakes (in batches, if needed). Store, lightly covered, on counter to be reheated later. Add olive oil and pine nuts to hummus and put out with crudités.
One hour: Roast chicken. Make salad. Make cocktails.
Half hour: Light candles. Start music.
When guests arrive: Boil water, warm pasta sauce and potato pancakes, and assemble pasta dish. Serve wine and appetizers. Offer dinner in two courses.
After dinner: Combine figs with honey and yogurt; serve with semolina cake and muscat.

even easier

If you have a few days to spare but not a lot of time to cook, mail-order Greek appetizers, such as spanakopita (spinach in phyllo triangles) and tiropita (feta cheese phyllo triangles). (See Resources.)

Forget cooking altogether and pick up a take-out feast from a Greek deli or restaurant or a Middle Eastern market. Choose dishes that are easily divided into snack-size portions, such as dolmas (grape leaves stuffed with rice or meat) and spanakopita (make sure to reheat before serving). Transfer Greek salad into a big bowl and sprinkle it with fresh feta cheese. Reheat Greek meatballs and sprinkle them with chopped fresh mint.

Don't make dessert from scratch. Serve store-bought baklava (walnut-and-phyllo pastries) with a light, sweet sauce (1 cup honey mixed with 1 cup lemon juice or rose water) or bite-size Mediterranean pastries (see Resources).

basics of greek entertaining

Dining customs: At a typical Greek dinner, guests nibble on a wide variety of small dishes. Since many Greek foods can be made in advance, it's fine to serve most lukewarm. The exception: Fresh fish, which should be grilled and served hot.

Common ingredients: Greek kitchen staples include olive oil, olives, lamb, fish, goat's- and sheep's-milk cheeses (such as feta), Greek yogurt, tomatoes, onions, garlic, bay leaves, capers, dill, fennel, oregano, thyme, lemon, honey, figs and phyllo. Greek yogurt, which can be made from cow's, sheep's or goat's milk, is creamier and thicker than other yogurts. It works as a savory dip (add chopped cucumber, garlic and fresh mint or dill) or a sweet finale (topped with honey, thyme and nuts).

Herbal remedy: Dried Greek oregano (which tastes different from traditional Italian oregano) often flavors fish, meat and sauces. It also spices up a quick Greek appetizer: Cut a pita into 6 pieces and drizzle them with olive oil. Add tomato cubes and Greek olive slivers, sprinkle with dried oregano and sea salt, and broil until crisp.

Classic main dishes: Grilled meat kabobs, gyros (roasted lamb, onions, peppers and cucumber-yogurt sauce in a small pita) and moussaka (Greek lamb casserole).

National beverages: Greece's two most popular drinks are ouzo, the traditional Greek aperitif, and coffee. Ouzo tastes like anise and is usually served "neat" or with water over ice, which makes it appear cloudy. Greek coffee (aka Turkish coffee) is a strong blend made sweet by adding sugar to the grounds while brewing.

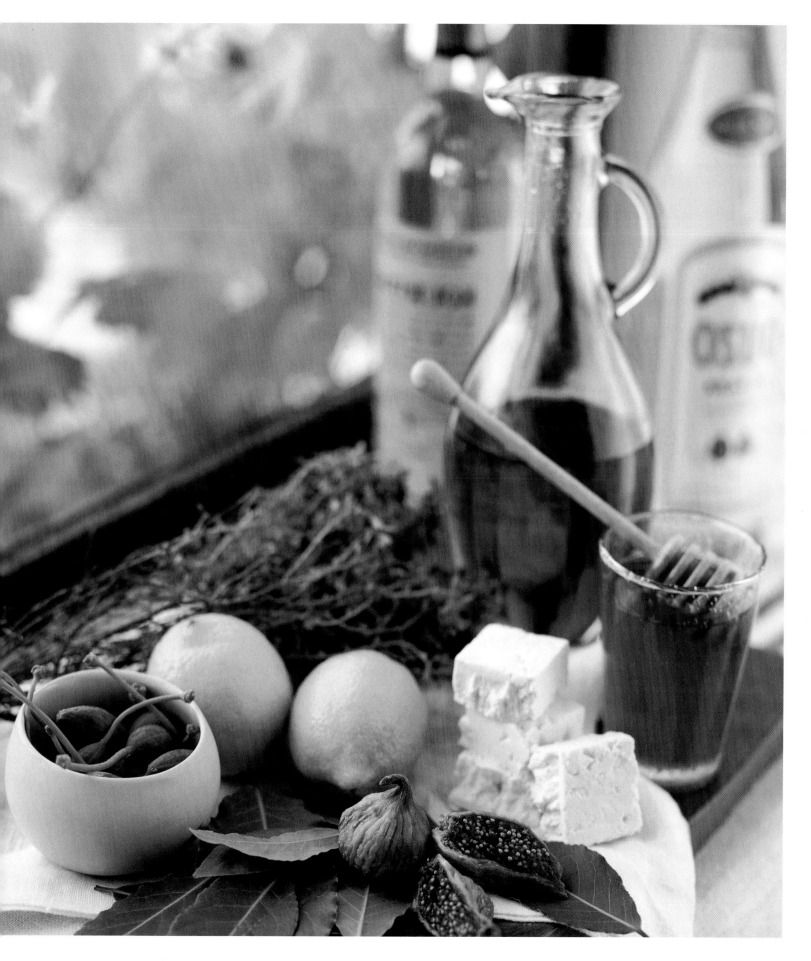

what to pour

Grapevine (serves 8). In pitcher, combine 4 cups chilled white grape juice, 1 cup chilled vodka, ¼ cup fresh lemon juice and 2 tsp grenadine. Mix and serve in ice-filled tumblers. Garnish with a few frozen grapes.

Wine picks: With appetizers, serve something with the gutsiness of retsina (the Greek white wine flavored with pine tree resin), such as Godeval Valdeorras from Spain or an Austrian Gruner Veltliner from Solomon. With the main course, pour a spicy California syrah from Ojai Vineyards or Qupe. With or after dessert, offer Muscat Vin de Glaciere from Bonny Doon in California or a muscat de Beaumes de Venise from Domaine de Durban in France.

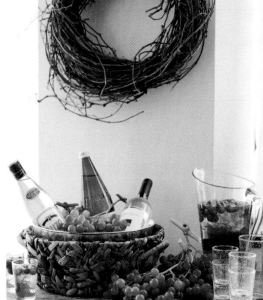

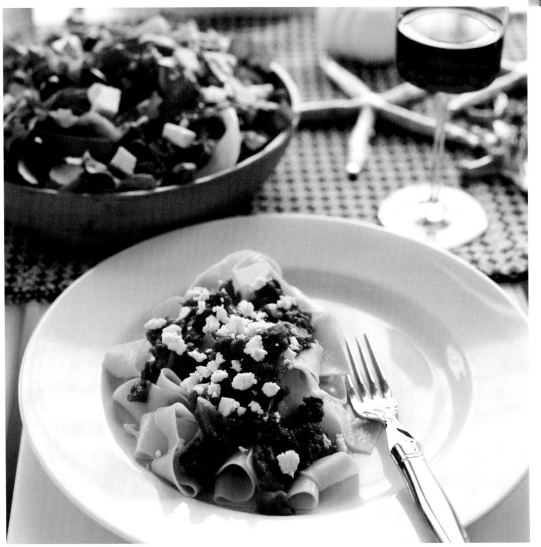

recipes

Hummus
(Makes 2 cups)
1¼ cups prepared hummus
⅓ cup plain yogurt
1 tbsp fresh lemon juice
½ tsp ground cumin
2 tbsp olive oil
2 tbsp toasted pine nuts

In small bowl combine hummus, yogurt, lemon juice and cumin. Before serving, drizzle with olive oil and sprinkle with pine nuts.

Grilled Eggplant with Feta, Mint and Chili
4 medium eggplant, trimmed and sliced
  ¼" thick
3 tbsp plus ¼ cup olive oil, divided
2 cups crumbled feta
1 jalapeño, seeded and minced
1 tbsp fresh lemon juice
3 tbsp fresh, chopped mint, divided

Prepare a charcoal grill with medium-hot coals or heat a gas grill to medium-high. Set eggplant on rack. Brush with 3 tbsp olive oil. Grill eggplant 4–5 min., turning once. You can also cook the eggplant in a ridged grill pan on the stove top. In small bowl mash together feta, remaining olive oil, jalapeño, lemon juice and 1 tbsp mint. Evenly divide feta mixture over eggplant and roll up. Place on serving platter and sprinkle with remaining mint.

Mini Dill Potato Pancakes

(Serves 8)

3 medium Idaho potatoes (about 2 lb.),
   baked
2 tbsp minced fresh dill
2 tbsp minced, fresh flat-leaf parsley
2 tbsp unsalted butter, melted
1 scallion, chopped
1 tsp lemon zest
Salt and pepper to taste
1 egg, lightly beaten
¾ cup matzo meal
¼ cup vegetable oil, divided

*Cut baked potatoes in half and scoop
out the inside. Discard the skins. In
medium bowl mash potatoes with dill,
parsley, butter, scallion and lemon zest.
Season with salt and pepper. Stir in the
beaten egg. Place matzo meal in a pie
plate. Using a tbsp potato mixture, form
it into small pancakes. Dredge in matzo
meal. Heat 2 tbsp oil in large nonstick
skillet over medium-high heat. Working in
batches, sauté the pancakes 3–4 min.,
turning once, or until golden. Add more
oil to skillet as necessary. Serve hot.*

Ultimate Greek Salad

(Serves 8)

1 medium red onion, thinly sliced
2 tbsp red wine vinegar
1 tbsp dried oregano
¼ tsp pepper
3 large plum tomatoes, cut into thin
   wedges
½ tsp sugar
¼ tsp salt
6 cups torn pieces romaine lettuce
1 small fennel, trimmed and sliced thin
½ cup extra-virgin olive oil
2 tbsp fresh lemon juice
½ cup pitted kalamata olives
½ cup crumbled feta

*Sprinkle onion with vinegar, oregano and
pepper. Cover with plastic wrap and set
aside for 1 hr. Place tomato wedges in
medium bowl and sprinkle with sugar
and salt. Cover with plastic, wrap and set
aside for 1 hr. Toss together lettuce, fennel, olive oil and lemon juice. Top with
red onion, tomatoes, olives and feta.*

Bay-Scented Chicken With Retsina and Dried Figs

(Serves 8)

12 bay leaves
2 cups full-bodied white wine or Greek
   retsina (can substitute any dry white
   wine)
2 cups dried mission figs
4 cloves garlic, smashed
1 small onion, halved
2 tbsp olive oil
2 tsp salt
1 tsp ground allspice
2 whole chickens, each cut into 8 pieces

*In medium bowl combine first 8 ingredi-
ents. Place each chicken in resealable
plastic bag. Evenly divide marinade
ingredients over chicken. Seal bag and
refrigerate 8 hrs. or overnight. Let chick-
en come to room temperature before
roasting. Heat oven to 375°F. Arrange
chicken pieces in single layer in large
roasting pan. Tightly cover
pan with foil and roast skin-side down
40 min. Remove foil and turn chicken
pieces over. Return to oven and continue
roasting 20 min. To serve, arrange chick-
en on serving platter and spoon juice
and figs around chicken.*

Greekish Lamb Pasta

(Serves 8)

2 tbsp olive oil
1 large onion, chopped
4 cloves garlic, minced
¼ lb. white mushrooms, cleaned,
   stemmed and chopped
1 lb. ground lamb
½ cup red wine
2 cans (28 oz. each) crushed tomatoes
   in purée
1 tbsp tomato purée
2 tbsp milk
1 tbsp dried oregano
1 tbsp sugar
Salt and pepper to taste
1 lb. cooked pasta
1 cup crumbled feta

*Heat oil in Dutch oven over medium-low
heat. Add onion, garlic and mushrooms;
sauté 12 min., or until wilted. Add lamb;
brown 7 min., or until no longer pink,
breaking up with a wooden spoon. Add
wine, tomatoes, tomato purée, milk,
oregano and sugar, scraping up any
browned bits from bottom of pot with
wooden spoon. Bring to simmer; cook
1 hr., or until thickened. Season with salt
and pepper. To serve, spoon sauce over
hot cooked pasta. Top with crumbled
feta.*

Sticky Semolina Cake

(Serves 8)

½ cup plus 6 tbsp sugar, divided
½ tsp fresh lemon juice
½ tsp orange blossom water
1½ cups semolina
1 cup drained yogurt
4 tbsp unsalted butter, melted
1 egg
1 tsp baking powder
½ tsp baking soda
½ tsp lemon zest
¼ tsp ground cardamom
16 whole blanched almonds

*Heat oven to 350°F. Line 8" x 8" baking
pan with foil. Lightly spray with nonstick
cooking spray. In small saucepan combine ½ cup sugar and ½ cup water. Cook
over low heat, stirring with wooden
spoon until sugar has dissolved. Stop
stirring and increase heat to medium.
Simmer 2 min. Remove from heat, stir in
lemon juice and orange blossom water;
let cool. Refrigerate 2 hrs. In food
processor combine semolina, yogurt,
butter, egg, baking powder, baking soda,
lemon zest and cardamom until smooth.
Spoon into prepared baking pan. With
sharp knife lightly divide batter into 16
squares. Place an almond in center of
each square. Bake 30–35 min. While
cake is hot, cut squares completely
apart and pour sugar syrup over hot
cake. Let cool in pan completely.*

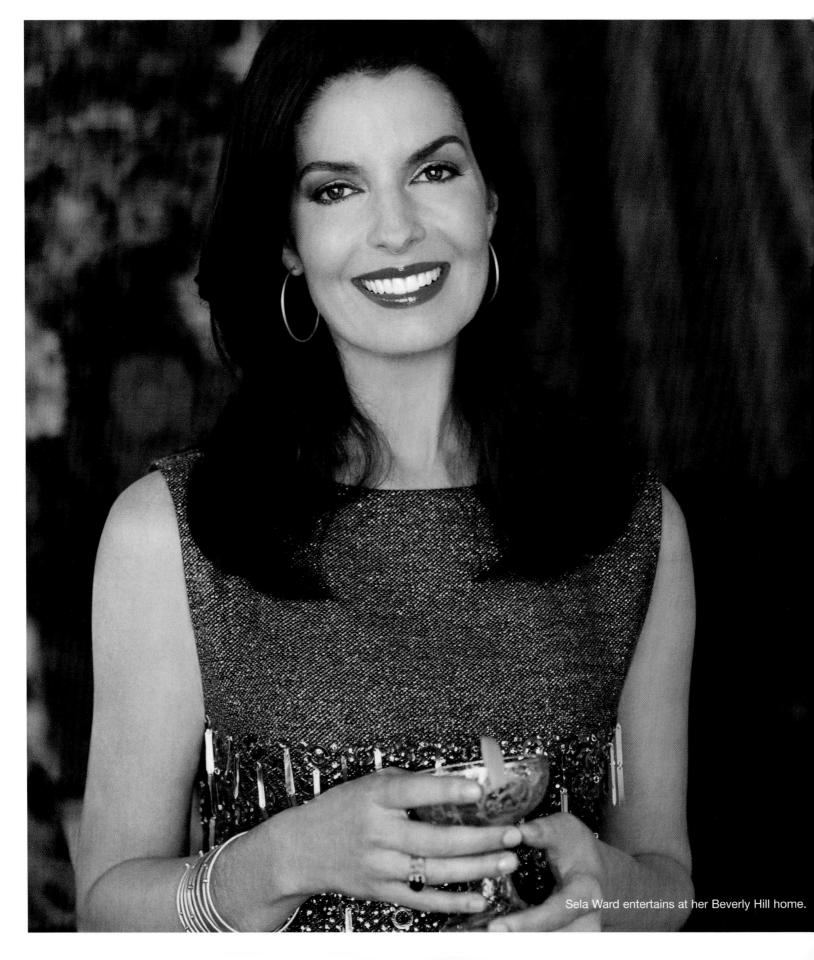

Sela Ward entertains at her Beverly Hill home.

holiday parties

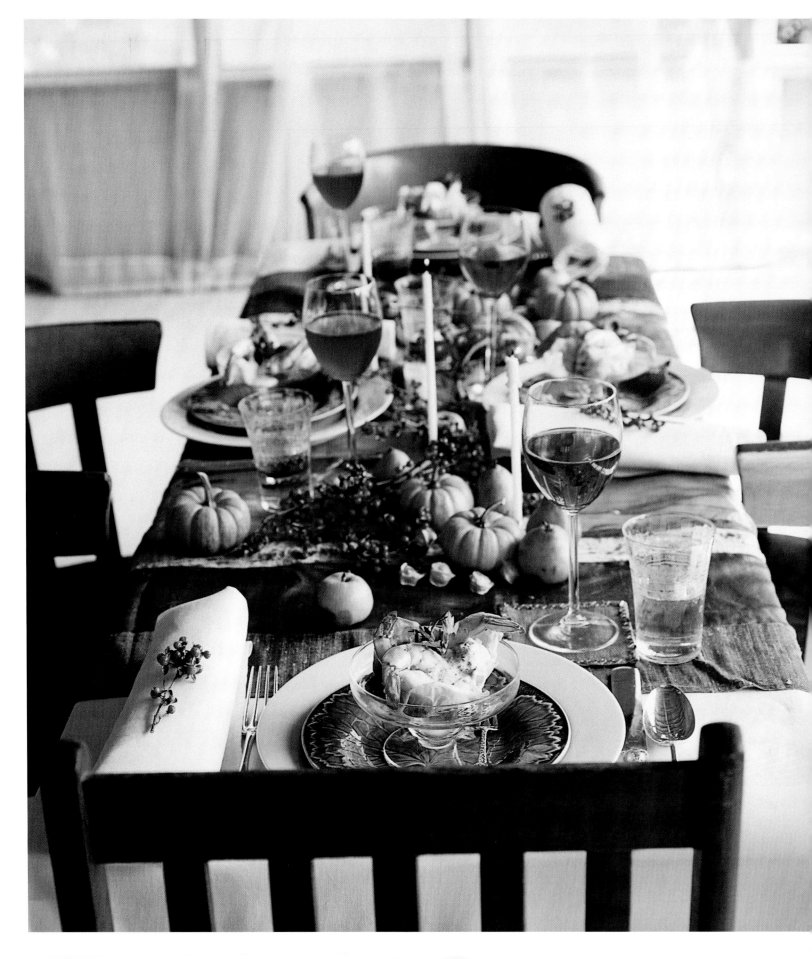

thanksgiving
dinner

This holiday dinner for eight is the ultimate comfort-food feast. The traditional menu, the familiar faces around the table, and even the football games make this a favorite holiday, for many. When hosting in your home, don't fuss too much over the details. Since most people long for their own family recipes, ask guests to bring their favorite dish or to share a recipe with you ahead of time. Instead of fancy decorations, use the season's fresh fruits, vegetables and branches to create a simple take on the classic cornucopia. Spend time and energy on what really matters—enjoying friends and family—and watch your house become the preferred destination for this annual pilgrimage.

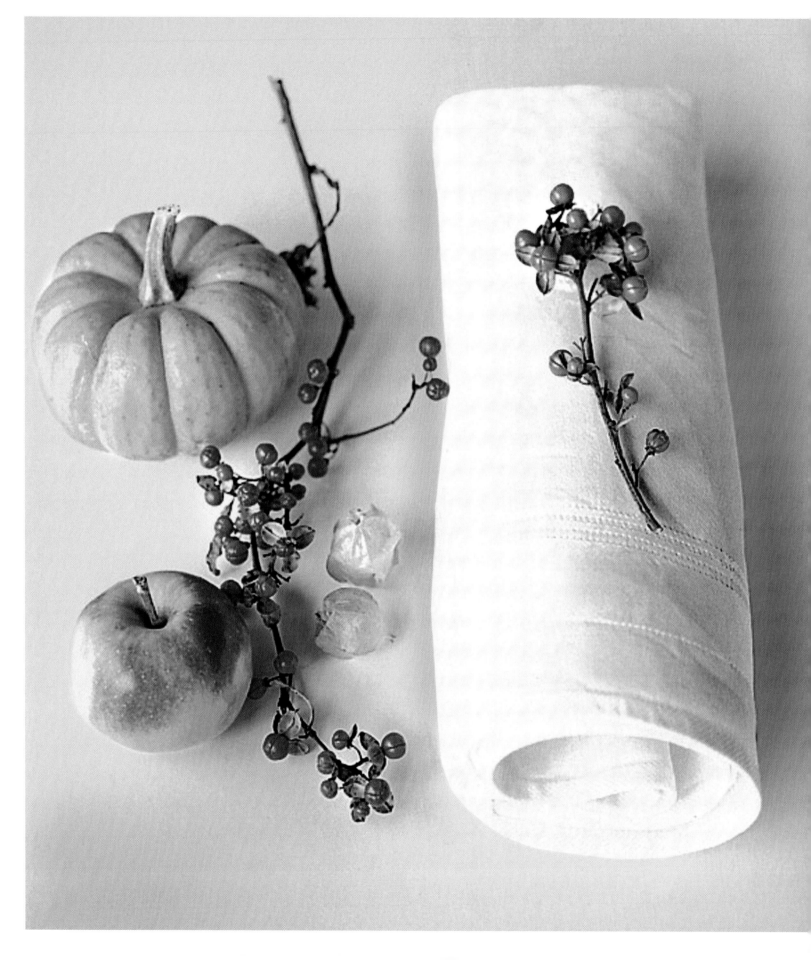

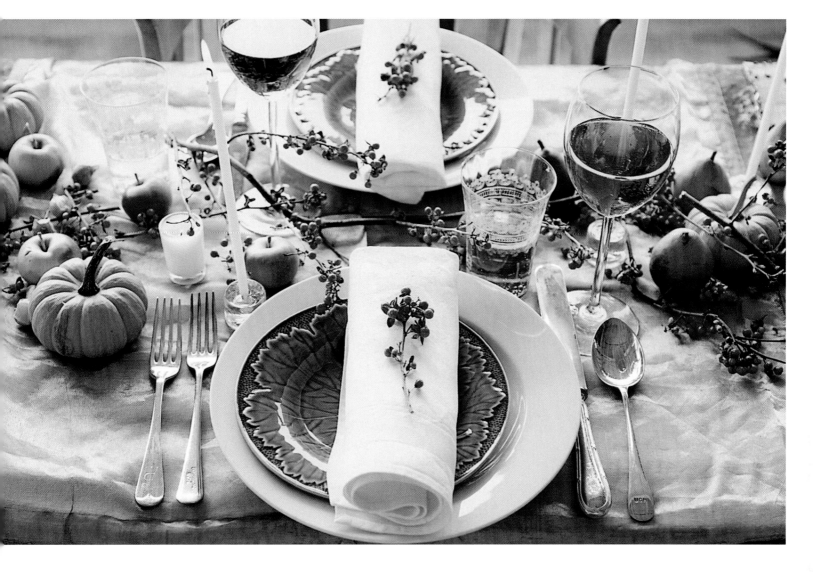

the menu

Signature drink: Classic kir
Hors d'oeuvres: Stuffed deviled eggs, smoked salmon on toast with dill, warm olives with citrus zest
Appetizer: Shrimp with green goddess dressing
Main course: Roast turkey with cornbread-and-sausage stuffing, bay-scented mashed potatoes, string beans braised in olive oil
Dessert: Pecan chocolate tart

setting the scene

The décor: Send your tablecloth and napkins (white is always classic and pretty, but they don't have to match exactly) to a dry cleaner the week before the dinner if they're not already beautifully ironed. For a really crisp look, ask for medium starch. Scatter crab or lady apples, Seckel pears, little pumpkins and gourds, and branches of bittersweet down the center of the table. Add tall, ultrathin tapers (15" candles) and 10 to 12 tiny votives to create a soft, flattering glow. Lay a white dinner plate at each place and top with colored salad plates if you have them. Arrange silver and glassware. Place a simply rolled napkin on each top plate and lay a sprig of bittersweet, a fresh herb (like rosemary or sage), dried wheat or even a pretty fall leaf on top.

The music: The idea of giving thanks has inspired many a pop song—why not stuff your guests with the gift of music as well as food by downloading songs for a Turkey Day–inspired CD? Our musical cornucopia would include various songs titled "Thank You" by an array of artists including Tori Amos, Ashanti, the Charlatans, Duran Duran, John Mellencamp, Alanis Morissette and Barry White; "Thankful" by Mary Mary and Me'Shell Ndegeocello; Bing Crosby's "I've Got Plenty to be Thankful For"; and Massive Attack's "Be Thankful for What You've Got."

countdown

Three weeks: Send invitations.
One week: Order turkey (if you want to serve an organic, free-range bird, you may need to order it two weeks or more in advance). Buy wine and music. Send table linens to the laundry. Buy (or borrow) any glasses and silverware you may need.
Two days: Buy groceries, and if you'd like, a large pumpkin to serve the soup in.
Day before: Set the table. Bake cornbread if you're making it from scratch.
Morning of: Chill wines (use a cooler if the fridge is too full). Arrange flowers.
Eight hours: Peel potatoes and trim green beans. Make egg-yolk mixture for stuffed eggs.
Five hours: Make stuffing; stuff and roast turkey.
Two hours: Cook and mash potatoes (reheat them before serving). Braise beans.
One hour: Stuff eggs; prepare salmon toasts and olives.
15 minutes: Light candles. Start music.

even easier

Substitute a ready-made snack such as a wedge of good aged cheddar cheese for the stuffed eggs. Buy precooked shrimp.
Instead of homemade cornbread for the stuffing, buy corn muffins or use a prepackaged mix such as Jiffy.
Not a gravy master? Readily available Knorr mix and Williams-Sonoma turkey gravy base are good substitutes. Add a touch of dry sherry or white wine to either.
Buy whole-berry cranberry sauce and add a spritz of fresh orange juice and some of the zest for a fresh flavor.
Buy a pecan pie and add a homemade touch by melting 4 oz. of good-quality chocolate and drizzling it on top.
Other easy desserts: Buy a pumpkin pie from your local bakery or farmstand and serve it with cinnamon-spiked whipped cream. Or toast slices of pumpkin bread and serve them with vanilla ice cream, hot caramel sauce and chopped pecans.

talking turkey

Buying: Unfrozen organic, free-range birds (which usually must be ordered a few weeks in advance from better grocers or butchers) taste fresher and are ready to roast; frozen turkeys require thawing according to package directions. Typically, there are two methods: To thaw the bird in the refrigerator, place it breast-side up, in the packaging, on a tray, and allow one day per every 4 lb. For faster thawing, submerge the turkey, breast down and packaging on, in cold water. Change the water every half hour to keep it cold. Allow 30 min. per 1 lb. of bird. When deciding how big a bird to buy, plan for 1 lb. of turkey per person, or 1½ lb. if you want lots of leftovers.
Brining: Brining a turkey before cooking can add flavor and keep the meat moist. To brine, submerge an unfrozen turkey in a large covered container of salted and seasoned water (⅛ cup salt per 1 gal. of water; seasonings vary—try ½ cup brown sugar, 1 tbsp peppercorns, plus a bay leaf and a sprig of thyme per gallon) for 10 to 12 hours. Rinse thoroughly before cooking. Do not brine self-basting or kosher turkeys; they've already been subject to a salty stock.
Roasting: Turn the page for a basic, foolproof recipe. For additional help, refer to a classic American cookbook or call Butterball's Turkey Talkline, open during November and December, at 800-288-8372.
Carving: After letting the roasted turkey sit for 20 min. place the platter on top of a damp dishtowel so it doesn't slip around while you carve. Use a sharp 8" knife to carve breasts first and legs last, always slicing against the grain. If your bird is dry or overcooked, remove the whole breasts off the bird and the dark meat off the bone. Place it in a disposable foil pan, bathe it in hot chicken broth, and reheat it in a 300°F oven for 15 min. Then slice and serve.

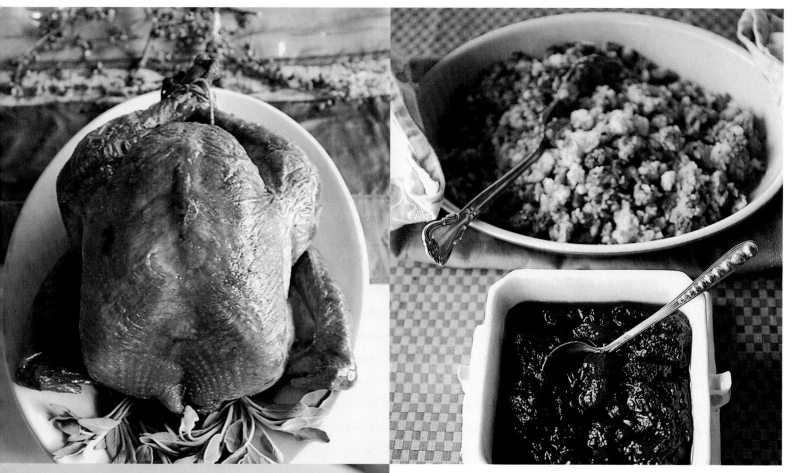

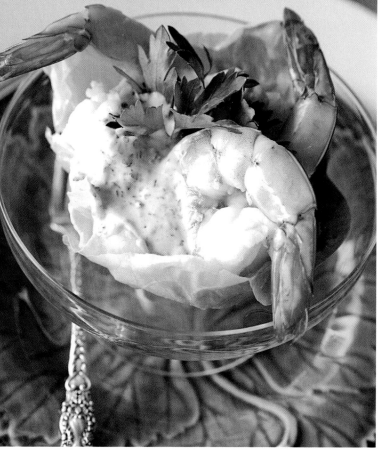

the most delicious party favor

Some people think that the best part of Thanksgiving is tucking into a turkey sandwich or a plate of reheated stuffing the next day, so be sure to share the leftovers with loved ones.

Pack up a small sampling of the meal in disposable plastic containers that can be warmed quickly in the microwave.

Place stuffing and mashed potatoes on the bottom and top them with turkey (and gravy), green beans and other side dishes. Cranberry sauce should travel separately in small resealable plastic bags.

what to pour

Classic kir: To make this classic pink aperitif, add a few drops of crème de cassis to a glass of crisp dry white wine such as a muscadet from France (the Loire Valley) from Metaireau, Domaine de la Quilla or Sauvion.

Wine picks: Pinot noir is the classic choice to drink with turkey. With dinner, serve a Carneros Creek or Iron Horse from California, or Louis Jadot from Burgundy, France.

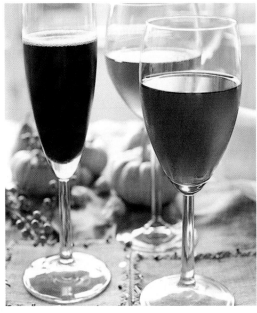

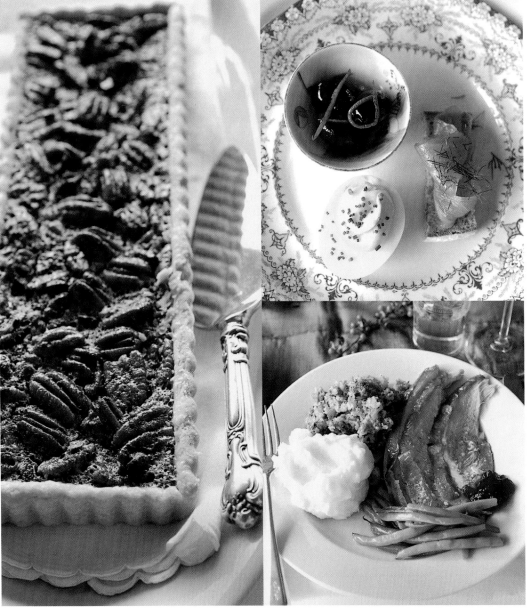

recipes

Warm Olives with Citrus Zest
(Serves 8)
2 cups kalamata olives
¼ cup extra-virgin olive oil
1 wide strip lemon zest, julienned
1 wide strip orange zest, julienned
¼ tsp fennel seeds
3 pinches dried red pepper flakes

Place all ingredients in small saucepan. Heat over medium-low heat until warmed through.

Smoked Salmon on Toast with Dill
(Makes 24)
4 oz. smoked salmon, cut into 24 pieces
5 slices good-quality bread cut into 24 1" x 2" pieces, lightly toasted
½ lemon
2 tbsp coarsely chopped dill

Place 1 salmon piece on each toast, squeeze on a few drops of lemon juice; garnish with dill.

Stuffed Deviled Eggs
(Makes 16)
8 eggs, hard-boiled, peeled and halved lengthwise
5 tbsp mayonnaise
2 tsp Dijon mustard
1 tsp fresh lemon juice

Salt and white pepper to taste
2 chives, finely chopped

Remove egg yolks from whites, leaving whites intact. Place yolks in medium bowl and mash with fork. Add mayonnaise, mustard, lemon juice, salt and pepper; mix well. Spoon mixture into whites; garnish with chives. Refrigerate.

Shrimp with Green Goddess Dressing
(Serves 8)
1 cup mayonnaise
½ cup sour cream
4 tbsp minced parsley
4 tbsp minced scallions
2 anchovy flat fillets, minced
1 tbsp white wine vinegar
1 tbsp fresh lemon juice
Salt and white pepper to taste
8 Bibb lettuce leaves
24 medium shrimp, peeled, deveined, simmered until pink (3–4 min.) and chilled
¼ cup flat-leaf parsley leaves

In medium bowl combine first ingredients (1–7); season with salt and pepper. Place a lettuce leaf on each of 8 salad bowls; arrange 3 shrimp on top; spoon dressing on. Garnish with parsley.

Roast Turkey with Stuffing
(Serves 8)
1 turkey (10–12 lb.), ready to stuff
3 tbsp butter, softened
Salt and pepper to taste
Stuffing (recipe follows)
1 bunch sage

Heat oven to 350°F. Rub turkey with butter, salt and pepper. Spoon hot stuffing into turkey cavity (bake extra stuffing in small baking dish 30 min. before turkey is done). Tie drumsticks with kitchen string; place turkey on rack in roasting pan. Roast 2–3 hrs., or until instant-read thermometer inserted 2" into flesh away from bone reads 170°F. The USDA recommends 180°F, but that can make white meat dry and stringy. Take turkey out when the breast meat is 170°F and

let residual heat bring it up to 180°F as the bird rests. Center of stuffing needs to be at least 165°F. Reserve cooked neck/giblets and pan juices for gravy. Loosely cover turkey with foil; let stand 20 min. Place turkey on bed of fresh sage on warm serving platter.

Turkey Gravy
(Serves 8)
1 cup dry white wine
6 tbsp all-purpose flour
4 cups turkey giblet stock, including reserved cooked neck and giblets
Salt and pepper to taste

Skim fat from pan juices, reserving ⅓ cup fat, and deglaze pan with white wine over moderately high heat, scraping up brown bits. Bring white wine to boil and remove pan from heat. In saucepan whisk together reserved fat and flour and cook roux over moderately low heat, whisking, 3 min. Add white wine mixture and stock or broth in a stream and simmer, whisking occasionally for 5 min. Season gravy with salt and pepper and transfer to hot gravy boat.

Cornbread-and-Sausage Stuffing
(Serves 8)
6 cups crumbled cornbread
¼ cup chopped parsley
1 lb. Italian sweet sausage, crumbled
2 tbsp butter
2 cups chopped celery (including leaves)
1 cup chopped onion
1 clove garlic, minced
Salt and pepper to taste

Place cornbread and parsley in large bowl. In large skillet over medium heat, brown sausage 8–10 min.; add to bowl, discarding most fat. In same skillet, melt butter; sauté celery, onion and garlic 10 min., until soft; add to bowl. Season with salt and pepper and mix well.

Bay-Scented Mashed Potatoes
(Serves 8)
5 large potatoes, peeled and quartered
4 fresh bay leaves

1 cup milk, hot
6 tbsp butter, melted, divided
Salt and pepper to taste

Add potatoes and bay leaves to large pot of salted water. Boil 20–30 min., until tender. Drain potatoes, discarding bay leaves. Mash roughly with potato masher or force through ricer. Stir in milk, 4 tbsp butter, salt and pepper. Beat until smooth and fluffy. Place potatoes in warm serving dish and drizzle remaining butter on top. Serve immediately.

String Beans Braised in Olive Oil
(Serves 8)
2 lb. string beans, trimmed
1 cup olive oil
Coarse salt to taste

In medium pot, place beans and oil. Cover and braise over medium-low heat 30–45 min., until very tender. Lift beans from oil and place on warm serving plate, spoon a little oil on top, and season with salt.

Pecan Chocolate Tart
(Serves 8)
½ cup sugar
2 tbsp flour
2 eggs, lightly beaten
1 cup light corn syrup
2 tbsp melted butter
1 tsp vanilla
Pinch salt
2 cups pecan halves
6 oz. bittersweet chocolate, chopped
1 homemade pie crust in 13" x 4" loose-bottomed tart pan or 9" frozen pie crust, thawed

Heat oven to 325°F. Combine sugar and flour. Add rest of filling ingredients; mix well. Pour into crust; bake 1 hr., or until knife inserted in center comes out clean.

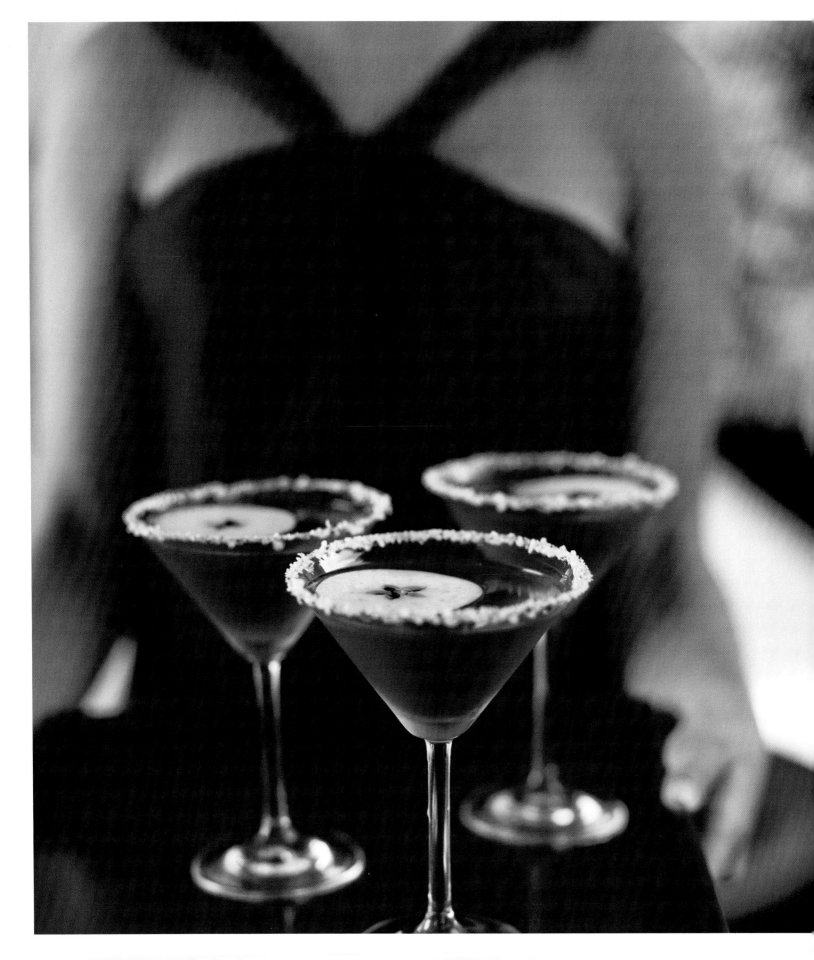

holiday cocktail party

This holiday season, give the most memorable gift of all: a giddy, glamorous cocktail party for 20 friends. Schedule the event for a Saturday night in December and mail invitations early to avoid the crush. Los Angeles event planner Jo Gartin, who planned Molly Shannon's wedding, offers an elegant spin on the classic holiday gathering with a gift-wrap theme that is reflected in everything from the invitations to the flower arrangements to the hors d'oeuvres. Instead of a traditional (and predictable) red-and-green theme, opt for a sleek red, white and silver palette. It's as modern as it is merrymaking.

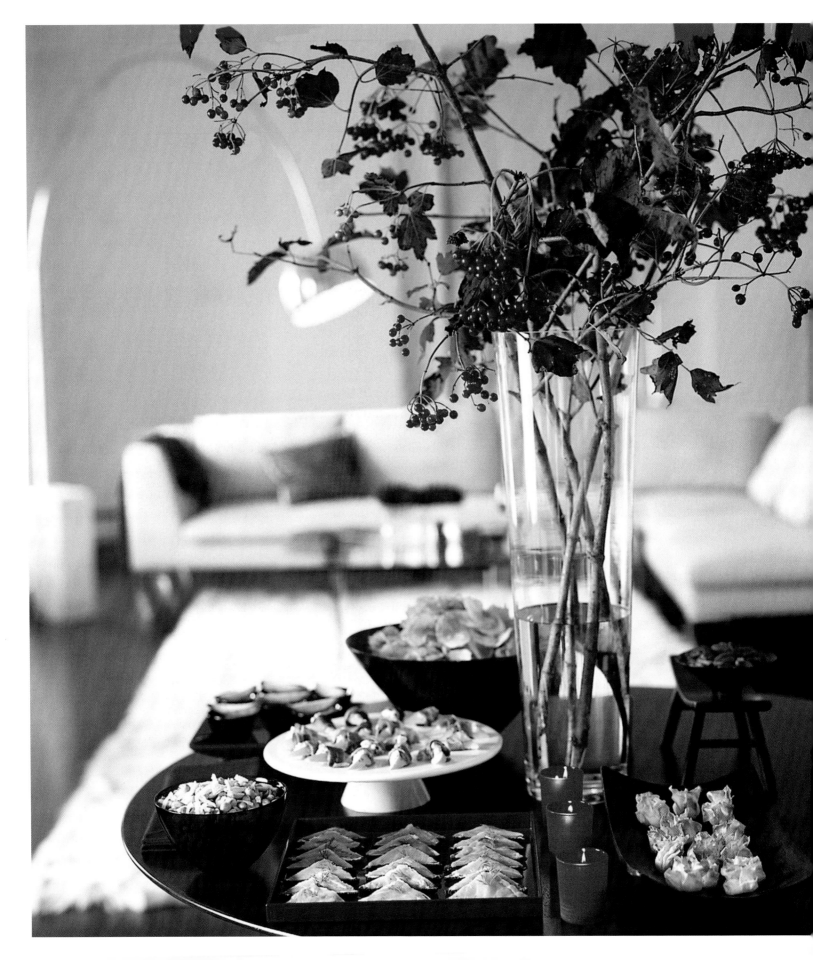

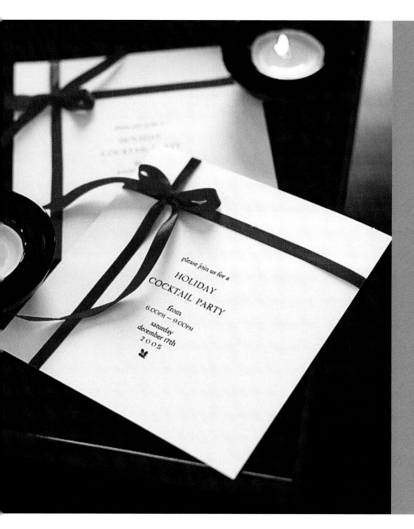

At an open house, where a large number of guests come and go over the span of four to six hours (usually from late afternoon into the evening), certain pointers come in particularly handy:

Stagger the party times. On invitations make half say 4 to 7 P.M., the other half 6 to 9 P.M. so everyone does not show up all at once.

Keep snacks simple. You can serve a few hot hors d'oeuvres if you're feeling ambitious, but supplement them with bowls of mixed smoked nuts, spiced popcorn and cheese platters.

Serve food buffet style. Use small serving platters and replenish them often, so food always looks and tastes fresh. Have plenty of glasses, plates and silverware.

Set aside extra space for coats and bags. Designate an entire bedroom or study, or rent a coatrack to place in the foyer.

the menu

Signature drink: Red apple martini
Hors d'oeuvres: Sweet potato soup shots, baked brie parcels, smoked salmon bites, prosciutto wraps, Parmesan popcorn, Cajun-spiced potato chips
Dessert bites: Assortment of holiday cookies, petits fours and candies

setting the scene

The invitation: Send a festive paper "present": Print or write party details on a square piece of white card stock. Tie a thin red satin or velvet ribbon in a crisscross around the "gift"; mail in a bright red envelope.

The décor: Create a clean, sophisticated combination of red, white and silver. Incorporate touches of high-shine black or red with a glossy lacquered tray or bowl. Arrange tall branches of winter berries in a cylindrical vase on the buffet table (use the dining room table, or a table set in the party area). Set up the bar on a long narrow table, such as a console or hall table, with access on all sides. Cluster different shades of red roses in low lacquered or silver boxes (to resemble gift boxes) and place them on the bar and on coffee and side tables. Scatter red votive candles on tables and windowsills. For areas not close to food, try candles scented with pine or mulling spices.

The menu: Set out snacks like popcorn and chips in small bowls or lacquered boxes (make popcorn special by tossing it with Parmesan and freshly ground pepper; sprinkle Cajun seasoning on chips). Place smoked salmon bites and prosciutto wraps on the buffet; either pass trays or set out small batches of hot hors d'oeuvres (like soup and baked brie parcels) and replenish as needed.

The music: Every major artist has recorded a holiday album, but our dream stocking would include classic carols by Bing Crosby. Other fun selections include the Brian Setzer Orchestra's *Boogie Woogie Christmas,* Ultra-Lounge's *Christmas Cocktails, The O.C. Mix 3: Have a Very Merry Chrismukkah,* and, for those who think they're just too cool for Christmas: *A Santa Cause—It's a Punk Rock Christmas.*

countdown

Three weeks: Mail invitations.
Two weeks: Buy candles, boxes, ribbon, liquor and all non-perishables. Order cookies and petits fours at the bakery.
One week: Buy music and wine.
Two days: Buy groceries and flowers. Buy candies at a gourmet shop.
Day before: Pick up holiday sweets at the bakery. Arrange and set out flowers. Make soup; cool, then refrigerate.
Morning of: Add spices to popcorn and potato chips. Assemble prosciutto wraps and salmon bites; chill. Chill white wine.
Four hours: Prep brie parcels (don't bake); cover and store at room temperature.
Two hours: Set up bar.
One hour: Crush candy canes for martini glasses. Mix pitchers of martinis; refrigerate.
30 minutes: Reheat soup and keep it on simmer. Set out other snacks. Light candles. Start music.
Party time: Bake batches of phyllo parcels; serve soup.
During party: Continue to serve soup (stir occasionally); heat and serve phyllo parcels. A few hours into the party, set out cookies, petits fours and candies.

even easier

Substitute ready-made pumpkin or sweet potato soup from a gourmet shop. Add a splash of sherry or white wine when reheating and top each cup with store-bought crostini and minced fresh parsley.
If you don't have dozens of sake cups on hand to serve the soup, use shot glasses or espresso cups. Ask a few friends to bring over extras.
Don't make the brie parcels. Set out a party-size brie *en croute* (a brie wheel wrapped in puff pastry and baked, available at gourmet stores) and have guests serve themselves.
Nix the prosciutto. Serve sliced pears with a creamy dip made from 1 pkg. of Boursin cheese mixed with 1 cup of sour cream.

more holiday party ideas

Typically, there are two prime Saturday evenings in December when everyone gives holiday parties. If those dates are already booked, try one of these alternatives:

Host a late-night dessert party. Along with sweet nibbles like cookies, chocolates and fresh berries, serve one big festive dessert such as a rich chocolate cake or traditional bûche de Noël. Serve sparkling wine, hot coffee and cocoa spiked with a splash of Kahlùa or Grand Marnier liqueur.
Throw a cocktail party during the week. Double up on hors d'oeuvres or serve a light buffet (roast a turkey breast or beef tenderloin, for instance); guests coming straight from work will be thrilled to see substantial snacks that can serve as a light dinner.
Take advantage of an unexpected party time. Throw a late-afternoon open house on the weekend and include children. Serve the same menu of cocktails and hors d'oeuvres but also offer a kid-friendly drink like cranberry juice mixed with lemon-lime soda, in kids glasses with the rims dipped in colorful sugar crystals.

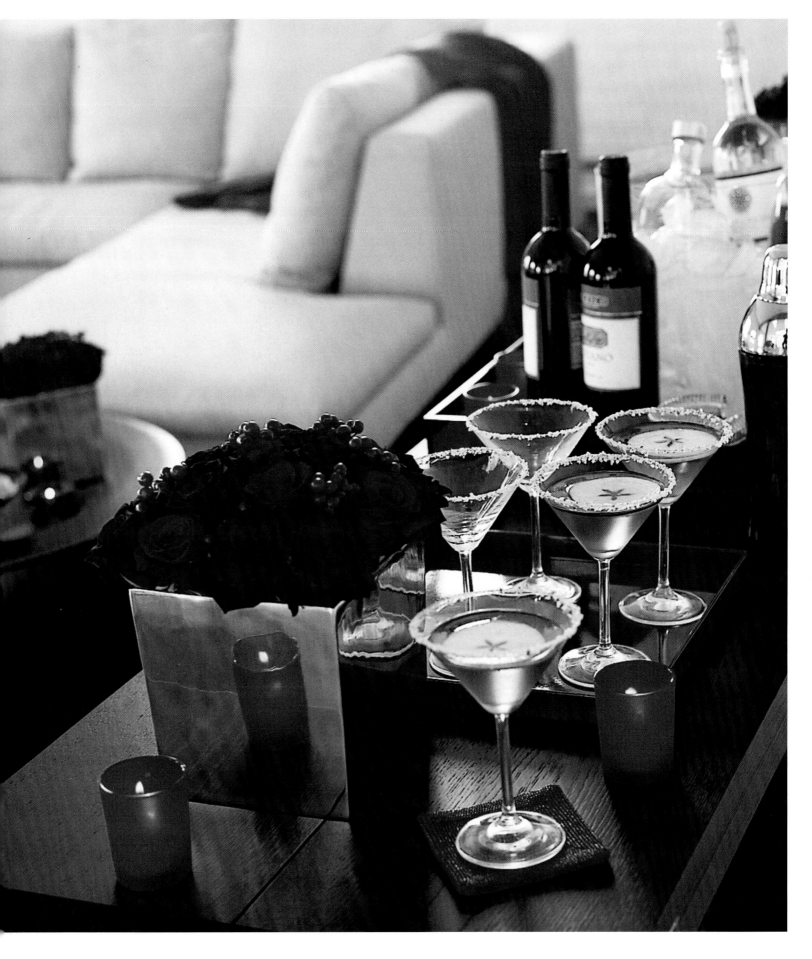

what to pour

Red apple martini (serves 20): Dip martini glass rims in a bowl of fresh lemon juice, then into a dish of finely crushed candy canes. Mix 5 cups vodka, 5 cups sour-apple schnapps and 7 cups apple juice; chill. When ready to serve, mix in an ice-filled shaker. Pour into glasses; garnish with very thin apple slices.

Wine picks: For a party this size, plan to serve 6 bottles each of red and white wine, but have more on hand. Reds: Penfold shiraz from Australia or a Guigal Côtes du Rhône from France. Whites: pinot grigio from Italy, from Venica or Livio Felluga. Stock a few bottles of sparkling wine as well; try Domaine Chandon, Napa Valley or Veuve Amiot from Saumur (the Loire Valley) or Roederer Estate brut from California.

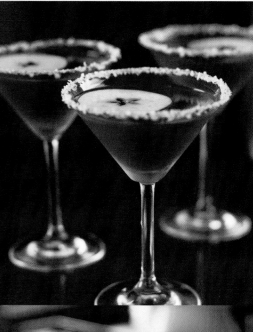

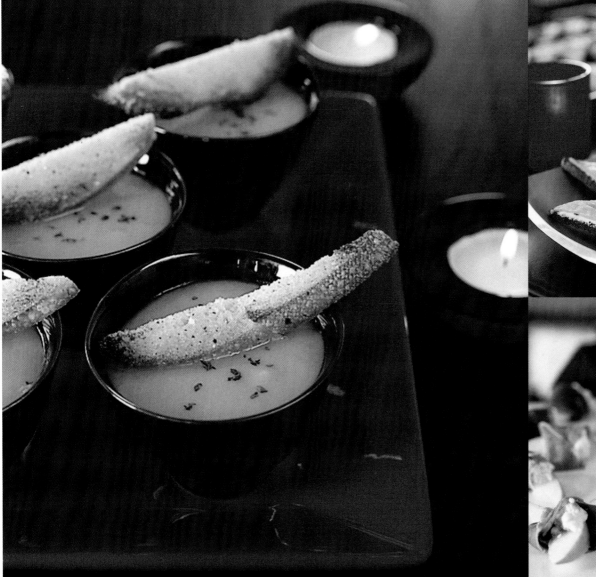

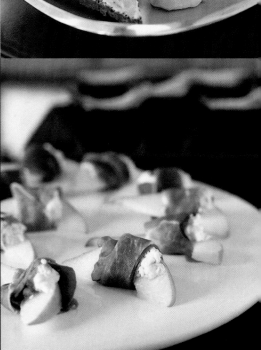

recipes

Sweet Potato Soup Shots
(Makes 40 4 oz. cups)
2 tbsp unsalted butter
1 large onion, chopped
2 cloves garlic, chopped
3½ lb. sweet potatoes, peeled and cubed
1½ lb. baking potatoes, peeled and cubed
2 containers (32 oz. each) chicken broth
1½ cups heavy cream
Salt and pepper to taste
Toasted baguette slices and minced
   fresh parsely for garnish

Melt butter in Dutch oven over medium heat. Add onion and garlic; cook 3–4 min. Add all potatoes, broth and 5 cups water. Bring to boil, reduce heat and simmer 25–30 min., or until tender. Let cool slightly, then, working in batches, purée soup in a blender. Return to heat. Stir in cream; heat through. Add salt and pepper; garnish with crostini and parsley.

Baked Brie Parcels
(Makes about 64 pieces)
1 pkg. (16 oz.) frozen phyllo pastry,
   thawed
⅔ cup unsalted butter, melted
1 lb. brie
1½ cups whole cranberry sauce

Heat oven to 400°F. Place 1 sheet phyllo on clean work surface; brush with butter. Top with another sheet; brush with butter. Repeat with 2 more sheets. Cut phyllo into 16 even squares. Scoop brie into small balls. Place 1 ball on square of phyllo; top with ½ tsp cranberry sauce. Bring up corners of pastry; twist to secure. Pinch edges together; place on baking sheet. Repeat. Bake 18–20 min., or until lightly golden.

Prosciutto Wraps
(Makes about 60 pieces)
⅓ lb. thinly sliced prosciutto, cut in
   long, narrow strips
6 ripe pears, washed, cored and sliced
   ½" thick (to prevent browning, gently
   turn pear slices in a bowl with juice of
   ½ lemon).
2 pkg. softened herb cheese (Boursin)
60 arugula leaves

Place 1 slice of prosciutto on work surface; top with pear slice, small dollop of cheese and arugula leaf. Wrap prosciutto around until secure.

Smoked Salmon Bites
(Makes 60 pieces)
30 slices cocktail pumpernickel bread,
   sliced in half on the diagonal
1 container (10 oz.) crème fraîche
⅓ lb. thinly sliced smoked salmon, cut
   into bite-size pieces
Dill sprigs for garnish

Spread crème fraîche in thin layer over each piece of bread. Top with smoked salmon and garnish with dill.

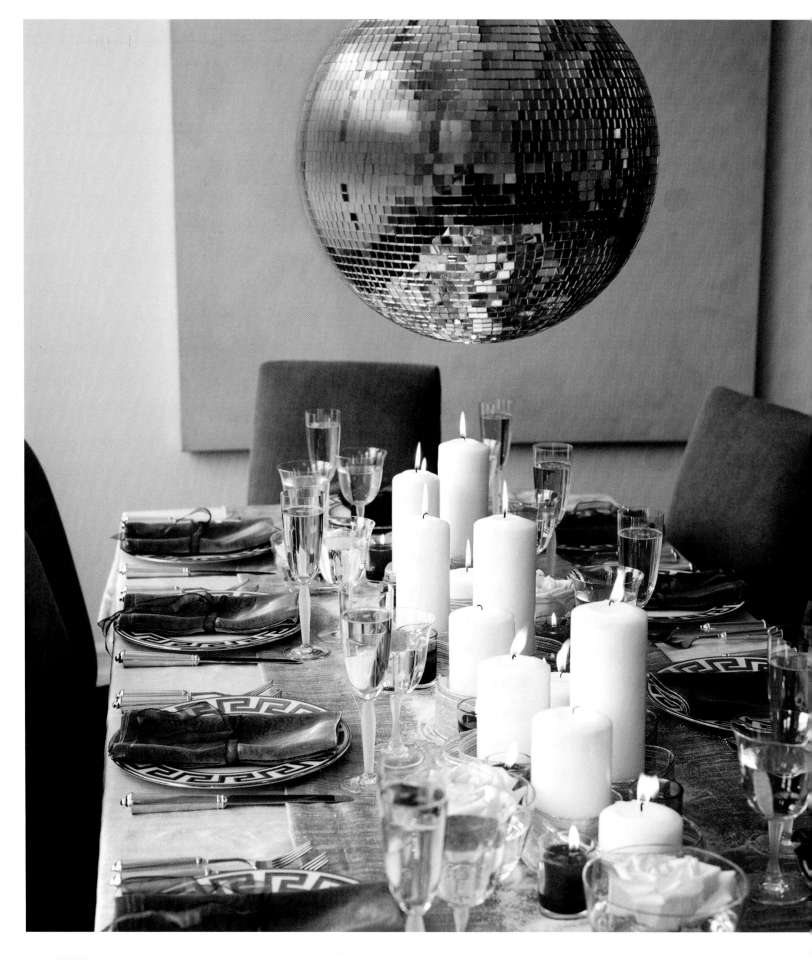

new year's eve supper

Everybody loves a bit of glamour and decadence on New Year's Eve. If painting the town red sounds more exhausting than fun, celebrate over a festive, hearty supper at home instead. Party planner Colin Cowie, who has pulled off stylish affairs for Tom Cruise, Jerry Seinfeld and Lisa Kudrow, put together this affair with one principle in mind: Creative presentation is more important than expensive ingredients. The best part? The whole meal, from the veal stew to the gooey chocolate dessert, can be prepared in a few hours (and much of it in advance), so you'll have plenty of energy to ring in the new year.

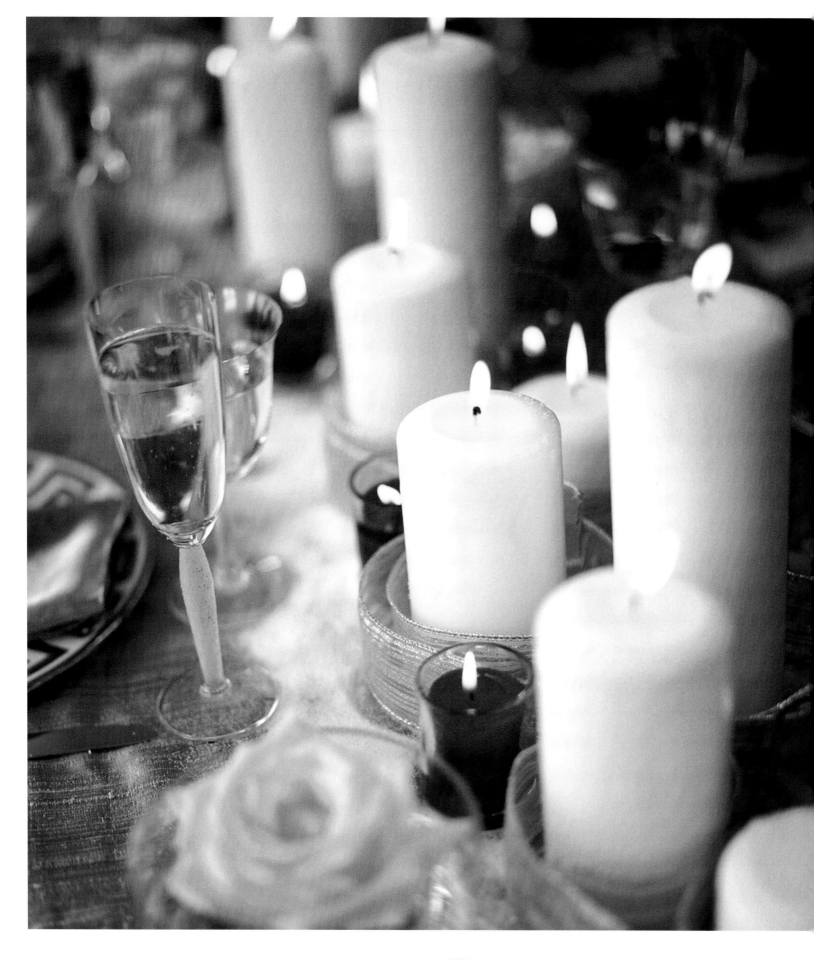

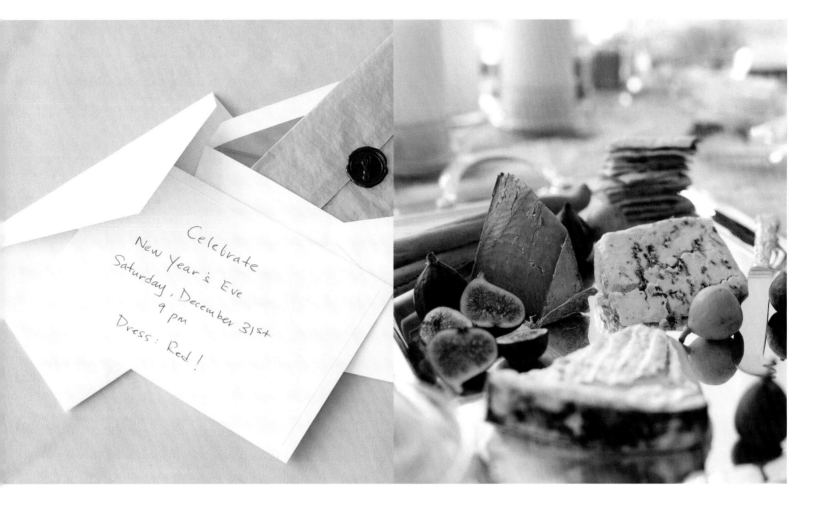

the menu

Signature drink: Champagne cocktail
Hors d'oeuvre: Shrimp cocktail ring
Salad: Endive salad served in coffee cups
Main course: Veal stew with baked spinach risotto
Cheese: Stilton, Camembert and cheddar wedges with flat-bread and fresh or dried figs, apples and pears
Dessert: Chocolate symphony

setting the scene

The invitation: Write in red ink on white cards; wrap them in silver tissue paper and close the tissue with red sealing wax (available at craft stores). For added glamour, Cowie suggests asking women to wear red. Invite guests for 9 P.M. Serve dinner at 10 P.M. and dessert at 11:15 P.M. to minimize lag time between the meal and the midnight festivities.

The tabletop: A silver cloth and platinum-accented white china set an elegant tone. Tie silver napkins with red ribbon. Down the center of the dining table, simulate snow by creating a "runner" of kosher salt; on top, set red votives and white pillars with silver ribbon running loosely around the candles (use double-sided tape to secure). Float white roses, stems removed, in shallow glass bowls.
The décor: Put a red lightbulb in your porch light. Inside, hang a disco mirror ball and set up a dance floor. Set up a bar to let guests make champagne cocktails or their own variations, by topping champagne with a splash of liqueur, like Chambord (raspberry), crème de cassis (currant), or Poire Williams (pear).
The music: It will always be fun to party like it's 1999. Prince provides a great soundtrack for any celebration. Ditto for Dee-lite and any disco—this is, after all, the one night of the year when even people who can't dance live it up like it's the grand reopening of Studio 54. Think disco box sets and greatest hits compilations from Abba, the Bee Gees, Donna Summer and KC and the Sunshine Band. A midnight medley of these bands is bound to inspire boogie woogie en masse.

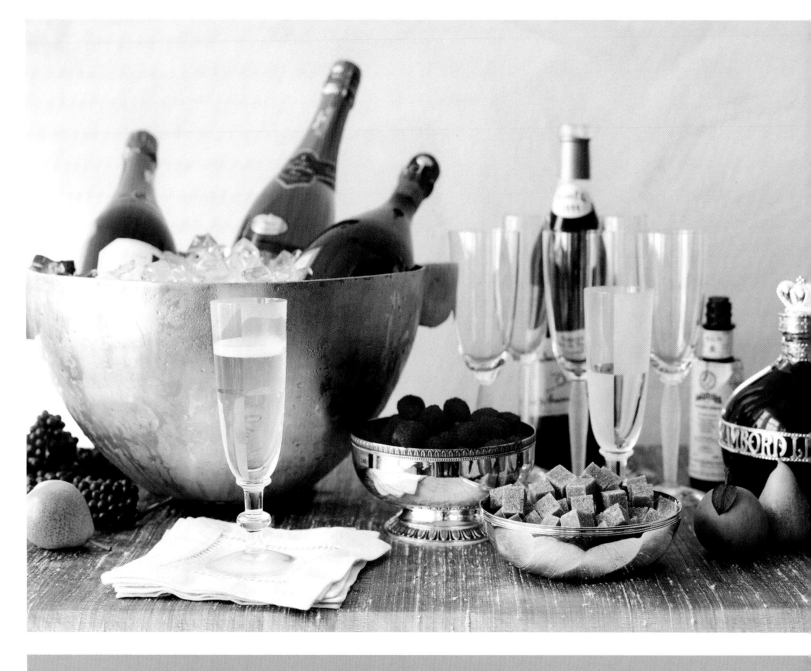

champagne essentials

From the moment guests arrive to the second the clock strikes midnight, follow these tips to keep the bubbly flowing.

If you want to splurge, buy French champagne such as Dom Perignon, Krug Grande Cuvée or Taittinger Comtes de Champagne (all at $100, but truly great). For moderately priced bottles try a sparkling wine such as Franciacorta from Italy or, from California, Schramsberg, Roederer Estate or Domaine Carneros. For a bargain, go with a sparkling crémant d'Alsace from Lucien Albrecht (France), Domaine Chandon Napa Valley or Mumm Napa blanc de blancs.

If you're mixing champagne into cocktails or punch, use sparkling wines under $15. Dry sparklers (bruts) work best with sweet liqueurs. **To chill a bottle,** place it in an ice bucket filled with equal parts ice and water for 25 min., or in the refrigerator for three to four hours. To open a bottle, remove the foil, place a napkin or dish towel on top and grip the cork. Ease it out while holding the bottom of the bottle with one hand. When pouring, hold the glass upright, pour a bit in and wait until the foam subsides, then top it off. **Count on** guests drinking two to four glasses of champagne in an hour (a bottle yields six glasses).

countdown

Three weeks: Send out invitations. Pick out something red to wear.

Two weeks: Buy music, candles, silver ribbon and any needed tabletop items.

One week: Shop for wines, liqueurs, cake ingredients and music.

Three days: Bake cake for dessert; wrap in foil and store in an airtight container.

Two days: Shop for groceries. Buy white roses.

Day before: Make veal stew; prepare vinaigrette. Boil shrimp, make sauce; refrigerate. Freeze ice ring for the shrimp cocktail and chill champagne. Set the table and create the centerpiece.

Morning of: Chill wine. Arrange flowers.

Five hours: Prepare risotto and set aside (do not bake). Cut cake into circles.

Three hours: Prep salad. Set up champagne bar; chill extra bottles on ice.

90 minutes: Go get glam—it's New Year's Eve!

30 minutes: Start music. Light candles. Dress salad and assemble in cups. Arrange shrimp and sauce on the ice ring.

During cocktails: Set up the cheese platter for later. Reheat veal stew on the stove; bake risotto.

During cheese course: Assemble dessert.

even easier

Can't get to the fish market? Buy cleaned, precooked shrimp for the cocktail ring. Bottled cocktail sauce is fine, but rev it up with extra horseradish and fresh lemon juice.

Instead of making the risotto, mix cooked orzo with chopped sautéed spinach and fresh grated Parmesan.

Don't bother baking. Buy a chocolate cake and pour chocolate or fudge sauce over it for dessert.

caviar wishes

To turn a special night into an unforgettable one, kick off the evening with caviar. Serve it on ready-made mini blinis (sold at many shops that stock caviar), toast points, melba rounds or in hollowed-out boiled new potatoes with a small dollop of crème fraîche. High-quality caviar doesn't require any other enhancement, but if you're serving a more affordable variation, you can complement the flavor by serving finely chopped red onion and chopped egg as condiments. Here's what you need to know:

What to buy: Beluga, osetra, and sevruga caviars, which all come from sturgeon, are considered the best caviars in the world and can cost up to several thousands of dollars a pound. The most expensive caviars come from Russia and Iran. Luckily, North American varieties are far more affordable (they cost a fraction of the price of Russian or Iranian caviar), are accessible and perfectly delicious. The most popular varieties are American sturgeon, lake sturgeon and Hackleback Sturgeon caviar (they're black in color) and salmon roe (red).

How much to buy: You'll need about ½ tsp per hors d'oeuvre; 1 oz. of caviar will make eight to 10 servings. If your guests are caviar fanatics who prefer to eat it by the spoonful, buy (much) more.

How to store it: Fresh caviar is considered the most delicious, classic kind; it's sweet, nutty, juicy, not at all fishy, and "pops" on the tongue. Pasteurized caviar, which is heated and then vacuum-packed, tastes less fresh and may be harder. Unopened fresh caviar can be stored in a refrigerator for up to six months, and unopened pasteurized caviar can be stored in the pantry for six months (and should be chilled before you serve it). Cover and refrigerate any leftovers promptly and eat them within a day or two. If caviar is left in the jar or tin, the surface should be smoothed and a sheet of plastic wrap should be pressed directly onto the surface before placing it back in the refrigerator. Never freeze caviar; it toughens the eggs and changes the flavors.

How to serve it: Gently lift and spread caviar with a spoon made from bone, tortoiseshell or mother-of-pearl (a metal spoon can impart a metallic taste). Caviar goes best with frozen vodka, champagne or sparkling wine.

what to pour

Champagne cocktail (serves 1): Drop a sugar cube in a champagne glass. Sprinkle with 1–2 dashes of bitters. Top with cold, dry champagne; a lemon twist garnish is optional.

Wine picks: With dinner, serve champagne with salad, then red wine for the main and cheese courses. Try a pinot noir from California (Chalone, Saintsbury or Au Bon Climat) to go with the delicate veal; count on 4 bottles for 12 guests. Return to champagne for dessert and the midnight toast.

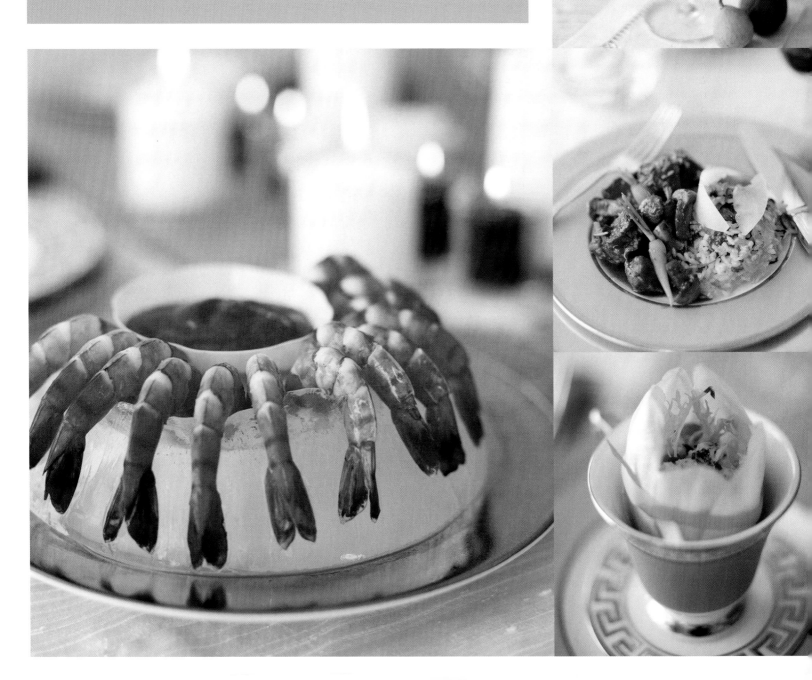

recipes

Shrimp Cocktail Ring

(Serves 12)

3 lb. jumbo shrimp, peeled and deveined (with tails intact)
2 cups ketchup
⅓–¼ cup prepared horseradish
2 tbsp fresh lemon juice
1½ tsp Worcestershire sauce

Fill 5½-cup ring mold with water; freeze overnight. In large pot boil salted water. Reduce heat to low and add shrimp. Cook until pink, 4–5 min. Drain; refrigerate. Turn mold upside down and quickly run it under hot water. Invert onto platter; return to freezer for 2 hrs. When ready to serve, put a bowl of cocktail sauce (a mixture of remaining ingredients) into the center of the mold and place shrimp over the edges.

Endive Salad

(Serves 12)

¼ cup red wine vinegar
2 tbsp grainy mustard
¾ cup grapeseed oil
¼ cup walnut oil
Salt and pepper to taste
6 large heads endive
1 large leek, green part only
2 bunches watercress, washed and trimmed
2 heads frisée, washed
⅔ cup pine nuts, toasted
6 oz. goat cheese

In small bowl combine vinegar and mustard. Slowly whisk in grapeseed and walnut oils; season with salt and pepper. Peel 8 leaves from each endive; set aside. Slice leek greens into 12 long strips; blanch. Slice remaining endive; mix with watercress, frisée, pine nuts and goat cheese; toss with dressing. To assemble: Cut 4 endive leaves to fit into cup, fill each with salad, and tie with leek strip.

Veal Stew

(Serves 12)

6 sprigs fresh thyme
3 sprigs fresh rosemary
3 lb. veal stew meat, cut into 1½ " pieces
Salt and pepper to taste
½ cup all-purpose flour
6 tbsp olive oil, divided
3 tbsp butter, divided
1 large onion, chopped
1 lb. baby carrots, peeled
3 cans (10 oz. each) chicken broth
1 cup dry white wine
2 tbsp tomato paste
1 pkg. (10 oz.) white mushrooms, halved if large
¼ cup chopped flat-leaf parsley
1 tbsp grated lemon peel

Wrap herb sprigs in cheesecloth; tie with cotton twine. Season veal with salt and pepper. Pour flour in large resealable plastic bag, add veal and shake to coat. Remove veal and shake off excess oil. Heat 2 tbsp oil and 1 tbsp butter in 8 qt. Dutch oven over medium-high heat. Working in batches, brown meat, adding oil and butter as needed. Reduce heat to medium. Add onion; cook 3 min., stirring, until almost tender. Add carrots, broth, wine, tomato paste and bouquet garni (herbs). Return veal to Dutch oven; heat to boil. Reduce heat to low; cover and simmer 40 min. or until veal is fork-tender, stirring occasionally. Add mushrooms; simmer 10 min. Remove bouquet garni. Stir in parsley and lemon peel. Serve hot.

Baked Spinach Risotto

(Serves 12)

2 tbsp olive oil
1 large onion, chopped
2¼ cups Arborio rice
1½ cups white wine
4½ cups vegetable broth
1 bag (6 oz.) fresh spinach, cleaned and trimmed
½ cup grated Parmesan cheese, divided
1 tsp salt
¼ tsp pepper

Heat oven to 375ºF. Heat oil in large saucepan over medium-high heat. Add onions; cook until soft, about 5 min. Add rice; stir to coat; cook 2 min. Stir in wine; cook until most is absorbed. Stir in broth; bring to boil. Reduce heat to low; simmer 6–8 min. Stir in spinach, ¼ cup Parmesan, salt and pepper. Spoon into 13" x 9" glass baking dish. Sprinkle with remaining cheese. Cover with foil; bake 30 min.

Chocolate Symphony

(Serves 12)

2 tbsp Dutch processed cocoa
⅛ tsp salt
1 cup whole blanched almonds
1 pkg. (6 oz.) semisweet chocolate morsels
2½ sticks unsalted butter, at room temperature
1 cup sugar
3 eggs
1 cup all-purpose flour
2 pints chocolate sorbet
12 chocolate truffles
⅓–½ cup prepared chocolate sauce

Heat oven to 350ºF. Heat ½ cup water to simmering. Stir in cocoa and salt; let cool slightly. Grease 10" springform pan. Grind almonds and chocolate separately in food processor; set aside. In a large bowl cream butter and sugar until soft and light. Add eggs one at a time, beating well after each addition. Stir in almonds and chocolate. Beat in flour. Add cocoa mixture; stir well. Pour into prepared pan; bake 35–45 min., until inserted wooden toothpick comes out clean. Cool in pan on rack 1 hr. Remove cake from pan; cool on rack 1 hr. more. With 2½" cookie cutter, cut 12 circles from cake. To serve, place each on a dessert plate; top with a small scoop of sorbet and a truffle, and drizzle with chocolate sauce.

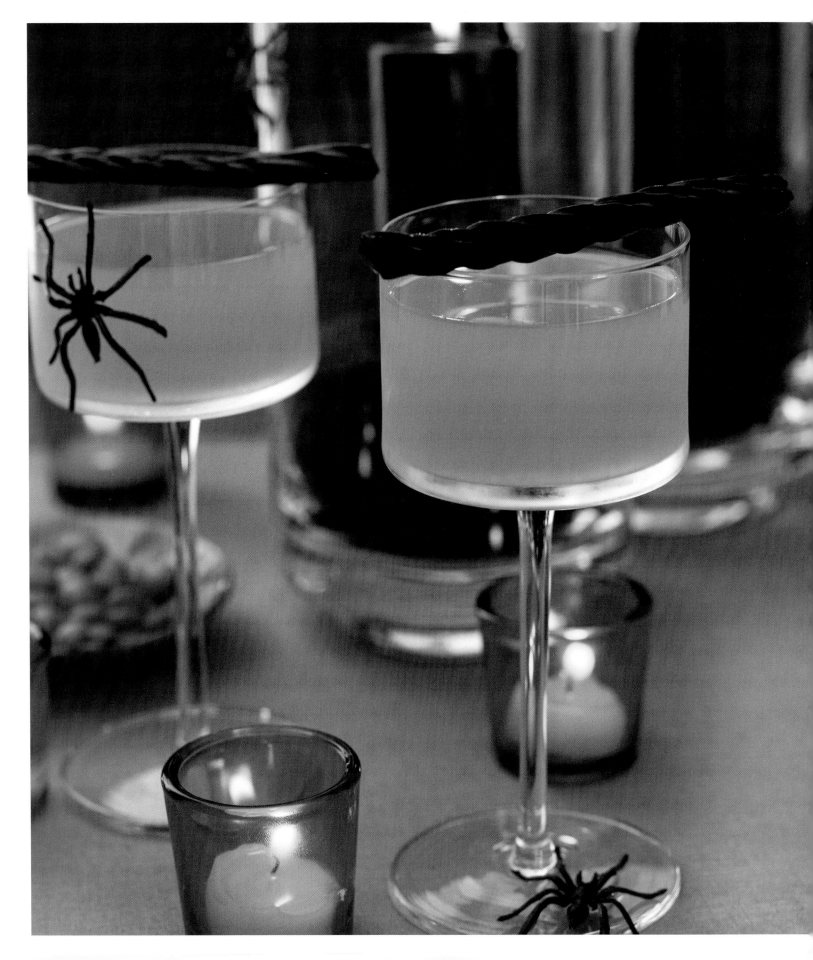

halloween
cocktail buffet

Don't let the junior set have all the fun on All Hallow's Eve. Grown-ups should have a wicked good time too. With that in mind, New York City event planner Bronson van Wyck, whose clients include Madonna and Sean Combs, skips the tricks and goes straight for the treats with a sophisticated party for 20. As a macabre twist on the usual costume attire, why not ask guests to come in the outfit they'd like to be buried in? Then strategically scatter some rubber spiders and snakes and serve up orange satin cosmos and a devilishly tasty buffet. Guests will be positively bewitched.

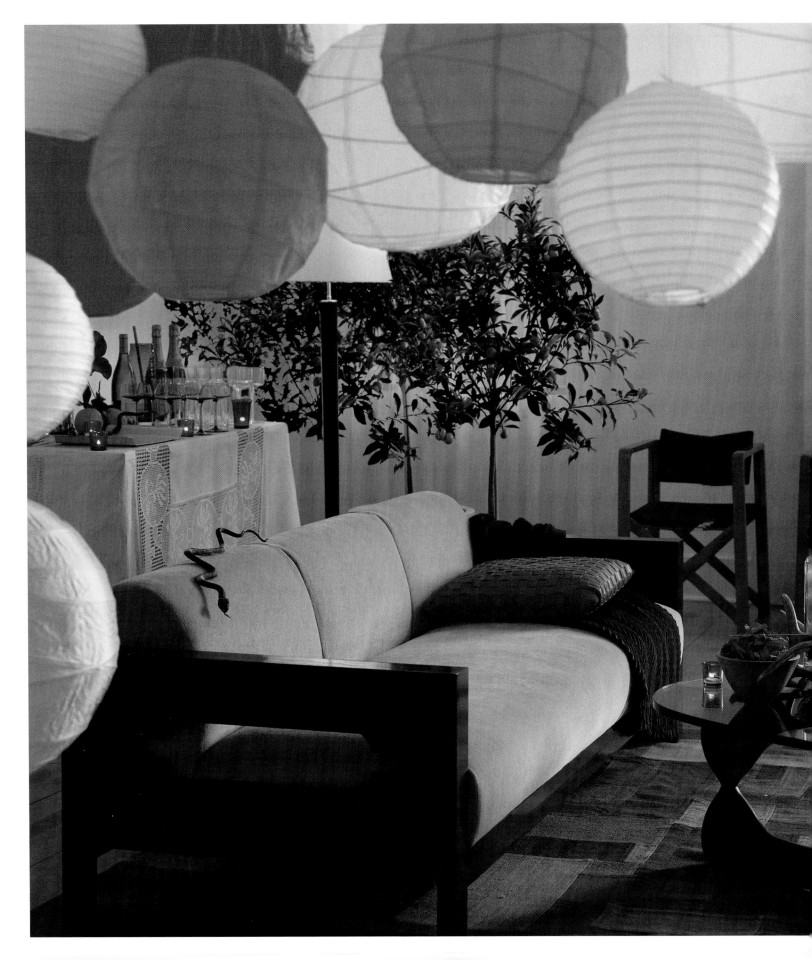

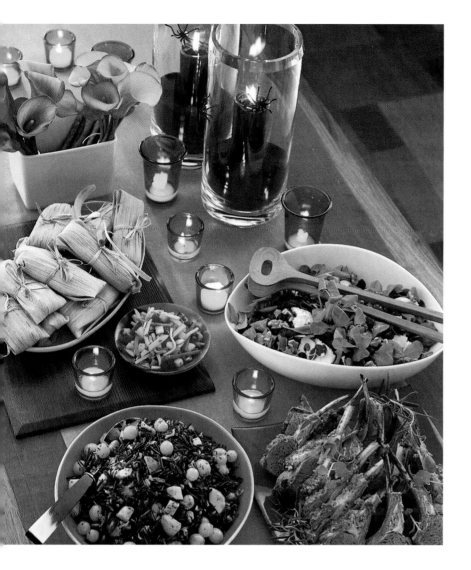

the menu

Signature drink: Orange satin cosmo
Snacks: Toasted orange pecans, black and orange caviar toasts, sweet potato chips
Cocktail buffet: Mustard-crusted mini lamb chops, tamales with mango-squash salsa, autumn mâche salad, wild rice with almonds, artichokes and grapes
Dessert: Mini carrot cupcakes and candy (of course)

setting the scene

The décor: Honor the holiday with an orange palette. Near the front door, create a lantern "garden" to welcome guests by dangling paper lanterns on fishing line at multiple levels. Design a core seating area; clear away unnecessary furniture. Make bouquets of rust- and mango-colored calla lilies; tie the stems with raffia and stand in vases just a bit shorter than the bouquet. Attach plastic spiders to hurricanes filled with black sand and black pillar candles, and scatter orange votive holders.

The menu: Set out bowls of chocolate espresso beans, orange M&M's, candied mango, orange pecans, sweet potato chips and a tray of toast points with crème fraîche and black and red (which is orangeish in color) caviar. Set up a self-serve bar. The buffet menu includes ready-made tamales; guests can simply untie the husks and eat the filling topped with mango-squash salsa. Mini lamb chops, wild rice and an autumn salad are also easy to eat (no knife required).

The music: How to inspire a spooky spirit faster than you can say boo? Michael Jackson's classic *Thriller* CD is still bound to get everyone moonwalking in the moonlight. Other haunting acts such as Siouxsie & the Banshees, the Cramps and Bauhaus (their greatest hit was titled "Bela Lugosi's Dead") will get guests into a gothic groove. Or download songs that are both chilling and very cool: "The Monster Mash," Nina Simone's "I Put a Spell on You" and Dusty Springfield's "Spooky."

countdown

Three weeks: Send invitations.
Two weeks: Order tamales if desired (see Resources). Buy black sand (from a pet store's aquarium section) for the hurricanes. Buy or order paper lanterns (see Resources).
Ten days: Buy black candles at a craft or candle store, buy rubber spiders and snakes at a toy store (to mail-order, see Resources). Buy candy and liquor.
One week: Buy wine and music.
Two days: Buy groceries.
Day before: Buy flowers. Bake orange pecans (and cupcakes if you're making them yourself).
Night before: Rearrange your living room for optimum mingling, hang the paper lantern "garden," and set up the buffet table. Prep cheese for the salad.
Morning of: Refrigerate wine. Arrange flowers.
Four hours: Make salsa. Make two batches of cocktails without ice (add at the last minute); chill. Stock bar.
Three hours: Prep lamb (don't cook) and salad ingredients (don't mix); refrigerate.
Two hours: Make rice; keep warm, covered on the stove.

One hour: Remove goat cheese discs from the refrigerator. Assemble the salad but don't dress it.
30 minutes: Steam tamales, spread caviar on toast points. Roast racks of lamb.
20 minutes: Set out bowls of candies, sweet potato chips and orange pecans, and trays of caviar toasts. Light candles. Start music. Carve lamb.
After guests arrive: Dress salad and set up the buffet an hour into the party. Later, serve cupcakes.

even easier

Instead of bouquets of calla lilies, tie tight bunches of orange tea roses with raffia and stand them in low clear glass vases.
Rather than making the orange pecans, toss ready-made spicy mixed nuts with finely chopped orange zest.
Don't bake the cupcakes. Buy carrot mini-muffins and top them with cream cheese frosting (and fake spiders).
Instead of making homemade salsa, spike a store-bought brand with fresh diced mango.

setting up the bar and buffet

Create a self-serve bar so guests can help themselves. Set out cocktail napkins, 40 glasses (2 per person), a pitcher of signature cocktails and 10 lbs. of ice. Refrigerate extra batches of cosmos and stash additional wine and ice in a cooler under the bar. Decorate the bar and buffet with calla lily bouquets and votives; if you have a big buffet table, van Wyck suggests visually anchoring it with a copper urn or tall clear vase filled with fall branches. Stock the buffet with 40 small plates, forks and napkins; have extras ready to go in the kitchen.
To restock the buffet: Keep lamb chops in foil in a warm oven and tamales in a steamer on the stove (have an extra bowl of salsa on deck too). Place rice in a covered pot in a pan of water on a warm stove burner. Store extra salad in the fridge, covered with a damp paper towel; add cranberries, goat cheese discs, walnuts and dressing right before serving.

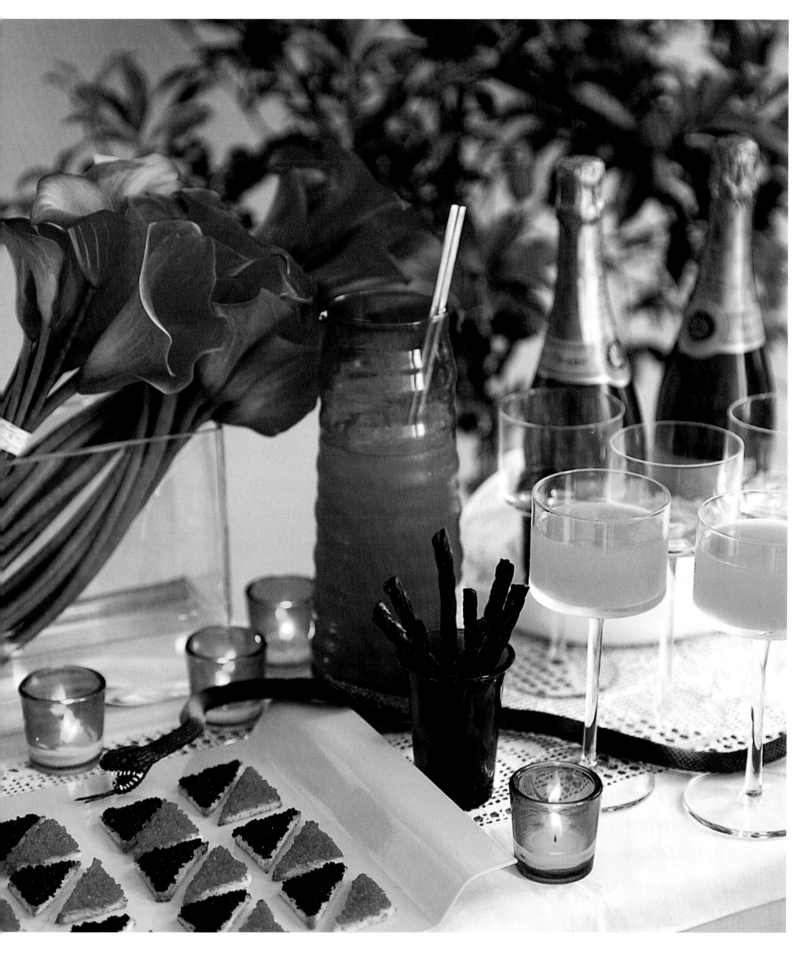

what to pour

Orange satin cosmo (serves 20): In large ice-filled pitcher stir together 8 cups vodka, 2½ cups mango juice, 2½ cups Cointreau or triple sec, 1¼ cup fresh lime juice and 7 tbsp superfine sugar. Mix well and strain into cocktail glasses. Garnish with black licorice sticks.

Wine picks: Pour crowd-pleasing, affordable chardonnays such as Acacia, Hess Select, Mt. Eden and Marimar Torres from California. For reds, Italian Barbera from Icardi or Clerico in Piedmont, Penfolds or Rosemount shiraz-cabernet from Australia.

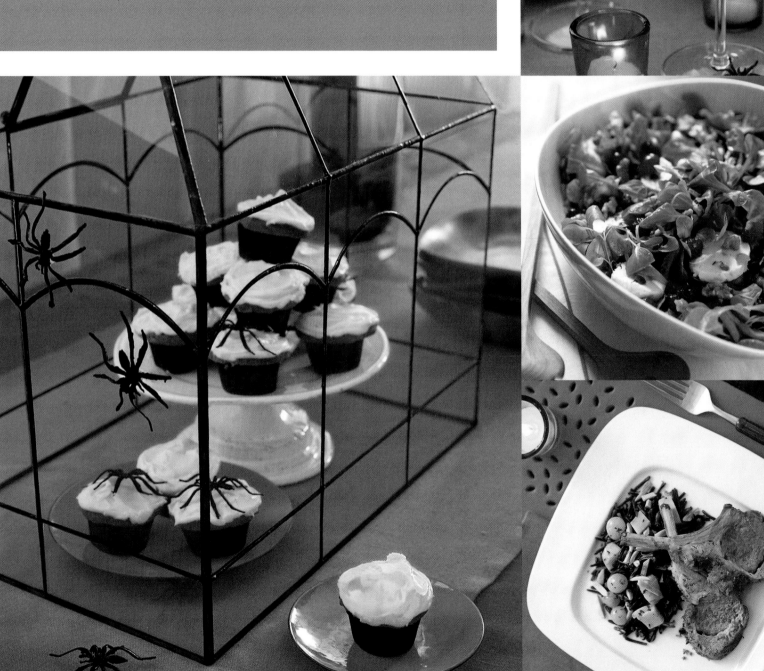

recipes

Toasted Orange Pecans
(Makes 8 cups)
3 cups sugar
1 cup fresh orange juice
2 tbsp orange zest
8 cups toasted pecan halves

Line 2 baking sheets with foil. In saucepan bring sugar, juice and zest to boil, while stirring. Boil 1 min. Remove from heat. Stir in pecans; pour onto baking sheets. Let stand until firm. To serve, break into pieces.

Mango-Squash Salsa
(Makes 5 cups)
3 yellow squash, julienned
2 medium ripe tomatoes, diced
1 large ripe mango, peeled and diced
½ cup diced red onion
½ cup julienned carrot
½ cup diced yellow pepper
½ cup minced cilantro
¼ cup olive oil
¼ cup fresh lime juice
1 jalapeño, seeded and minced
Salt and pepper to taste

In medium bowl combine all ingredients. Cover with plastic wrap; refrigerate.

Autumn Mâche Salad
(Serves 20)
2 cylinders (11 oz. each) goat cheese
⅓ cup olive oil
2 tbsp chopped fresh thyme
16 oz. fresh or frozen cranberries
1 cup fresh orange juice
1 cup light brown sugar
½ cup each cider vinegar and red wine vinegar
2 cloves garlic, minced
1 tbsp Dijon mustard
1 cup canola oil
Salt and pepper to taste
20 cups mâche (lamb's lettuce) or other greens, cleaned
1½ cups toasted walnuts

Slice goat cheese into 20 disks; place on baking sheet. Sprinkle with oil and thyme. Cover with plastic wrap; refrigerate overnight (bring to room temperature before serving). Place cranberries, juice, sugar and cider vinegar in saucepan; bring to boil. Reduce heat; simmer 15 min. Let cool. With slotted spoon remove berries and set aside. Add red wine vinegar, garlic and mustard to liquid. Whisk in canola oil and salt and pepper. To serve, place mâche in serving bowl, then top with cheese, cranberries and walnuts. Drizzle with dressing.

Mustard-Crusted Mini Lamb Chops
(Serves 20)
5 cups fresh bread crumbs
½ cup mixed chopped parsley, thyme and oregano
5 large cloves of garlic, minced
10 racks (6–7 bones in each) baby lamb chops, trimmed
Salt and pepper to taste
5 tbsp olive oil, divided
5 tbsp unsalted butter, divided
10 tbsp Dijon mustard

Heat oven to 450°F. In bowl combine bread crumbs, herbs and garlic. Season lamb with salt and pepper. Heat 1 tbsp oil and 1 tbsp butter in skillet over medium-high heat. Working in batches (add oil and butter as necessary) sear racks on all sides; let sit 4–5 min. Spread 1 tbsp mustard on each; press bread crumb coating over meaty side of lamb. Roast on baking sheet 15–18 min. for medium-rare. Let sit 5–10 min. before carving.

Wild Rice with Almonds, Artichokes and Grapes
(Serves 20)
10 tbsp unsalted butter, divided
4½ cups wild rice
6¾ cups chicken broth
3 cans (14 oz. each) artichoke hearts, drained and diced
3 cups small, seedless green grapes
1½ cups toasted slivered almonds
Salt and pepper to taste

In large skillet melt 5 tbsp butter over medium-high heat. Add rice; toss to coat. Add broth; increase heat and bring to boil. Reduce heat; simmer, covered, 50 min., or until rice is cooked through and liquid is gone. Meanwhile heat remaining butter in separate large skillet over medium-high heat. Add artichokes and grapes; sauté until hot. Add to rice along with almonds. Season with salt and pepper; stir well.

Mini Carrot Cupcakes
(Makes 12 cupcakes)
2 oz. white chocolate
1 pkg. cream cheese, softened
½ cup unsalted butter, softened
2 tsp vanilla extract, divided
½ tsp orange extract
4 cups confectioners' sugar
2 tbsp heavy cream
2 eggs, lightly beaten
1⅛ cups white sugar
⅓ cup brown sugar
½ cup vegetable oil
2 cups shredded carrots
½ cup crushed pineapple
1½ cups all-purpose flour
1¼ tsp baking soda
½ tsp salt
1½ tsp ground cinnamon
½ tsp ground nutmeg
¼ tsp ground ginger

Heat oven to 350°F. In small saucepan melt white chocolate over low heat. Stir until smooth; cool to room temperature. In bowl beat together cream cheese and butter. Mix in white chocolate, 1 tsp vanilla extract and all orange extract. Gradually beat in confectioners' sugar. Mix in heavy cream. In large bowl, beat together eggs and sugar and mix in oil and 1 tsp vanilla. Fold in carrots and pineapple. In separate bowl mix flour, baking soda, salt, cinnamon, nutmeg and ginger. Mix flour mixture into carrot mixture. Transfer to greased muffin cups and bake 25 min. Cool completely before topping with icing. Garnish with plastic spiders.

Actress Selma Blair at the annual Children's Action Network benefit, hosted by Carrie Fisher at her Spanish-style hacienda in Los Angeles.

occasions and theme parties

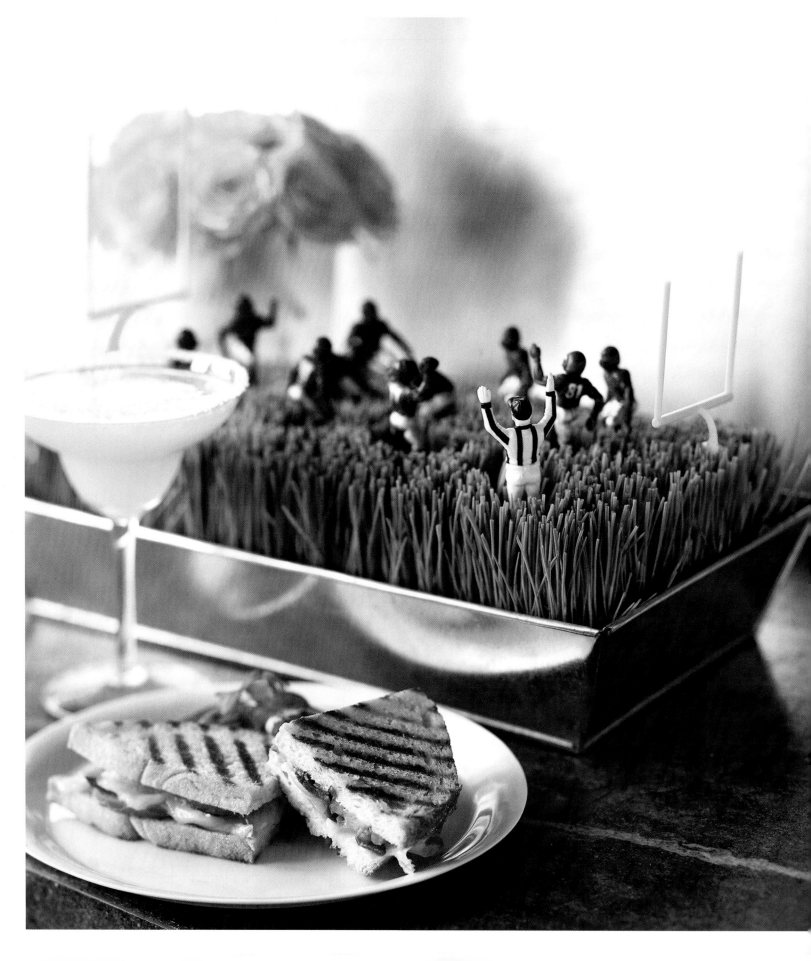

super bowl party

Want your Super Bowl party to rival a Tom Brady Hail Mary pass for excitement? Deep-six the six-foot subs and follow the playbook of Los Angeles event planner Marianne Weiman-Nelson of Special Occasions. She has concocted a **fool-proof bash** bursting with team spirit, **pregame munchies** and a lively **South-western buffet**. Die-hard fans can join a football pool, and guests who can't tell a tackle from a tight end will cheer for the half-time **sundae bar**. And thanks to these easy decorating ideas and recipes, you'll be relaxing with a cold beer well before kickoff.

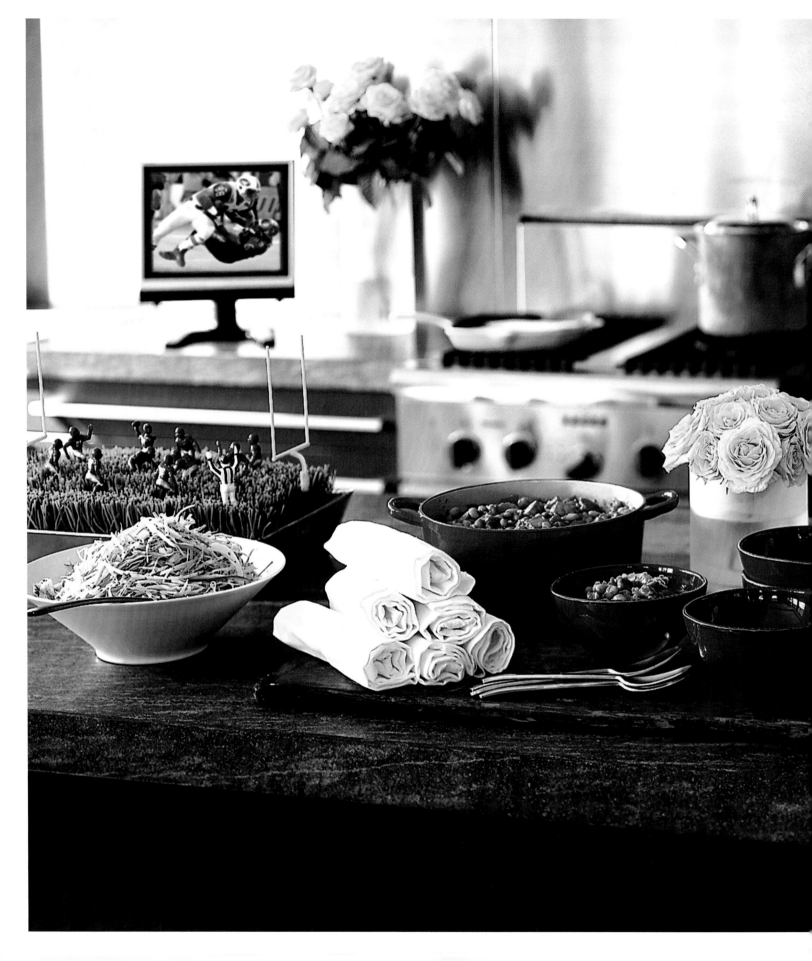

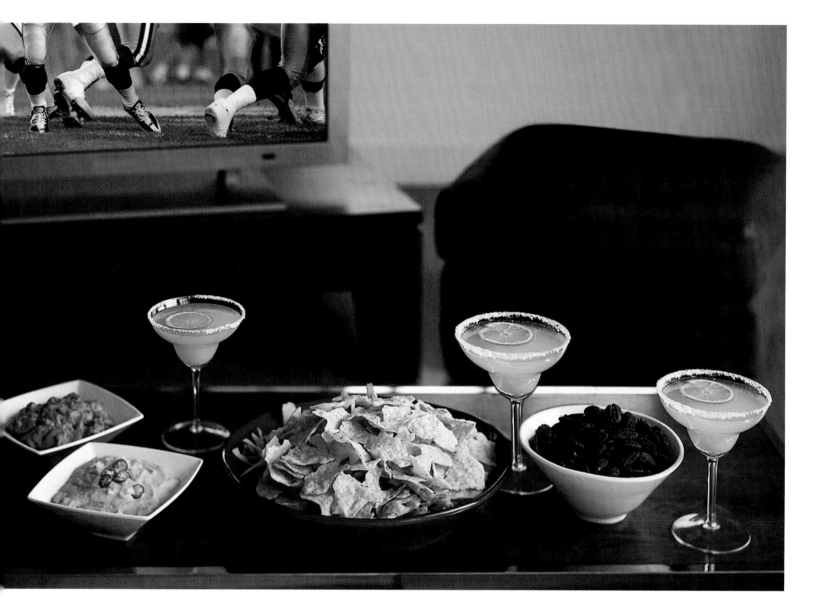

the menu

Signature drink: The kickoff
Hors d'oeuvres: Sugar-and-spice pecans, tortilla chips with jalapeño-bean dip, salsa and guacamole
Buffet: Panini with chorizo green chile and cheese, chili with turkey and white beans, jicama-citrus slaw
Dessert: Ice cream sundaes with chocolate-butterscotch bars

setting the scene

The invitation: Write on card stock glued to the back of mini football pennants representing the teams playing in the big game (available at sporting goods stores or from Wincraft

Sports; see Resources). Check nfl.com for kickoff time, and start your party an hour beforehand.
The décor: A kitchen buffet setup lets you concentrate on the game along with your guests; place dishes on a counter, island or table, and have a small television tuned into the game so nobody misses a crucial play. Transform flats of wheatgrass (available from florists for about $20) into playing fields with miniature plastic football players and goalposts (available at Kaskey Kids; see Resources). Add a floral grace note with cheerful yellow or orange roses bunched in simple frosted-glass vases. Set out a tray of football novelty candies (available at Dylan's Candy Bar; see Resources) as favors.
The menu: Guests can help themselves to turkey chili, chorizo-chili panini and jicama slaw. At halftime set up the ice cream sundae bar.

countdown

Three weeks: Send invites.
Two weeks: Order pennants for invitations.
One week: Order roses and wheatgrass flats from your florist. Buy wine.
Three days: Buy beer and nonperishables.
Two days: Buy groceries and make chocolate-butterscotch bars.
One day: Make chili, jicama slaw and pecans. Pick up roses and wheatgrass.
Morning of: Prepare ingredients for panini. Chill beer and white wine. Prep jalapeño-bean dip but do not bake.
Four hours: Arrange roses. Set up a separate bar area.
One hour: Make two batches of kickoff cocktails in pitchers; refrigerate them until guests arrive.
15 minutes: Bake dip and set it out with chips, salsa and guacamole. If you're using a baby keg, tap it now.
Party time: Set up the kitchen buffet and turn on the TVs.
During halftime: Set up the sundae bar. Put out a tray of party favors.

even easier

Speed up the spiced nuts with this quick recipe: Add ¼ cup brown sugar and 1 tsp cayenne pepper to an 8 oz. package of peanuts; bake them for 15 min. at 400ºF until they're lightly browned.

Buy smoked turkey breast or rotisserie chicken for the chili, or get takeout chili from a Tex-Mex restaurant.

Instead of making the sandwiches yourself, buy a platter of preassembled gourmet deli sandwiches (make sure they're not too thick) and grill those.

In place of sundaes, serve pies from a bakery with vanilla ice cream at halftime. Instead of homemade chocolate-butterscotch bars, serve a plate full of old-school favorites like Oreos, Nutter Butters and Chips Ahoy (don't worry: The crowd will still go wild).

for your viewing pleasure

Just because your eyes glaze over when you see a packed football stadium on TV doesn't mean you can't learn to love the game. A straightforward book such as *Football for Dummies* (amazon.com) is a handy guide for anyone who can't get past the coin toss. Once you know the rules and become familiar with the players, the sport will be far more interesting—really!

Up the ante at your party. Organize a football pool and have guests chip in a dollar (or more, if you've invited a bunch of gamblers).

Don't forget that the commercials can be as entertaining (if not more so, for some) than the football game. Keep the volume up during the breaks.

a panini primer

Paninis, or hot, pressed sandwiches, are a snap to make at home.

Weiman-Nelson uses a Krups panini press, but a George Foreman grill yields similar results, as will a handled iron weight, sold at cooking supply stores, used to "press" the panini as it cooks in a pan. Most presses have nonstick surfaces, so no oil is needed, but it's a good idea to spritz bread with olive oil spray or brush with butter before cooking for extra crispiness. Don't stick a hoagie in a panini press; a thinner sandwich with fewer layers cooks best. On average, panini cook in 2 or 3 min., depending on thickness.

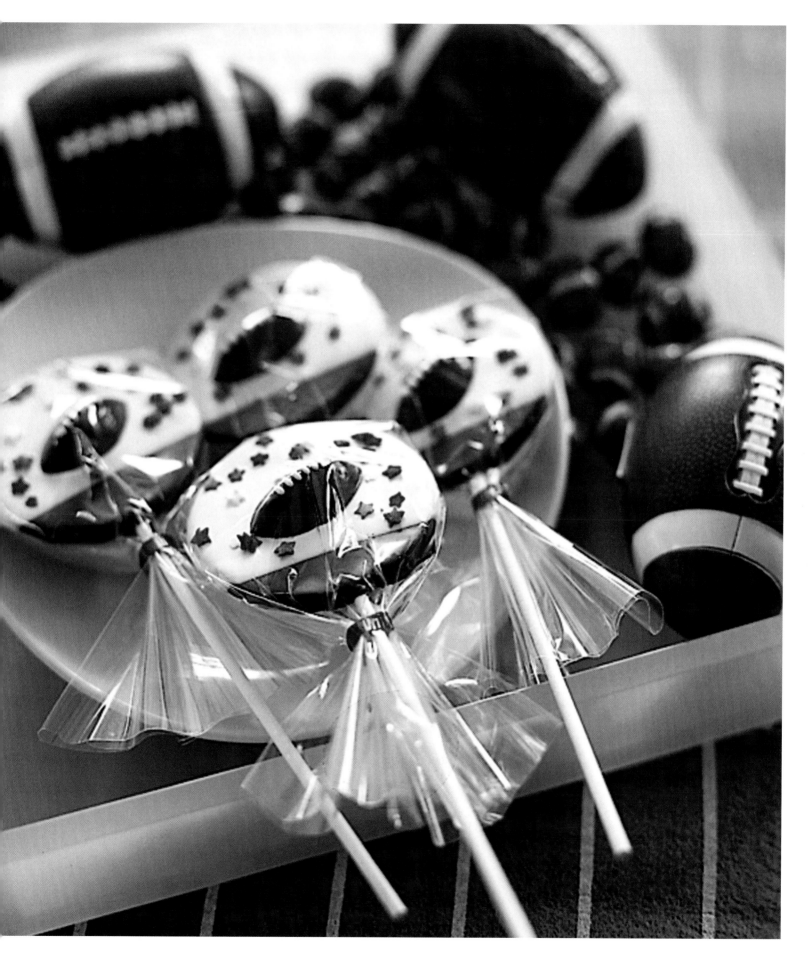

what to pour

The kickoff (serves 12): Combine 1½ cups tequila, ¾ cup triple sec, 7½ cups fresh orange juice and 6 tbsp fresh lime juice; chill. To serve, add ice to pitcher and pour into glasses rimmed with coarse salt. Garnish with lime wheels.

Beer chasers: For a quaff with less kick, serve a selection of microbrews, or get baby or pony kegs, which are more manageable than the larger frat-party versions.

Wine picks: Pour Terazzas Malbec from Argentina, or a beaujolais from Georges DuBoeuf.

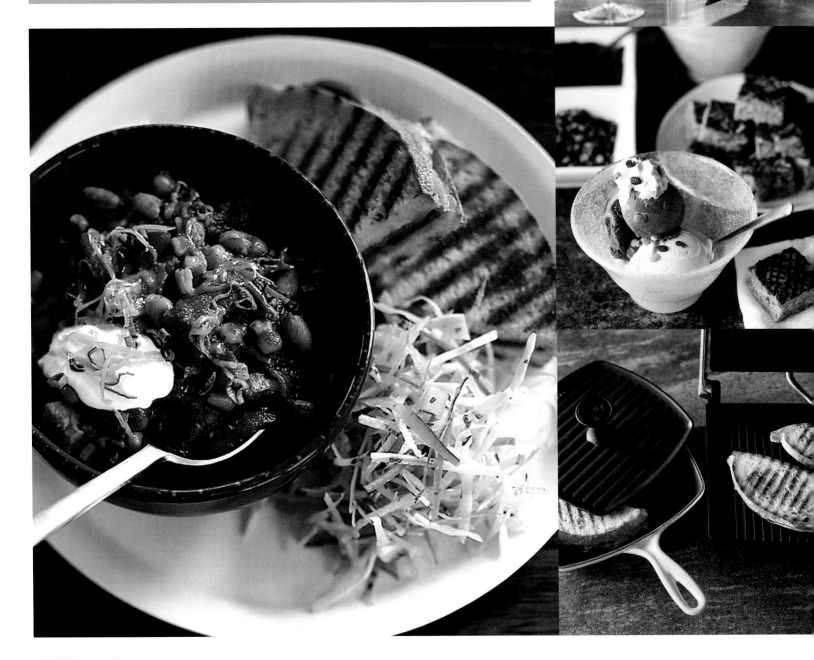

recipes

Sugar-and-Spice Pecans
(Makes 5 cups)
4 tbsp sugar, divided
½ tsp salt
½ tsp ground cinnamon
½ tsp ground ginger
½ tsp chili powder
½ tsp ground cumin
½ tsp ground cayenne
2 egg whites
5 cups pecan halves

Heat oven to 375°F. In small bowl combine 2 tbsp sugar, the salt and all spices. In medium bowl beat egg whites until frothy; add spice mixture. Stir in pecans and toss until evenly coated. Lightly coat 2 baking pans with nonstick cooking spray; spread nuts in single layer. Bake 10 min. Sprinkle with remaining sugar; bake 10 min. more, or until golden. Store in airtight container.

Jalapeño-Bean Dip
(Makes 3¾ cups)
2 cans (15½ oz. each) cannellini beans, drained and rinsed
1 can (4 oz.) chopped green chiles, drained
½ cup chopped onion
¼ cup pickled jalapeños plus 1 tbsp liquid
2 cloves garlic
½ lb. cheddar, cut into small cubes

Heat oven to 375°F. In food processor purée first 5 ingredients. Spoon into small casserole dish; top with cheese. Cook 20 min., or until cheese melts. Serve hot with tortilla chips.

Panini with Chorizo, Green Chile and Cheese
(Makes 12)
24 slices good-quality sandwich bread
⅓ cup roasted-garlic paste
1 pkg. (8 oz.) dried chorizo sausage, very thinly sliced after casing removed
3 cans (4 oz. each) whole green chiles, cut into strips
1½ lb. Monterey Jack, sliced
8 tbsp (1 stick) unsalted butter, melted
Salt and pepper to taste

Spread bread slices evenly with garlic paste. Top half the slices with chorizo, chiles and cheese, and cover with remaining bread slices; press together. Brush outsides with melted butter. Grill 2–3 min., or until cheese melts. Serve hot.

Chili With Turkey and White Beans
(Makes 14 cups)
3 tbsp olive oil
2 medium onions, chopped
4 cloves garlic, chopped
1 each red, yellow and green peppers, chopped
1 jalapeño, seeded and chopped
2 tbsp chili powder
2 tsp ground cumin
½ tsp salt
½ tsp black pepper
4 cups chicken broth
3 cans (14½ oz. each) diced tomatoes
6 cups diced, cooked turkey (or chicken)
3 cans (15½ oz. each) cannellini beans, drained and rinsed
Grated cheddar, sour cream, chopped cilantro and scallions for garnish

Heat oil in heavy-bottom pan over medium-high heat. Add onions, garlic, peppers and jalapeño. Cook 5–7 min., or until soft. Add spices, salt and pepper; stir. Add broth and diced tomatoes; bring to boil. Reduce heat; stir in turkey and beans. Simmer 30 min. Garnish as desired.

Jicama-Citrus Slaw
(Serves 12)
1½ cups fresh orange juice
6 tbsp fresh lime juice
¼ cup chopped fresh cilantro
⅓ cup olive oil
Salt and pepper to taste
1 medium green cabbage, shredded
2 stalks celery, chopped
2 carrots, shredded
1 green pepper, seeded and julienned
1 small jicama, peeled and julienned

In small bowl whisk together juices, cilantro, oil, salt and pepper. In bowl toss vegetables with dressing, salt and pepper. Cover; let sit 2 hours before serving.

Ice Cream Sundae Bar
(8 servings)
4–6 different flavored pints ice cream
1 bottle fudge sauce
1 can whipped cream
1 bag each chocolate and toffee chips

Let guests assemble their own sundaes in glass bowls.

Chocolate-Butterscotch Bars
(Makes 12)
½ cup light corn syrup
½ cup sugar
½ cup chunky peanut butter
3 cups cornflakes
⅔ cup butterscotch morsels, melted
2 squares (1 oz. each) semisweet chocolate, melted

Lightly coat 8" x 8" baking pan with nonstick cooking spray. In saucepan bring corn syrup and sugar to boil; stir until sugar dissolves. Remove from heat; add peanut butter and cornflakes. Spread mixture evenly in pan; smooth butterscotch on top. When cool, drizzle with chocolate.

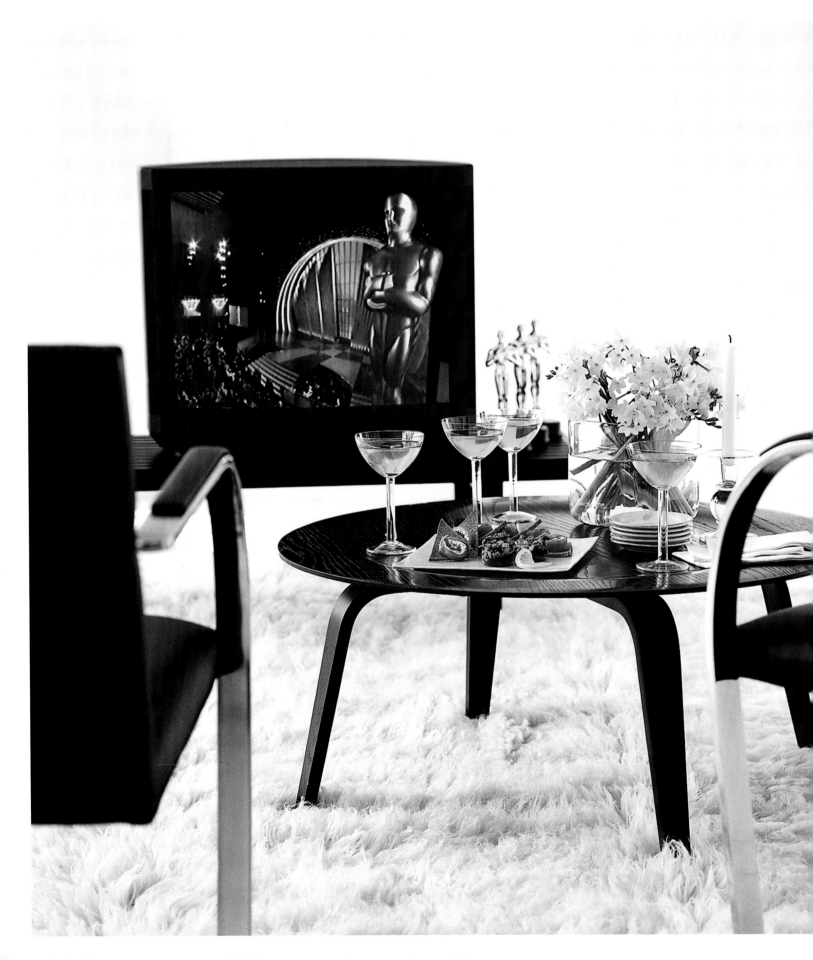

oscar party

Lights! Camera! Pizza! That's no way for any-one to watch the Academy Awards. If you can't make it to the Kodak Theatre this year, create your own glamour on Oscar night with a **vintage Hollywood bash at home.** Here, Robyn Leuthe and Tom Bryne (who produced an Oscar shindig for Dreamworks) design an evening that takes guests back to an era when a sidecar was a de rigueur cocktail: **the glamorous fifties.** In addition to sleek decorations and a decadent meal—eaten in front of the television, of course—they suggest **trivia and prizes that will keep guests on their toes** from arrivals to after-parties coverage on TV. So invite your own Rat Pack over and let the fun begin.

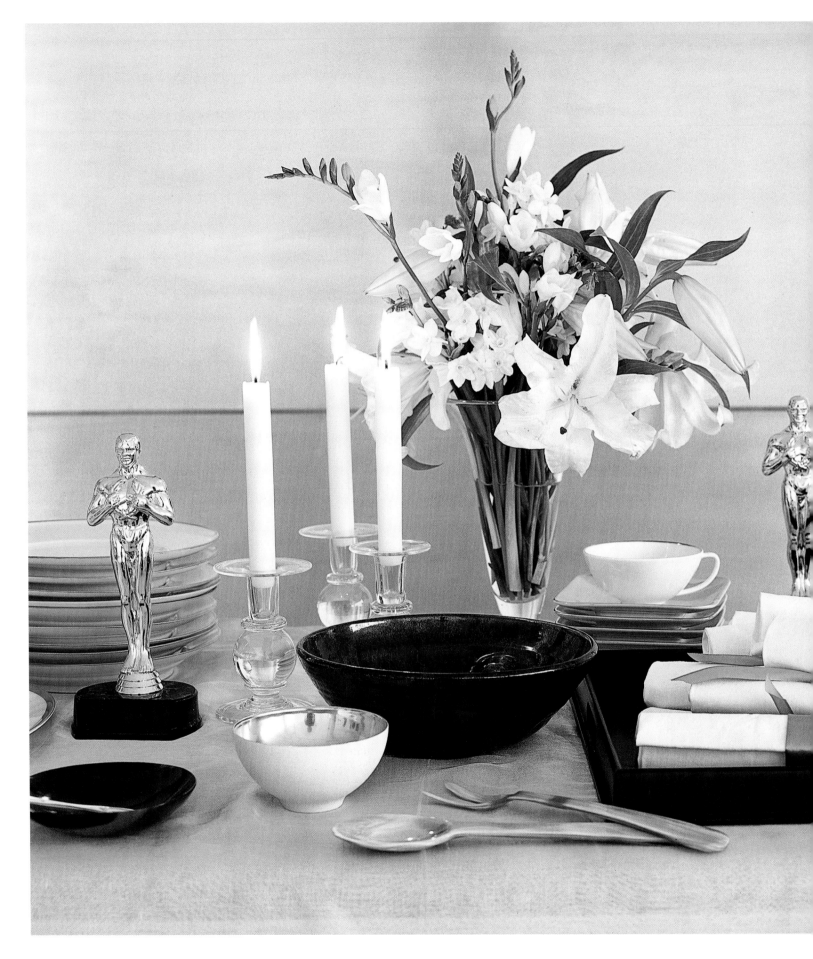

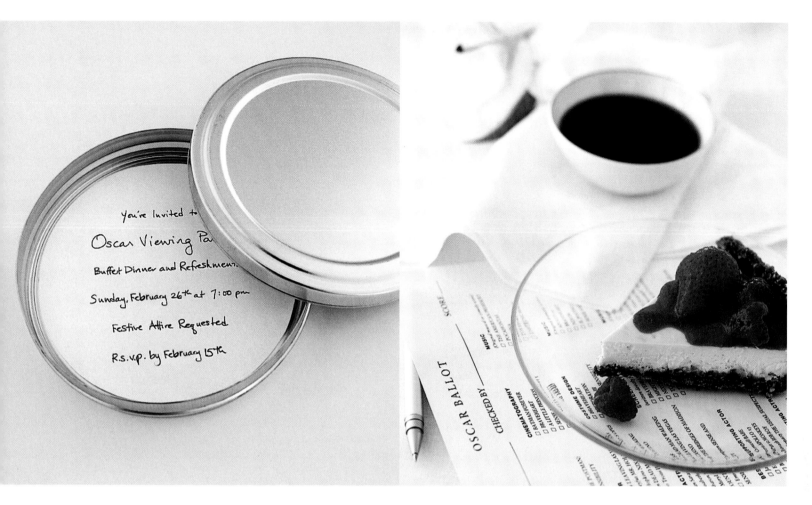

The invitation reads: You're Invited to / Oscar Viewing Pa... / Buffet Dinner and Refreshmen... / Sunday, February 26th at 7:00 pm / Festive Attire Requested / R.s.v.p. by February 15th

the menu

Signature drink: Sidecar
Hors d'oeuvres: Smoked-salmon roulades and crabmeat-stuffed mushrooms
Main course: Beef tenderloin with horseradish sauce, Gruyère-Parmesan scalloped potatoes and chopped-vegetable salad
Dessert: Cheesecake with crushed berries

setting the scene

The invitation: Send invites in film canisters (available at FPC; see Resources) with an awards ballot tucked inside. Copy the nomination list of the top categories from the newspaper or download it from oscar.com. Ask guests to show up a half-hour before airtime (or earlier, for red-carpet arrivals) with completed ballots, and to dress a bit glamorously.
The décor: A gold, white and black palette accented with old-fashioned crystal pieces (bought or borrowed) like vases, candlesticks, ice buckets and coupe-style champagne glasses establishes an Old Hollywood ambience. Use a gold runner or a black tablecloth on the buffet table; tie napkins with gold ribbon. Move the biggest television into the living room so there'll be plenty of seating. Clear off coffee tables and side tables to make room for plates and glasses.
The flowers: Leuthe suggests vases of varying heights with white flowers—white tulips and white freesia, for example—on the buffet, and lower arrangements on the coffee table.
The music: Entertain guests with best song nominees from years past. Some classics to download: "Streets of Philadelphia," *Philadelphia* (1993); "Let the River Run," *Working Girl* (1988); "Endless Love," *Endless Love* (1981); "Nobody Does It Better," *The Spy Who Loved Me* (1977); "Theme from Mahogany," *Mahogany* (1975); "The Way We Were," *The Way We Were* (1973); and "Moon River," *Breakfast at Tiffany's* (1961).

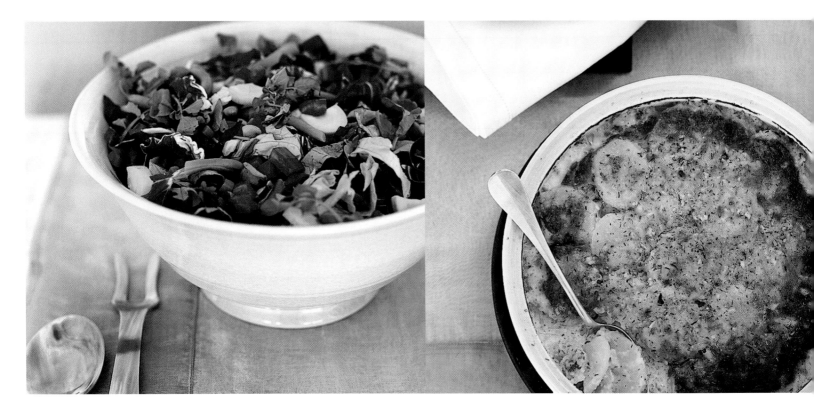

countdown

Three weeks: Mail invitations.
Two weeks: Order flowers from your local florist.
One week: Prepare contest materials; buy prizes. Buy music and wine.
Two days: Pick up flowers; buy food and beverages.
One day: Roll silverware; tie napkins. Prep potatoes and make cheesecake.
Morning of: Chill wine. Arrange flowers.
Six hours: Set up buffet table. Arrange living room for optimum TV viewing.
Four hours: Chop vegetables; make salad dressing. Make crab filling.
Two hours: Make roulades. Sauté and fill mushroom caps.
One hour: Chill champagne; mix sidecars.
45 minutes: Bake potatoes.
15 minutes: Bake mushrooms. Light candles.
One hour before dinner: Roast tenderloin.
15 minutes before dinner: Reheat gratin, dress salad and slice beef. Set out buffet.

even easier

Make bouquets from easy-to-find white roses instead of white freesia.
Buy frozen hors d'oeuvres such as smoked salmon puffs, wild-mushroom phyllo triangles and cheese soufflés in pastry cups and heat them in the oven (see Resources).
Instead of making salmon roulades, set out smoked salmon, sliced miniature pumpernickel bread and ramekins of crème fraîche or sour cream, chopped dill and red onion. Guests can make their own.
Don't roast the beef tenderloin yourself; purchase a ready-cooked one at a gourmet shop or grocery, slice and serve.
Buy a cheesecake with a graham cracker crust and cover it with fresh raspberries.

and the winner is...

Oscar ballots: Place a tray for completed ballots near the front door (make sure everyone signs her name). After guests arrive, pass out pens and have each guest pick another guest's ballot to score during the show.
Trivia contest: During commercials, test guests' Tinseltown knowledge with trivia questions. Examples: What does Oscar stand on? (A film reel.) What film and sequel both won a best picture Oscar? (*The Godfather* and *The Godfather Part II*.) What was the first X-rated film to win best picture? (*Midnight Cowboy*.) For more ideas, look on oscar.com or pick up a copy of *Hot Young Hollywood Trivia Challenge* (Renaissance Books).
Prizes: A bottle of Laurent-Perrier brut—the champagne often served at the Governors Ball, the after-party hosted by the Academy—is an apt gift for the ballot winner. Give trivia champs gift certificates to a local movie theater and/or a DVD of a past best picture winner like (like *From Here to Eternity, Out of Africa, Shakespeare in Love* and *Casablanca*).

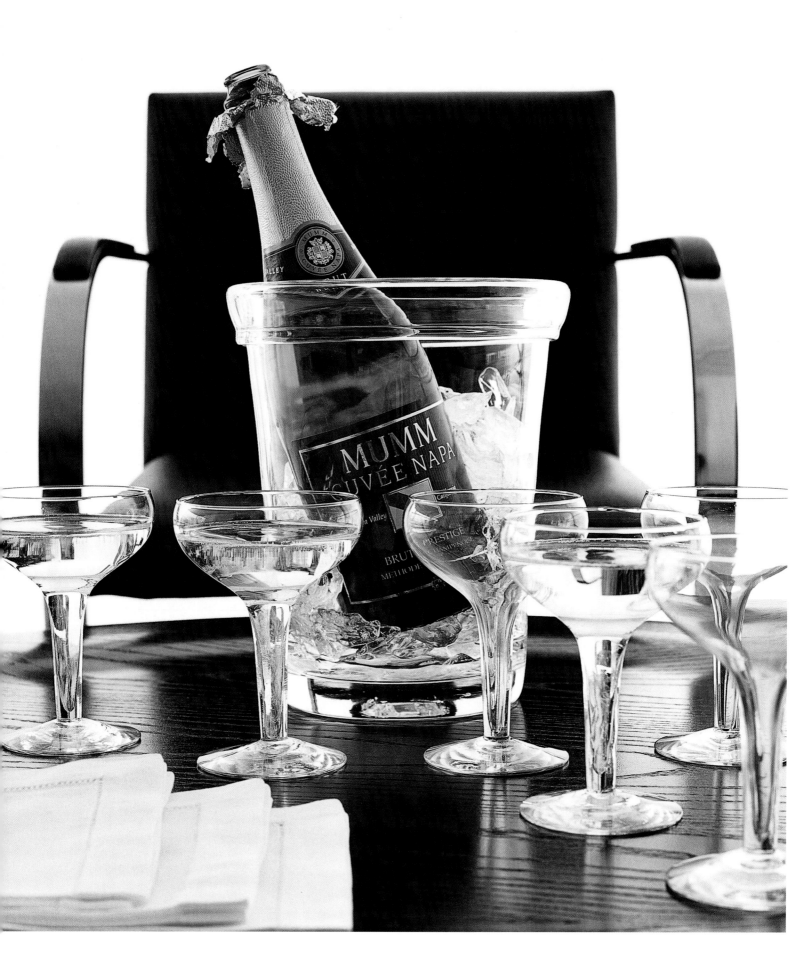

what to pour

Sidecar (serves 12): Mix 1½ cups triple sec, 1½ cups brandy and ½ cup fresh lemon juice with ice. Shake, strain and pour into martini glass (sugared rim optional).

Wine picks: With the hors d'oeuvres, pour a riesling such as Bonny Doon Pacific Rim from California or Chateau St. Michelle from Washington State, or a Soave by Gini or Pra from Italy. With the beef, cabernet sauvignon from California, such as Montelena Calistoga Cuvée, St. Clement or Phelps; or from Spain a Muga Rioja or Emilio Moro from the Riberta del Duero region. Both are elegant reds with smooth tannins. Toast the best picture award with a glass of champagne (Mumm brut Napa).

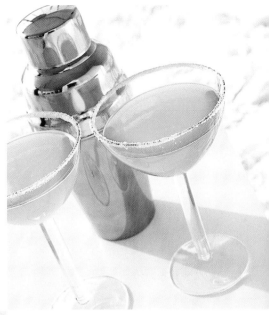

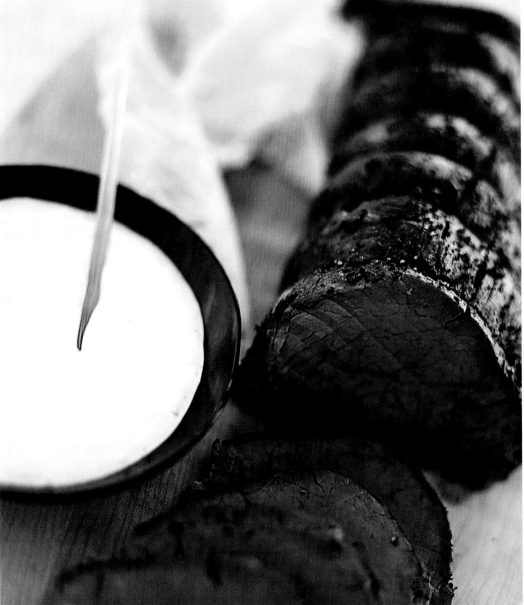

recipes

Smoked-Salmon Roulades
(Serves 12)
1 8 oz. container whipped cream cheese, at room temperature
¼ cup chopped fresh chives
½ tsp salt
¼ tsp pepper
1 lb. smoked salmon, thinly sliced
3 tbsp chopped fresh dill

In small bowl combine cream cheese, chives, salt and pepper. On clean work surface place 11½" x 30" sheet of plastic wrap, with shorter sides positioned to the right and left. Carefully center a piece of salmon vertically on plastic wrap about 3" from the short side at left. Continue to lay pieces of salmon, overlapping each other by about 1", until all salmon is used. Finished salmon layer should measure about 6" x 24" and should end about 3" from right edge of plastic wrap. Using a cake-frosting metal spatula, gently spread cream cheese mixture over salmon. Sprinkle with dill. Starting at long side, roll up salmon into a log and wrap in plastic. Secure ends. Place on baking sheet and refrigerate until serving time. Then unwrap the salmon roll and slice into ½" thick pieces, which will resemble pinwheels. Arrange on platter and accompany with toast points if desired.

Crabmeat-Stuffed Mushrooms

(Serves 12)

36 large mushrooms
6 tbsp butter, divided
2 cloves garlic, minced
1 lb. lump crabmeat, picked over for shells
¾ cup fresh bread crumbs
½ cup grated Parmesan
2 tbsp chopped fresh flat-leaf parsley
½ tsp salt
¼ tsp pepper

Remove stems from mushrooms; reserve caps and finely chop stems. In large skillet melt 4 tbsp butter. Sauté stems and garlic 4–5 min. Stir in crabmeat, bread crumbs, cheese, parsley, salt and pepper. Cook until heated through, about 3 min. Spoon mixture into large bowl; let cool. With paper towel wipe skillet clean. Melt remaining butter in skillet. Working in batches sauté mushroom caps 5–6 min., until tender. Heat oven to 350ºF. Evenly divide crabmeat mixture into mushroom caps. Coat baking sheet with nonstick cooking spray. Place mushrooms on sheet. (Mushrooms can be refrigerated at this point and baked before serving.) Bake about 15 min., until heated through.

Beef Tenderloin

(Serves 12)

4–6 lb. fillet of beef, trimmed and tied
2 tbsp olive oil
2 tsp salt
1 tsp pepper

Heat oven to 450ºF. Rub beef with oil. Sprinkle with salt and pepper. Place roasting pan in oven for 5 min. Reduce temperature to 400ºF. Remove pan from oven and place seasoned beef in pan. Roast until instant-read thermometer inserted in thickest part of meat reads 135ºF for medium-rare or 140ºF for medium (30–45 min.). Remove from oven and cover loosely with foil. Let rest 15 min. Remove strings and slice. To serve, arrange slices on platter. Serve at room temperature with grainy mustard and horseradish sauce. Mix 1 cup sour cream, 1 cup horseradish, 1 cup mayonnaise and 1 tbsp fresh lemon juice; add salt and pepper to taste.

Chopped-Vegetable Salad with Mustard Vinaigrette

(Serves 12)

¼ cup red wine vinegar
2 tbsp Dijon mustard
1 cup olive oil
Salt and pepper to taste
¼ lb. green beans, trimmed and cut into ½" pieces
2 carrots, peeled and diced
6 vine-ripened tomatoes, chopped
1 medium head radicchio, cored and chopped
1 medium head Boston lettuce, chopped

In small bowl combine vinegar and mustard. Slowly whisk in olive oil. Season with salt and peppe; set aside. Blanch beans and carrots. In large bowl combine beans, carrots, tomatoes, radicchio and lettuce with ½–⅔ cup vinaigrette. Adjust seasoning with more salt and pepper.

Gruyère-Parmesan Scalloped Potatoes

(Serves 12)

7 baking potatoes (about 2½–3 lb.), peeled
1½ cups grated Gruyère (about ¼ lb.)
3 large shallots, peeled and chopped (about 1 cup)
½ cup grated Parmesan
2 tsp dried thyme
Salt and pepper to taste
2 tbsp unsalted butter, softened
2 cups heavy cream

In large pot of salted water boil potatoes until tender, 25–30 min. Drain. Slice potatoes ¼" thick when cool enough to handle. Heat oven to 350ºF. In medium bowl combine Gruyère, shallots, Parmesan, thyme and salt and pepper to taste. Rub the inside of 4 qt. gratin dish with butter. Arrange potatoes in layers, sprinkling each layer with cheese mixture. End with layer of cheese on top. Pour heavy cream over potatoes. (Potatoes can be prepared up to this point and refrigerated; add an extra 10–15 min. to the baking time.) Bake 50–60 min., until top is golden. (Potatoes can be set aside at this point, for up to 1 hour. To reheat, bake 15 min.) Let sit 10 min. before serving.

Crushed Berries

(Serves 12)

Place this recipe on top of a completely cooled homemade or store-bought cheesecake.

2 cups raspberries
½ cup plus ⅔ cup sugar, divided
3 cups strawberries, hulled and quartered

In bowl of food processor combine raspberries and ½ cup sugar. Pour into strainer. Using rubber spatula, press raspberry mixture through to remove seeds. Add strawberries to raspberry mixture. Refrigerate until ready to serve.

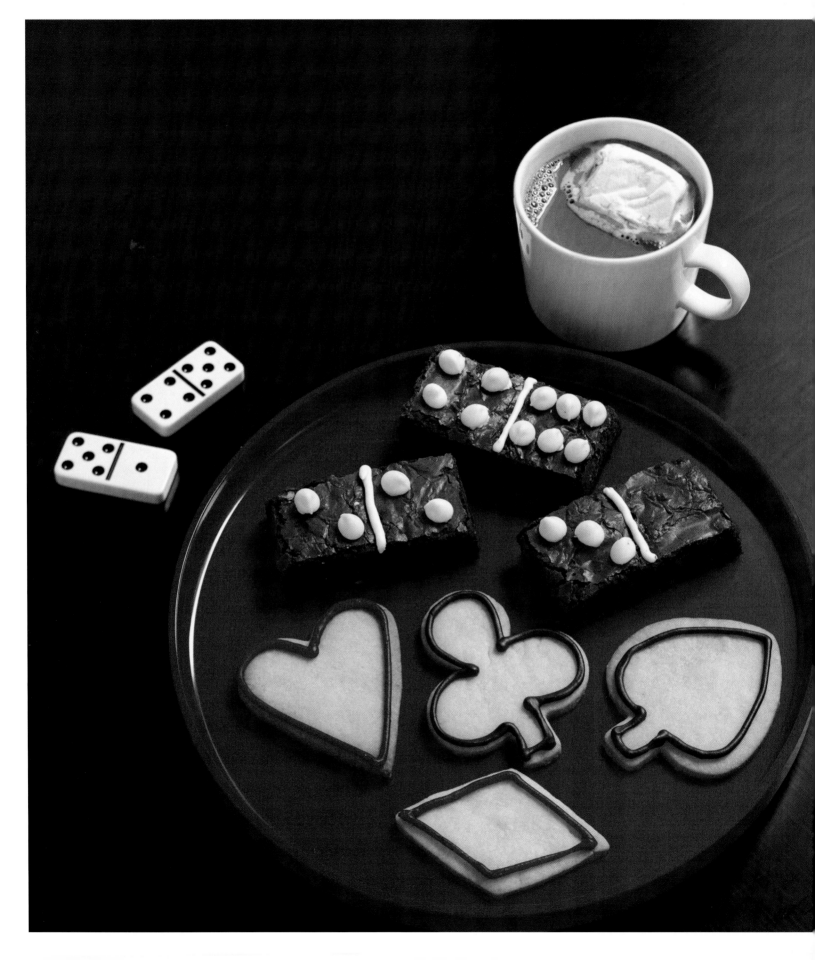

game night

On a chilly night, channel your inner card shark and invite friends over for an evening of fun and games. Follow tips from Beverly Hills event planners Marianne Weiman-Nelson and Alyse Sobel of Special Occasions (they coordinated the weddings of Anne Heche and Lisa Rinna). Decorate tables in casino colors of red and black. Bring out board games, cards and dice. And stack the odds in favor of a good time with comforting casual fare like pigs in a blanket, mini grilled-cheese sandwiches and domino brownies. With a setup this playful, everyone's a winner.

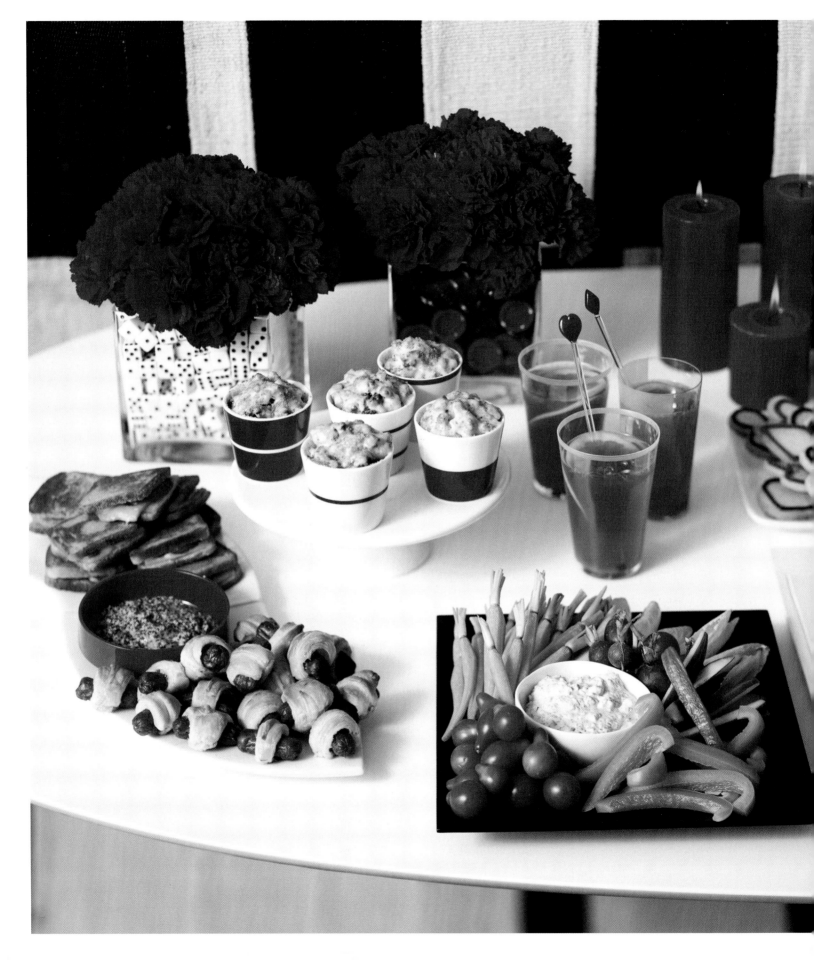

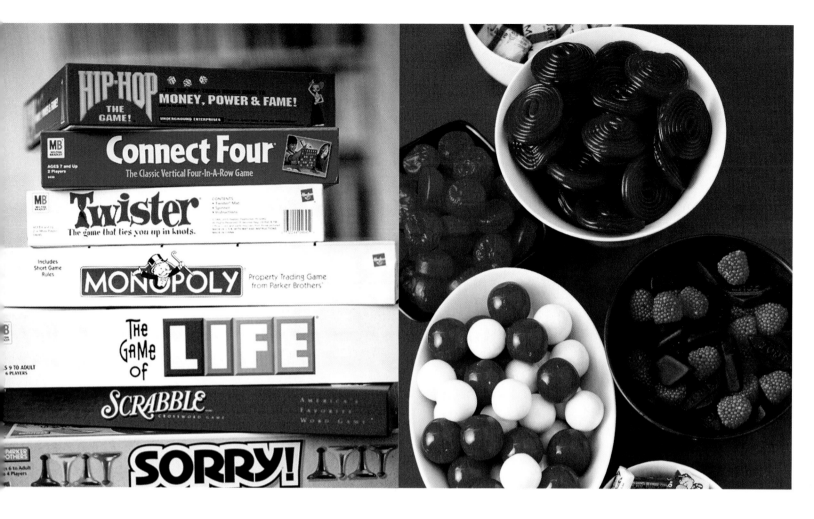

the menu

Signature drink: Players' punch
Casual dinner: Crispy popcorn shrimp, mini grilled-cheese sandwiches, chicken-apple-sausage pigs in a blanket, macaroni-and-cheese cups, crudités with avocado dip
Dessert: Domino brownies and sugar cookies with hot chocolate

setting the scene

The décor: Think retro casino. Put chairs at card tables or toss big, comfortable pillows around a coffee table. For each eye-catching tabletop bouquet, tightly arrange red carnations in a three and one quarter inch square glass vase; then nestle that into a six-inch-square glass vase (GM Floral; see Resources). Fill the space between the vases with dominos or checkers (Gamedaze; see Resources). Group together red pillar candles.

The menu: On a buffet table, set out platters of food along with napkins, forks, spoons and plates. Arrange glasses and pitchers on the table too. For dessert, bring out hot cocoa, domino brownies and homemade sugar cookies decorated like playing cards (playing-card cookie cutters available at Broadway Panhandler; see Resources).

The music: Think "Viva Las Vegas"—not just the Elvis movie soundtrack but gambling tunes. Set a campy casino vibe with greatest hits collections from the likes of Liberace, Wayne Newton and Sammy Davis Jr. There are even newly remastered *Live From Las Vegas* CDs from Rat Packers Dean Martin and Frank Sinatra. Or download your own Sin City–style soundtrack: The Rolling Stones' "Tumbling Dice," Peggy Lee's "Big Spender," Abba's "Take a Chance on Me," B.B. King's "Bad Luck," Basement Jaxx's "Good Luck," Frank Sinatra's "Luck Be a Lady," Rod Stewart's "Lady Luck," The Who's "You Better You Bet," Jackson 5's "I'll Bet You," The Cocteau Twins' "Heaven or Las Vegas," Emmylou Harris's "Ooh Las Vegas," The Thrills' "Your Love is Like Las Vegas," Sheryl Crow's "Leavin' Las Vegas," and, of course, Kenny Rogers' "The Gambler"—remember, you gotta know when to hold 'em, and you gotta know when to fold 'em.

the rules of the games

Board games: Monopoly, Trivial Pursuit, Scrabble, Life, Connect Four, Sorry!
Preparation: Place the board on a table or floor, surrounded by seats or cushions. Add a dictionary for Scrabble challenges.
Players: Most board games accommodate two to eight people. If you have more guests, set up extra games (have friends bring them).

Activity games: Twister, charades, Cranium, Celebrity, Pictionary, Scruples
Preparation: Clear plenty of space—these games can be action-packed. Have large pads and pencils on hand. Keep in mind that Twister's mat requires extra sideline room for spreading out.
Players: Good for teams, most can be played with any number of people.

Card games: Poker, bridge, blackjack, gin rummy, Uno
Preparation: All of these games use a standard deck of cards, except Uno, which requires its own cards. Supply pads and pencils to keep score and poker chips for poker.
Players: Gin rummy demands two people or two teams of two. Bridge requires two teams of two. Play blackjack, Uno and poker with two or more.

Dice and dominoes: Liar's dice, dominoes, mah-jongg, Boggle
Preparation: Play on a table or hard, flat surface. For liar's dice, provide five dice and one cup for each participant. Boggle requires pads and pencils for all.
Players: Two to six people can play Boggle; liar's dice requires two or more; mah-jongg is played with groups of four people; two or more can play dominoes.

Need more suggestions? *Hoyle's Rules of Games* (amazon.com) is full of good ideas.

countdown

Three weeks: Send invitations. Buy swizzle sticks (available at Mixology's; see Resources) for drinks and, if you need them, individual ramekins or ovenproof mugs for mac and cheese.
One week: Order flowers. Buy wine, music, candles, pads and pencils.
Two days: Shop for groceries. Make sure avocados for crudité dip are nearly ripe (not hard).
Day before: Pick up flowers. Bake brownies. Prep (don't bake) macaroni and cheese; refrigerate.
Morning of: Make flower arrangements, chill wine.
Six hours: Make punch and lemon aioli. Cut crudités. Refrigerate all.
Three hours: Prepare pigs in a blanket and mini cheese sandwiches (do not grill); refrigerate.
Two hours: Prepare (but don't cook) shrimp.
One hour: Bake pigs in a blanket and macaroni and cheese; keep them warm in the oven. Make avocado dip.
30 minutes: Cook shrimp. Grill cheese sandwiches. Set out food and drinks.
10 minutes: Light candles. Start music.
During party: Serve hot chocolate, brownies and cookies.

even easier

Instead of buying nesting vases and game pieces for the flower arrangements, place red carnations in simple low glass vases and scatter a few game pieces that you already own (checkers, chess pieces, dice, Monopoly pieces) across the buffet table.
Halve bakery brownies and decorate with white frosting from a tube and white chocolate chips to resemble dominos.
Instead of making your own macaroni and cheese, use a good boxed version such as Simply Organic or Annie's, and sprinkle with good-quality cheddar before serving.
Serve store-bought checkerboard cookies or Pepperidge Farm's classic Chessman cookies.

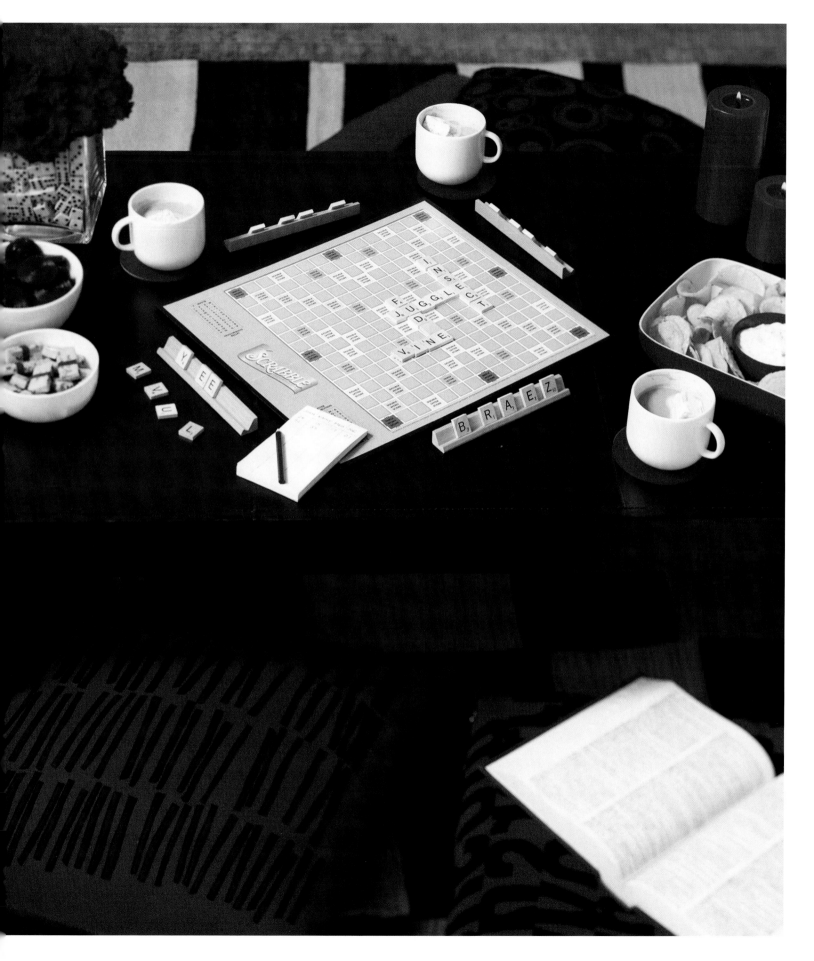

what to pour

Players' punch (serves 12): In large pitcher combine 6 cups cranberry juice, 3 cups orange juice, 3 cups vodka, 3 tbsp sugar and 1½ tsp pumpkin pie spice. Refrigerate for at least 2 hours to allow flavors to meld. When ready to serve, pour into ice-filled highball glasses and garnish with orange wheels and a swizzle stick for that Las Vegas look.

Wine picks: Serve a refreshing white, such as pinot blanc from Chalone or Au Bon Climat in California, or a sauvignon blanc from South Africa from Neil Ellis or Mulderbosch.

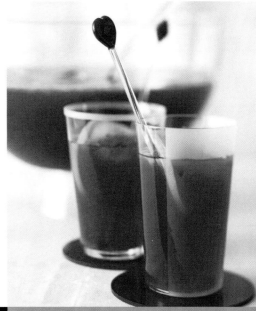

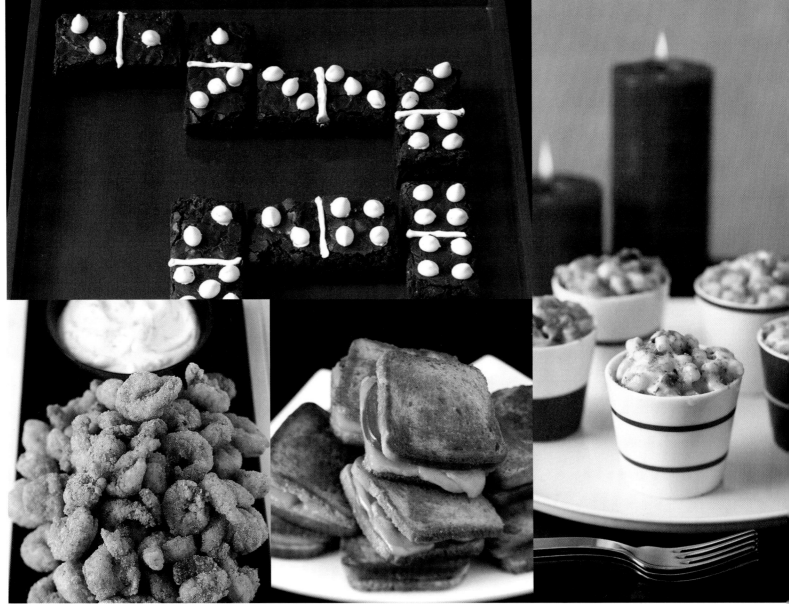

recipes

Avocado Dip

2 ripe avocados, pitted, peeled and
   mashed
1 cup sour cream
1 tbsp lemon juice
1 tbsp chopped fresh parsley
1 clove garlic, minced
Salt and pepper to taste

*For dip: Mix all ingredients. Press plastic
wrap directly on top of dip to prevent
avocado from blackening. Refrigerate
until serving time. For the crudités: 2 lb.
total fresh vegetables, such as cherry
tomatoes, carrots, sliced peppers, radishes,
cucumbers and endive leaves.*

Mini Grilled-Cheese Sandwiches

(Makes 24)
10 tbsp unsalted butter, divided
4 tbsp vegetable oil, divided
1 medium shallot, chopped
1 clove garlic, chopped
½ lb. sliced mushrooms
Salt and pepper to taste
48 slices rye cocktail bread
2 large plum tomatoes, sliced
½ lb. sharp cheddar, thinly sliced

*Heat 1 tbsp butter and 1 tbsp oil in
medium skillet over medium heat. Add
shallot and garlic; sauté 1 min. Add
mushrooms; cook until tender, 3–4 min.
Season with salt and pepper. Top bread
with mushrooms, tomatoes or both;
cover with cheese and bread slice. Press
together. In large skillet heat 3 tbsp butter
and 1 tbsp oil over medium heat. Brown
sandwiches in 3 batches until golden;
turn once. Serve hot.*

Chicken-Apple-Sausage Pigs in a Blanket

(Makes about 35 pieces)
1 pkg. frozen puff pastry, thawed
½ cup grainy Dijon mustard
1 pkg. (12–13 oz.) chicken-apple
   cocktail sausage links

*Heat oven to 350ºF. Unfold pastry
sheets on lightly floured surface. Cut
each into 6 rectangles, then each of
those into 4 long triangles (there will be
dough left over). Spoon small amount of
mustard onto wide end of pastry and
top with a sausage; roll, pressing gently
to seal. Place rolls 2" apart on baking
sheet. Bake 12–15 min., or until golden.
Serve warm.*

Crispy Popcorn Shrimp

(Serves 12)
1 cup all-purpose flour
1 tsp sugar
1 tsp salt
½ tsp onion powder
½ tsp garlic powder
½ tsp black pepper
½ tsp ground cayenne pepper
½ tsp dried thyme
1½ cups milk
2 eggs, lightly beaten
2 lb. medium shrimp, peeled, deveined
1½ cups unseasoned bread crumbs
2 cups vegetable oil (if frying)

*In medium bowl combine first 8 ingredi-
ents. Make a well in the center and
gradually whisk in milk and eggs. Let
stand 30 min. Working in batches, stir
shrimp into batter; remove with slotted
spoon, letting excess batter drip back
into bowl. Coat shrimp with bread
crumbs. If you want to fry the shrimp:
Heat oil to 350ºF in deep saucepan.
Working in batches, add shrimp to hot
oil. Fry 2–3 min., or until golden. Remove
with slotted spoon to baking sheet lined
with paper towels. Repeat until done. If
you want to bake the shrimp: Heat oven
to 450ºF. Place wire rack on baking
sheet; lightly spray with nonstick vegetable spray. Put shrimp on rack in single
layer. Bake 12–15 min., or until golden.
Serve hot with lemon aioli dip: In small
bowl combine 2 cups mayonnaise, 5
cloves minced garlic, 1 tbsp fresh lemon
juice, 1 tsp lemon zest, and salt and
pepper to taste.*

Domino Brownies

(Makes 24)
8 tbsp (1 stick) unsalted butter, softened
2 cups sugar
4 oz. (4 squares) unsweetened chocolate,
   coarsely chopped and melted
3 eggs
1 cup all-purpose flour
Pinch of salt
1 tsp vanilla
White chocolate chips and white frosting
   in tube for decoration

*Heat oven to 350ºF. Spray 13" x 9"
baking pan with nonstick cooking spray.
In large bowl beat butter and sugar
together with electric mixer. Stir in melted
chocolate; beat in eggs until well combined, then stir in flour and salt. Add
vanilla. Scrape batter into prepared pan.
Bake until wooden pick inserted in center comes out clean, about 25 min. Cut
into rectangles measuring about 3" long
by 1" wide. Place on wire rack to cool.
Add frosting lines (as shown opposite);
top with white chocolate chips to resemble domino patterns.*

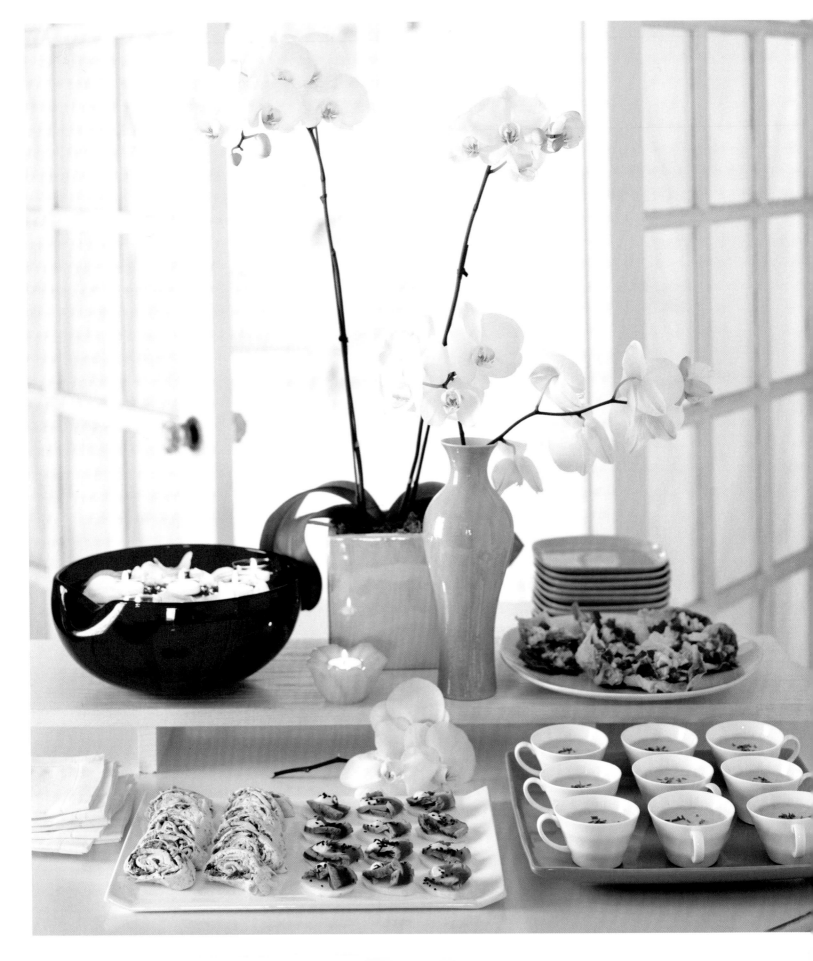

afternoon spa party

Here's a novel idea: Skip the endless errands and really relax this weekend by pampering yourself with a **spa-theme gathering** for eight girlfriends. Alexis Ufland, founder of SPArty On-Location Spa Parties—who has served up soothing experiences to Kim Cattrall, Justin Timberlake and the Dixie Chicks—suggests **bubbly blue cocktails** and light, **flavorful snacks** along with an appetizing menu of at-home spa services ranging from **manicures to reflexology** to heavenly neck and shoulder massages. Need any more convincing? If not, sit back, take a sip of punch, and start destressing and beautifying.

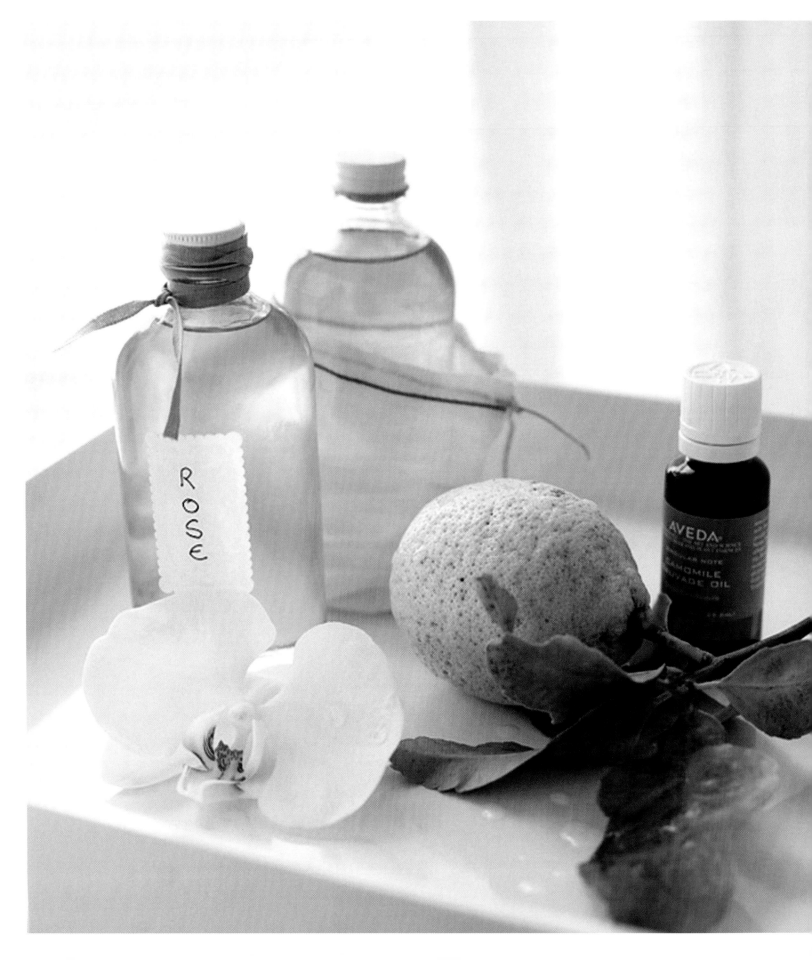

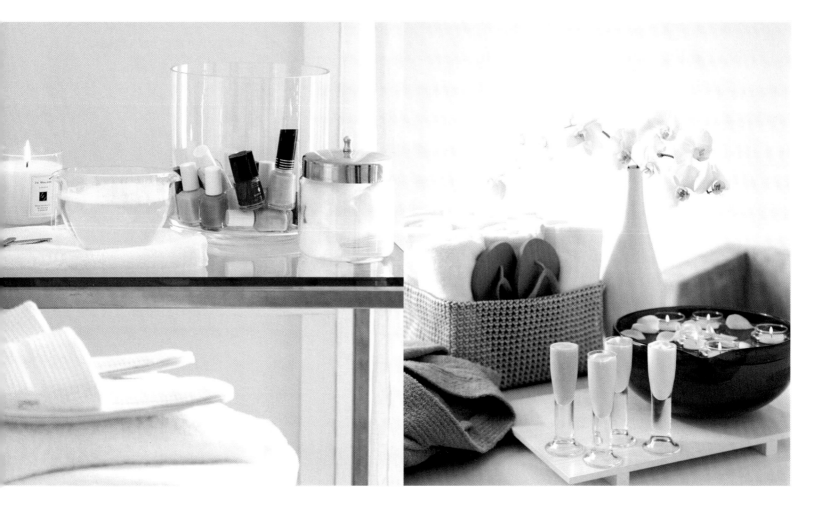

the menu

Signature drink: SPArty punch
Small bites: Asparagus-leek soup, seared tuna on daikon, chicken wraps with roasted tomato and goat cheese, vegetable salad cups with tarragon-yogurt dressing
Mini desserts: Fruit smoothies, lemon squares, berry bowls, chocolate truffles

setting the scene

The invitation: Splurge on Swarovski crystal–studded spa invitations by Twinklecards (see Resources). Less expensive options: any plain cards with watery hues or printed invitations with a bathtub or beauty motif. Ask guests to bring flip-flops and a robe or their favorite nail polish shade.
The décor: Turn your pad into a serene haven with soft lighting and a palette of aqua and white. Make the living room your main area: Set a large blue bowl filled with water on the coffee table, and float white rose petals and white votives in it. Add soothing aromatics with scented candles or by burning your favorite essential oil with water in a Sensory Stone burner. Set up a narrow table with a chair on either side as a manicure area and arrange a few comfortable chairs for reflexology or upper-body massages. In an adjoining room, make space for massage tables.
The menu: Set up a buffet table with two or three potted white orchids and another bowl of floating rose petals and votives. Place snacks on white and blue platters; serve asparagus-leek soup in demitasse cups. Halfway through the party, serve sweets: chocolate truffles, bakery-bought lemon squares cut into quarters, berry bowls (strawberries, raspberries and blueberries in little glass bowls), and a tray of fruit smoothies in shot glasses.
The music: Some of the best spas in the world play the worst music. Don't make that mistake. Skip clichéd New Age-y tunes in favor of truly cool chill-out music that never goes out of style: atmospheric and soothing songs by Brian Eno, the Cocteau Twins, Sigur Rós, Air or Moby.

countdown

Three weeks: Send invitations and book appropriate therapists (for details see box at right).
One week: Order flowers. Buy wine, music and decorating items.
Three days: Buy bar items and truffles.
Two days: Buy groceries.
Day before: Pick up flowers. Buy lemon squares at a bakery. Prep vegetables for salad cups; refrigerate.
Morning of: Marinate tuna. Chill wine. Set up spa stations and bar area. Arrange flowers.
Three hours: Bake tomatoes and sauté chicken for wraps; set aside.
Two hours: Sear tuna; set aside. Make soup.
90 minutes: Make chicken wraps and seared tuna on daikon. Fill berry bowls. Mix punch.
30 minutes: Make vegetable salad cups. Plate cold appetizers. Light candles. Start music.
During party: Heat and serve soup. Later, set out berry bowls, truffles, lemon squares (cut into mini-squares). Blend fruit smoothies and serve them in shot glasses with straws cut in half.

even easier

Rather than making the tuna on daikon and the chicken wraps, order sushi from a Japanese restaurant: two orders each of tuna, cucumber and California rolls (there are six pieces per roll).
Replace the fruit smoothies with mini sorbet parfaits. Layer small scoops of three different flavors in shot glasses (use a melon baller); make them the morning of the party and keep them in the freezer.
If there isn't enough time (or money) to book several kinds of aestheticians, hire at least one masseuse and one manicurist. Or set out callus removers, nail files, and a selection of polishes and have guests do their own manicures and pedicures.

spa party pampering

Treat friends to a truly relaxing afternoon. Pick one of these options and watch them unwind.

Treatment: Neck and shoulder massages
Staff: Two masseuses for one hour (each charges about $100 an hour)
Equipment: Give staff hair bands; have them circulate casually as partygoers relax.
Setup: None

Treatment: Full-body massages (30 min.)
Staff: Two masseuses, two hours (each charges about $100 an hour)
Equipment: Masseuses should provide tables, sheets, towels and hair caps.
Setup: Designate two private spaces to hold three-by-six-foot massage tables.
-
Treatment: Reflexology, 15-minute foot treatments
Staff: One reflexologist for two to three hours (each charges about $100 an hour)
Equipment: Same as above, plus one footstool with towels on top for therapist
Setup: Create an out-of-the-way treatment station within the party area, ideally in a reclining or comfortable chair.

Treatment: Manicures (quick file and optional cuticle trimming, hand massage and polish)
Staff: Two manicurists for two hours (each charges about $90 per hour)
Equipment: Manicurists should bring basic utensils. You may have to provide hand towels, finger bowls and polishes.
Setup: Design manicure stations, ideally at narrow tables with chairs facing each other across them.

Treatment: Eyebrow shapings
Staff: One shaper for two hours (about $80 to $100 an hour)
Equipment: Have the shaper bring supplies.
Setup: Create a station using a bar stool or high chair so the aesthetician can stand. Keep a hand mirror nearby for guests to admire their newly groomed brows.

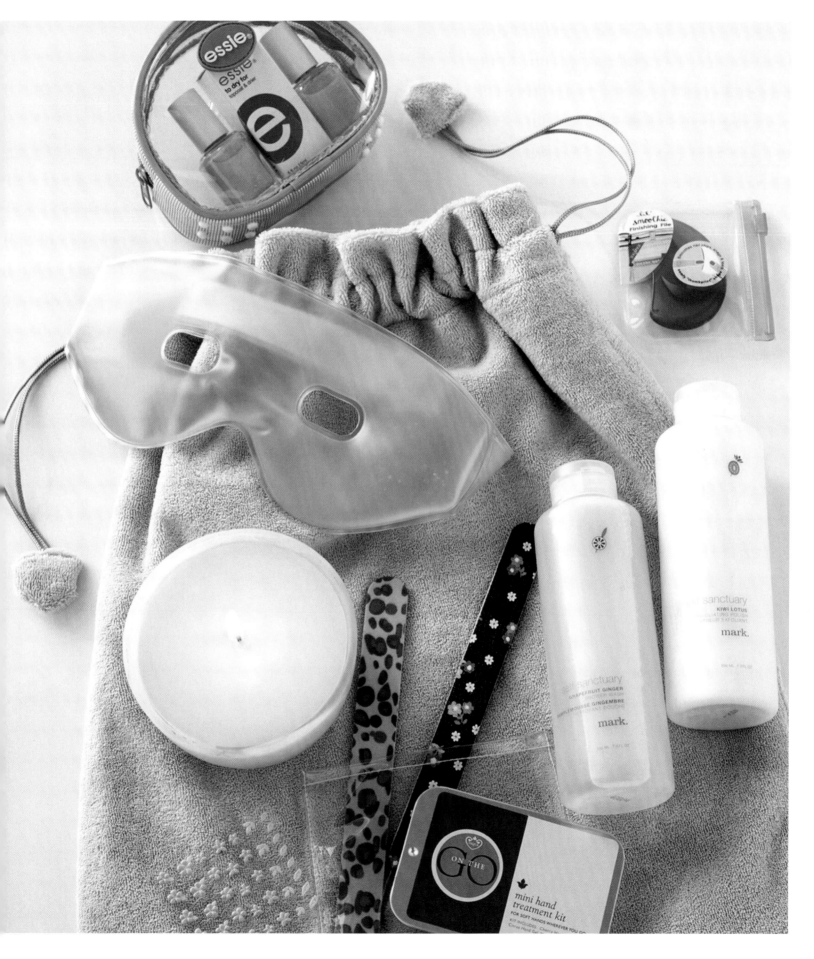

what to pour

SPArty punch (serves 8): Pour into an ice-filled punch bowl: 4 cups chilled club soda, 1 cup chilled blue curaçao, 2 cups each chilled vodka and white cranberry juice, and lemon and orange slices.

Wine picks: Serve a riesling from Austria, such as Brundlmeyer or Salomon, or from Alsace, France, such as Trimbach or Hugel.

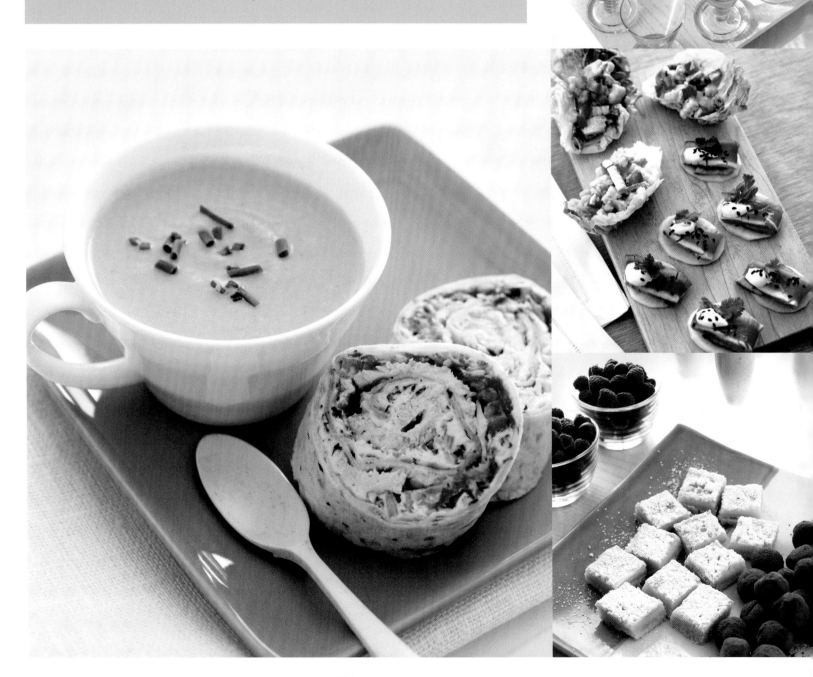

recipes

Asparagus-Leek Soup

(Serves 8)

2 tbsp unsalted butter
3 medium leeks, cleaned and chopped (white part only)
2 garlic cloves, minced
4 cans (14½ oz. each) chicken broth
2 bunches asparagus, trimmed and cut in 1" pieces
½ cup heavy cream (can substitute plain low-fat yogurt)
Salt and pepper to taste
Minced chives for garnish

Heat butter in large pot over medium heat. Add leeks and garlic; sauté until softened, 5–7 min. Add chicken broth and asparagus and bring to boil; reduce heat and simmer 12–15 min. With hand-held immersion blender, purée until smooth. Stir in cream. Season with salt and pepper; garnish with minced chives.

Seared Tuna on Daikon

(Serves 8)

2 tbsp soy sauce
2 tbsp sesame oil
1 tbsp fresh lemon juice
½ tsp pepper
½ lb. sushi-quality tuna
½ cup sour cream
2 tsp wasabi paste
Salt
1 daikon radish (about 6 oz.), peeled and sliced diagonally (can substitute unpeeled cucumber)
Minced cilantro and/or black sesame seeds for garnish

Combine soy sauce, sesame oil, lemon juice and pepper in resealable plastic bag. Add tuna and refrigerate, turning several times, 1–2 hrs. In bowl combine sour cream and wasabi paste; chill. Coat nonstick skillet with nonstick cooking spray and heat over medium-high heat. Remove tuna from marinade and season with salt. Sear tuna for about 2 min. on each side. Cool. Cut tuna against the grain into thin slices; top each piece of daikon with wasabi cream, then tuna and a final dollop of cream. Garnish.

Chicken Wraps with Roasted Tomato and Goat Cheese

(Serves 8)

3 large plum tomatoes, sliced
2 tbsp olive oil, divided
Salt and pepper
¾ cup (about 5⅓ oz.) goat cheese, softened
2 tbsp minced chervil
2 boneless, skinless chicken breasts (about ¾ lb.)
1½ cups shredded romaine lettuce
4 8" flour tortillas

Heat oven to 300ºF. Line sheet pan with foil; place tomato slices in single layer. Drizzle with 1 tbsp olive oil and sprinkle with salt and pepper. Bake until slices have shriveled slightly, about 30 min. In small bowl combine goat cheese and chervil. Heat remaining 1 tbsp oil in medium nonstick skillet over medium-high heat. Add chicken and sauté 8–10 min., turning once. Place chicken on cutting board and let rest 5 min.; cut into very thin slices. To assemble, heat each tortilla for 10 seconds in microwave to soften, then place on a clean work surface. Spread with cheese, then top with lettuce, tomato and chicken. Roll tortillas tightly; wrap in plastic wrap and chill. When ready to serve, remove from plastic; cut diagonally into 1" pieces.

Vegetable Salad Cups with Tarragon-Yogurt Dressing

(Serves 8)

½ cup plain low-fat yogurt
¼ cup mayonnaise
2 tsp minced fresh tarragon
1½ tsp white wine vinegar
1 tsp Dijon mustard
Pinch cayenne pepper
2 ears corn, kernels removed (or substitute 1½ cups frozen corn, blanched briefly)
3 oz. sugar snap peas, trimmed and sliced in 1" pieces
1 avocado, halved, seeded, peeled and diced
Salt and pepper to taste
8 Bibb lettuce leaves, cleaned
Chopped tomato for garnish

In small bowl combine yogurt, mayonnaise, tarragon, vinegar, mustard and cayenne pepper. In large bowl combine corn kernels, sugar snap peas and avocado. Pour dressing over vegetables and toss to coat. Season with salt and pepper. To serve, spoon vegetables into lettuce leaves and garnish with chopped tomato.

Mini Fruit Smoothies

(Makes 8 3 oz. servings)

1 pint ice cream, softened
½ cup milk
⅔ cup chopped fruit

Combine all ingredients in blender. Blend until smooth. For strawberry smoothies, use strawberry ice cream and fresh strawberries; for mango smoothies, use mango ice cream or sorbet with fresh mango; for pineapple smoothies, try pineapple-coconut ice cream and fresh pineapple. Serve in shot glasses.

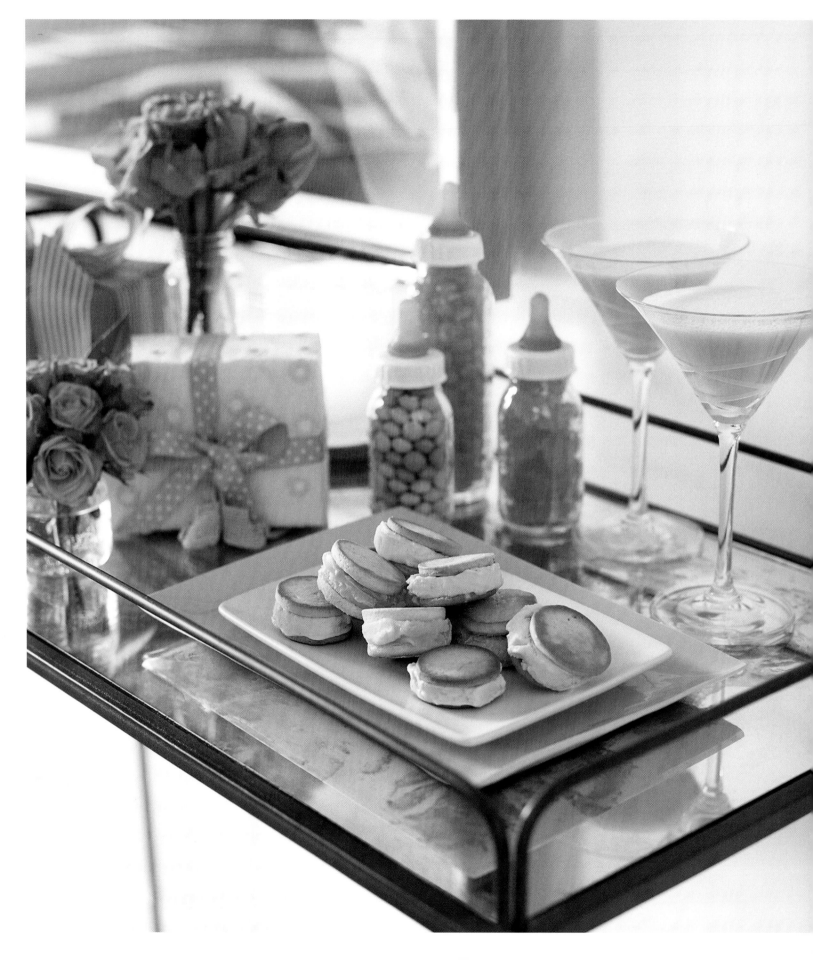

baby shower

Usually, baby showers are all-girl affairs punctuated by afternoon tea, games and gifts. The next time you celebrate an upcoming arrival, why not put a modern spin on the traditional gathering? Nicky Reinhard and Ann David of David Reinhard Events in New York City (who orchestrated Jessica Capshaw's wedding) have created a coed cocktail reception for 20 that is fun, sexy and far from predictable. With a fresh pistachio and orange palette and baby-size snacks by N.Y.C. caterer Olivier Cheng (who has whipped up feasts for Michael Douglas and Catherine Zeta-Jones), this is one shower that's fun for the hot mama-to-be and the cool daddy too.

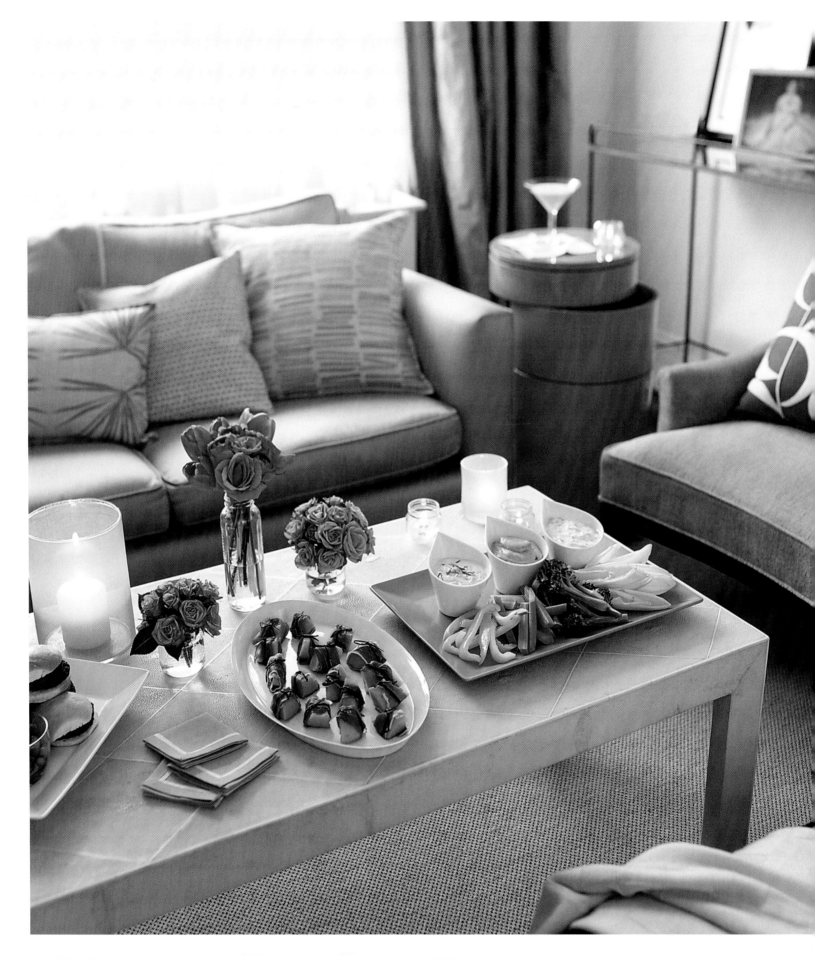

baby shower basics

David and Reinhard suggest throwing the party seven or eight months into the honoree's pregnancy (if it's a surprise, have someone book the couple for a false occasion). Set the tone with chic invites such as custom-printed Silhouette cards (photo on page 143) by Petite Alma (see Resources). If it's not a surprise, ask the parents-to-be to draw up a guest list six weeks in advance.

For a coed party, make sure to invite the couple's parents and siblings; likewise the mothers and sisters if it's an all-girls event. Encourage the soon-to-be-parents to register for gifts before invitations go out, ideally at stores easily accessible for local and out-of-town guests (list stores on the invites).

Plan to pay for the party, but rather than doing all the organizing yourself, you could select a host committee and recruit people to help plan and serve.

Set up a gift table near the door (make sure the mom-to-be decides in advance whether to open presents at the party). If gifts are opened, assign someone to make a list of who gave what. If not, send gifts home with the honorees (be sure not to separate cards from gifts).

Skip girlie games and go with fast, fun options. Ask guests to bring their own baby pictures, throw them in a bowl, and have each person pick one and guess who's who. Ditto with baby pictures of celebrities (see starswelove.com for a good downloadable selection).

the menu

Signature drink: Orange dream
Hors d'oeuvres: Melon-and-prosciutto rolls, chicken salad lettuce cups, crudités with a trio of dips, grilled cheddar-and-turkey-bacon sandwiches, mini burgers with red-hot smoky ketchup
Dessert: Mini ice-cream sandwiches

setting the scene

The décor: Just say no to baby blue and pale pink. Decorate with a contemporary palette of pistachio green and creamy orange with lively mint and mango accents. Place tight arrangements of citrus-colored blooms (ranunculus, tulips, roses, anemones or poppies) in glass baby bottles and arrange them on side and coffee tables. Add tea lights in baby food jars and serve green and orange M&Ms or jelly beans in glass baby bottles, silver baby cups and bowls with baby spoons. Design a self-serve bar stocked with orange dream cocktails, white wine, beer and a pitcher of fruity mocktails (equal parts chilled mango or passion-fruit juice, club soda and white grape juice; serve over ice with an orange wedge). For a warm, peachy glow, wrap hurricanes or vases with sheer tangerine vellum.

The menu: Bite-size comfort foods that riff on pregnancy cravings—such as tiny burgers with ramekins of cornichons and mini grilled cheddar-and-turkey-bacon sandwiches—will also appeal to nonexpectant friends (and guys). Set out or pass hors d'oeuvres on sleek clear, white, or mango- or mint-colored square trays. Toward the end of the party, bring out the mini mango-sorbet and pistachio-ice-cream sandwiches.

The music: Download the red-hot mama-to-be a homemade CD that includes Little Richard's "Baby," Prince's "Baby," Imperial Teen's "Baby," Bebel Gilberto's "Baby," Aretha Franklin's "Oh Baby," the Supremes' "Baby Love," Dusty Springfield's "Oh No, Not My Baby," Donna Summer's "Love to Love You Baby," Suzanne Vega's "As a Child," Carole King's "Child of Mine," Eurythmics' "Beautiful Child," Annie Lennox's "Little Bird," "Sweet Child O' Mine" by Guns 'N Roses and also covered by Sheryl Crow, and the Pretenders' "Kid."

countdown

Three weeks: Send invitations.
Two weeks: Purchase candy. Buy or borrow serving and décor items.
One week: Buy wine, music, candles, vellum and vases. Order flowers.
Two days: Buy groceries.
Day before: Buy bar items; pick up flowers. Make dips and ketchup. Prep burgers, crudités and sandwiches; refrigerate all.
Morning of: Arrange flowers, candles and décor items in the living room and entry. Make ice-cream sandwiches; freeze. Chill wine.
Three hours: Make melon-and-prosciutto rolls, as well as the chicken salad and dressing; refrigerate.
Two hours: Make a pitcher of cocktails; freeze. Set up bar.
One hour: Finish chicken salad cups. Cook burgers and sandwiches; keep them warm in the oven.
15 minutes: Start music. Light candles. Set out snacks.

even easier

Rather than making curry dip from scratch, enliven a store-bought version: Cut two parts hummus with one part plain yogurt; season with salt, pepper and Madras curry powder to taste.

Instead of making burgers, order them from your favorite local burger joint. Get them a little rare and without buns, heat them in the oven on a baking sheet, then quarter and serve them on store-bought biscuits or mini buns. Likewise, order in grilled-cheese sandwiches from a good diner or coffee shop (request cheddar and turkey bacon); warm them in the oven.

Skip assembling ice-cream sandwiches and do a self-service setup: Put out pints of softened ice cream with platters of cookies and invite guests to make their own sandwiches.

Forget about the ice cream altogether and serve pretty store-bought sweets: Pastel cupcakes and petits fours and exotic chocolates always please a crowd.

extra etiquette: bridal shower and engagement party

Many of the same rules apply when giving a bridal shower or engagement party, but there are slight adjustments:

Set the date for a bridal shower about six weeks before the wedding, so the bride isn't too busy or stressed out (confirm the date with her first!).
Plan to foot the bill, or enlist co-hosts to help coordinate the party, do prep work and split costs. Bridesmaids and the mother of the bride can also volunteer to chip in.
Consult the bride on the guest list to determine whether it's friends only or includes relatives. All shower participants should also be wedding guests. Always invite the female members of the wedding party as well as the bride's mother, sisters of the bride and groom, and the bride's future mother-in-law.
Bridal shower gift etiquette is the same as baby shower etiquette: Gifts can be opened at the party or afterward in private. Small, less expensive items from the wedding registry are appropriate gifts, but so are treats specifically for the bride-to-be: lingerie, a spa certificate or something to wear on her honeymoon.
An engagement party celebrates an upcoming marriage and allows the bride and groom's friends and families to get to know each other. It generally takes place within two months of the announcement, and is traditionally hosted by the bride's parents or friends of the couple. Everyone invited to an engagement party should also be invited to the wedding. The host should say a few welcoming words at some point during the party, and the couple should thank the host and guests for coming. Guests often bring small presents to engagement parties, but they aren't required (and shouldn't be opened at the party). Place gifts, with cards attached, in an out-of-the-way spot.

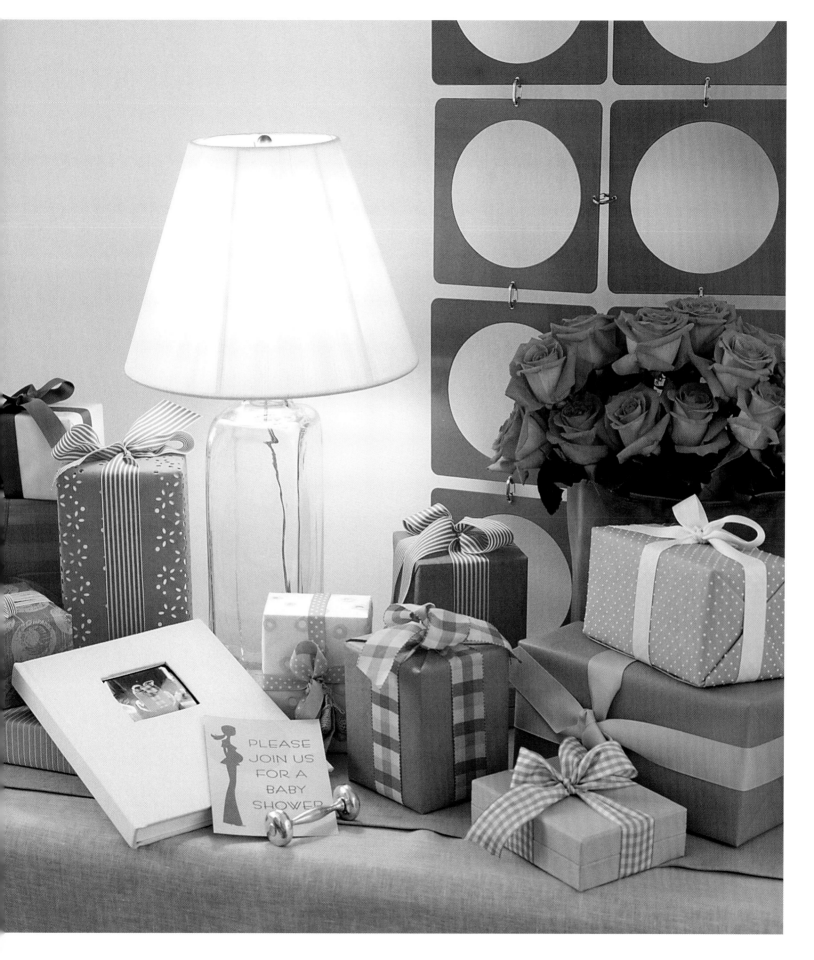

PLEASE
JOIN US
FOR A
BABY
SHOWER

what to pour

Orange dream (serves 10). In blender, blend 4 cups ice cubes; 2 cans (6 oz. each) frozen orange juice concentrate, thawed; 1 pt. orange sorbet; 1 pt. vanilla ice cream; 1 cup orange-flavored vodka; 1 cup vanilla-flavored vodka until creamy. Make 2 batches for 20 guests. Freeze if not serving immediately. Pour into pitcher, serve in cocktail glasses.

Wine picks: Offer a Solo Rosa rosé from California, or a rosé like Domaine de l'Hortus, Domain Tepier or Pradeaux, from France; a California zinfandel, such as Ravenswood Vintner's Blend or Seghesio; a California pinot noir, such as Castlerock; or Mas de Guiot, a grenache-syrah blend from Provence.

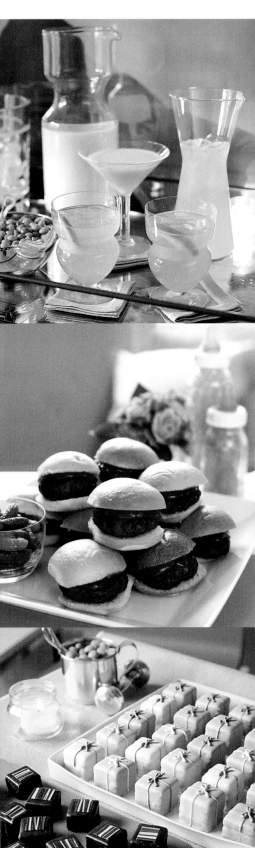

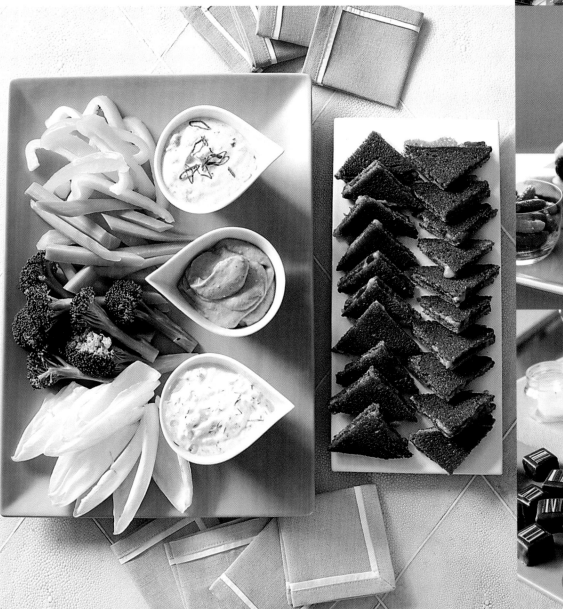

recipes

Melon-and-Prosciutto Rolls
(Serves 20)
2 melons (cantaloupe or honeydew)
½ lb. thinly sliced prosciutto, cut into strips
2 bunches fresh chives, trimmed and blanched

Seed and remove rind from melons; cut into 2" chunks. Wrap with prosciutto and tie with chives (or skewer with toothpicks).

Chicken Salad Lettuce Cups
(Serves 20)
½ cup soy sauce
¼ cup rice wine vinegar
2 tbsp Dijon mustard
2 tbsp minced ginger
1–2 tsp crushed red pepper flakes
¼ cup vegetable oil
2 tbsp sesame oil
8 cups shredded cooked chicken
3 cups shredded radicchio
60 Bibb lettuce leaves
Chopped scallions and toasted sesame seeds for garnish

In small bowl combine first 5 ingredients. Whisk in oils. In large bowl mix chicken and radicchio. Add dressing; toss well. To serve, spoon salad into lettuce leaves; top with scallions and sesame seeds.

Avocado-Tomatillo Dip
(Makes 4 cups)
1 lb. fresh tomatillos (about 10–12), husked, washed and finely chopped
1 cup chopped cilantro
4 cloves garlic, coarsely chopped
2 jalapeños, seeded and coarsely chopped
2 ripe avocados, pitted, peeled and mashed
⅔ cup sour cream
2 tbsp fresh lime juice
Salt to taste

Blend first 4 ingredients to coarse purée.

In medium bowl combine with avocados, sour cream and lime juice. Season with salt.

Cucumber-Yogurt Dip
(Makes 4 cups)
4 containers (8 oz. each) plain yogurt
2 large cucumbers, peeled, seeded and grated
2 cloves garlic, minced
2 tbsp fresh lemon juice
2 tbsp fresh minced dill
Salt to taste
2 tbsp olive oil

Thicken yogurt by placing it in sieve lined with coffee filter overnight in refrigerator. In medium bowl mix with cucumber; garlic, lemon juice and dill. Season with salt; chill. Drizzle with oil before serving.

Curry-Chutney Dip
(Makes 4 cups)
4 containers (8 oz. each) plain yogurt
1 cup mayonnaise
¼ cup mango chutney (such as Major Grey's)
2 tbsp minced cilantro
2 scallions, chopped
2 tsp fresh lime juice
½ tsp red pepper sauce
2 tbsp vegetable oil
2 cloves garlic, minced
2 tbsp curry powder

Prep yogurt as in preceding recipe; mix with next 6 ingredients. Heat oil in small skillet over medium-low heat. Add garlic; sauté 1 min. Add curry powder; cook until fragrant, about 30 seconds. Remove from heat; cool. Stir into dip. Chill. For the crudités: 2 lb. total fresh vegetables, such as sliced peppers and carrots, broccoli spears and endive leaves.

Grilled Cheddar-and-Turkey-Bacon Sandwiches
(Serves 20)
2 loaves (1 lb. each) thinly sliced wheat bread
½ cup grainy mustard
1 lb. sharp cheddar, thinly sliced
2 lb. turkey bacon, cooked
10 tbsp butter, melted

Heat oven to 450°F. Spread half the bread slices with mustard; top with 1 slice cheese and 1½ slices bacon. Top with another cheese slice and piece of bread. Brush baking sheet with some melted butter. Place sandwiches on sheet; brush tops with butter. Bake 5 min., or until lightly browned. Turn; brush again. Return to oven 3–4 min. To serve, remove crusts and cut each sandwich into 4 triangles.

Mini Burgers with Red-Hot Smoky Ketchup
(Serves 20)
1½ cups ketchup
1 tbsp chipotle in adobo plus 1 tbsp sauce
1 tbsp fresh lime juice
2 tsp ground cumin
4½ lb. ground beef
1 tbsp salt
1 tsp pepper
40 small dinner rolls
1 jar cornichons

In bowl combine ketchup, chipotle, lime juice and cumin; chill. Heat oven to 350°F. Season beef with salt and pepper; form into 40 2" burgers. Place on baking sheet; bake 8–9 min., or until done. Top with ketchup; serve on rolls with cornichons on the side.

Mini Ice-Cream Sandwiches
(Makes 40)
1 pt. mango sorbet
1 pt. pistachio ice cream
80 small cookies (like Nilla Wafers, Pepperidge Farm Mini Chessmen and small shortbread)

Scoop 2 tsp sorbet or ice cream on 40 cookies; top with another cookie. Smooth edges. Freeze on baking sheets 1 hr., or until ready to serve.

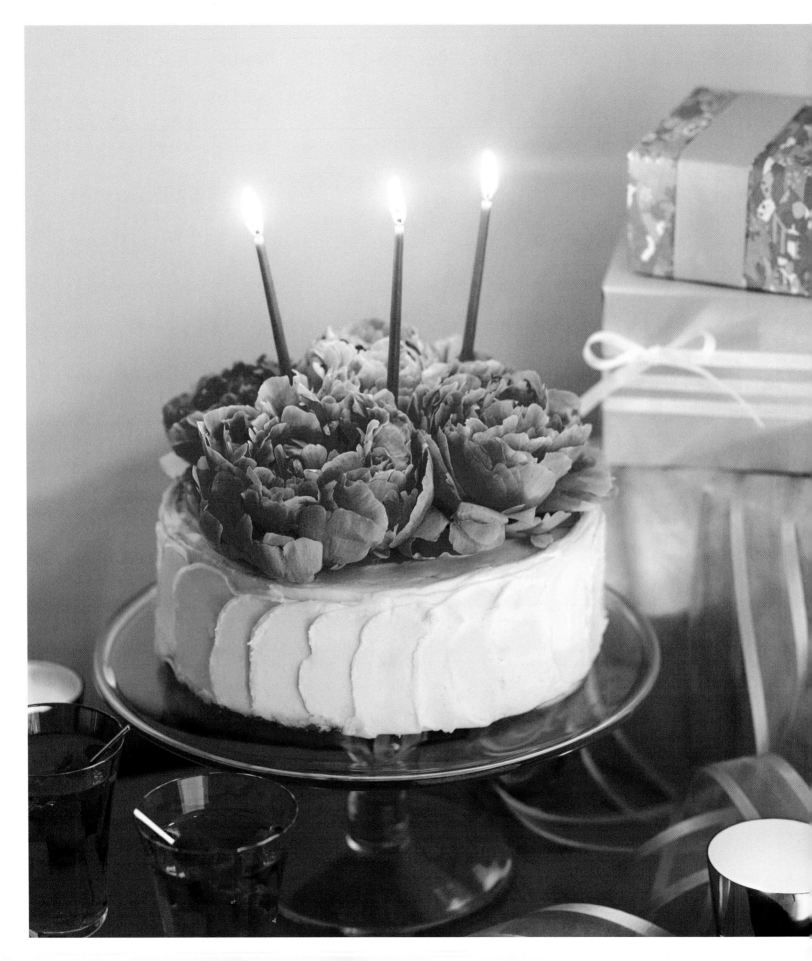

birthday
dinner party

Make your best friend feel extra special this year with an all-girl birthday party dinner. L.A. event and wedding producer Diann Valentine (who has planned events for Toni Braxton and Lela Rochon) puts a glamorous spin on the event. Start with a pink and chocolate-brown color scheme and bubbly cocktails, then have a light family-style meal. Finish with a shamelessly decadent cake—served with presents, of course—and see how a get-together with friends helps keep a birthday girl young at heart.

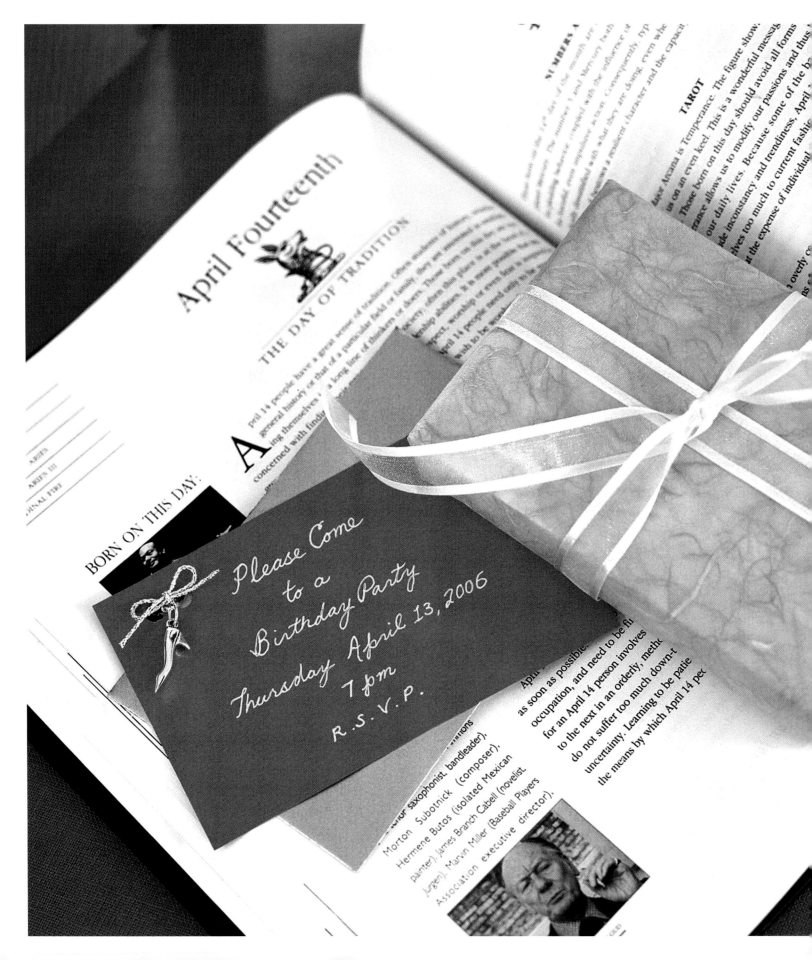

surprise-party pointers

A surprise party is probably the most unforgettable gift you can spring on a friend. For a seamless operation, try these maneuvers:

Don't give the party on the honoree's actual birthday. Throw her off by hosting it one or two weeks earlier.

Send a ruse invitation to the honoree inviting her to a fake event at a mutual friend's home. Word the invitation so that she'll dress appropriately for the kind of party you're throwing for her.

Have the honoree pick you up at your house (where the real sparty is). Make the time on her invitation a half-hour later to minimize the chance of her bumping into a friend at your front door. Have guests park out of sight, and set the gift table away from the front door.

It's the oldest trick in the book, but it works: Have guests hide behind furniture in the party area and jump out yelling "Surprise!" when the guest of honor enters the room.

Friends often avoid the birthday girl when they know they are about to surprise her. Remind them to call and inquire about her birthday plans or to send a card, so she doesn't get suspicious.

the menu

Signature drink: Pink halo
Hors d'oeuvres: Potato chips with crème fraîche and salmon caviar, green crudités with creamy horseradish dip
Main course: Garlic chicken piccata, spinach salad, spring vegetable risotto, roasted cherry tomatoes
Dessert: Red velvet cake

setting the scene

The invitation: Send pink note cards with details written in metallic silver ink; attach a small silver charm to each (available at Artbeads.com; see Resources) and ask guests to wear them to the party. When each guest RSVPs, ask for her birthday and write it down.

The décor: Start with a palette of pinks (ballet slipper, bubblegum, fuchsia) and browns (from taupe to chocolate). Decorate your living room with votives and small, tight bouquets of pink peonies in low glasses or silver vases. Set up a small bar on a credenza with sparkling water, white or rosé wine and pink halo cocktails. In the dining room, set the table with a pink cloth and pink napkins and taupe or cream-colored china. Buy the book *The Secret Language of Birthdays: Your Complete Personology Guide for Each Day of the Year* (available at amazon.com). Make color copies of the pages representing each guest's birthday, and use them as place markers or party favors. Scatter tea lights in silver holders across the dining table. In the center of the table, place tightly arranged peonies in glass or silver vases (low enough that guests can easily converse over them). Hang a festive cascade of ribbons from the back of each chair.

The menu: As guests arrive, offer crudités in the living room and pass potato chips topped with salmon caviar. For dinner, serve the spinach salad, risotto, roasted tomatoes and garlic chicken family-style. Afterward, honor the birthday girl with a delectable red velvet cake with cream cheese frosting, a traditional Southern favorite. Top the cake with tiny pink tapers (not short birthday candles) and pink peonies (put plastic wrap across the top of the cake and place flower heads on it; if necessary, anchor them with toothpicks).

The music: Download a special gift that the birthday girl can play every year: a festive soundtrack for blowing out the candles that includes Stevie Wonder's "Happy Birthday," the Beatles' "You Say It's Your Birthday," R. Kelly's "It's Your Birthday," Blur's "Birthday," Sugarcubes' "Birthday," Pet Shop Boys' "Birthday Boy," Altered Images' "Happy Birthday," Cibo Matto's "Birthday Cake," Loretta Lynn's "Happy Birthday," and the most popular hip-hop birthday song ever, 50 Cent's "In Da Club."

birthday extras: parties, gifts and toasts

To make the most of your birthday soirée, incorporate one or more of these ideas:

Consider having guests go in on one spectacular present. Tally how many people want to participate, decide on a price, ask friends and family for tips on a gift, collect contributions, and buy it. Pass around a card for everyone to sign.

Poll friends to assess whether the honoree would appreciate a surprise (some wouldn't!). If it's a go, remind guests to keep the secret, avoid sending revealing e-mails that could be forwarded, and book the honoree for a faux outing so she doesn't make other plans.

During dessert invite guests to take turns describing the thing they love most about the birthday girl, or to recount their fondest memories.

To stay sane divvy up party responsibilities. Ask a few friends to lighten your load by sending invitations, buying flowers or wine, or bringing a specific dish.

countdown

Five weeks: Order charms for invitations.
Three weeks: Send invitations.
One week: Buy wine, candles, vases, music, ribbons; order flowers and cake (if not making it).
Two days: Buy groceries.
Day before: Pick up and arrange flowers. Decorate chairs. Buy bar items. Make dip and prep crudités; refrigerate.
Morning of: Chill wine. Set table and set up bar. Bake or pick up and decorate the cake. Make roasted cherry tomatoes.
Four hours: Assemble, but don't dress, spinach salad; chill, covered with a damp paper towel.
Two hours: Prep, but don't bake, chicken. Prep asparagus, leeks and garlic for risotto.
One hour: Arrange crudités and dip on a platter. Make caviar chips. Start the risotto; continue to add broth and stir.
15 minutes: Make two pitchers of pink halo cocktails. Light candles. Start music.
When guests arrive: Serve drinks and hors d'oeuvres. Put chicken in the oven.
Dinnertime: Finish risotto and dress salad.
After dinner: Serve cake and offer toasts and gifts.

even easier

Pop open festive rosé champagne instead of making cocktails (try Schramsberg brut rosé).

Mix in or substitute less expensive and more available pink carnations or roses, as peonies can get pricey. Be sure to buy roses that are at least partially in bloom.

If you can't find salmon caviar, top chips and crème fraîche with pieces of smoked salmon.

Skip stirring the risotto. Make orzo (rice-shaped pasta) and mix in sautéed chopped asparagus, fresh chopped parsley and chives; finish with a drizzle of olive oil, grated Parmesan, salt and pepper.

Instead of baking it yourself, buy red velvet cake with cream cheese icing from a local bakery (if they don't have a recipe, tell them it's yellow cake with red coloring and cocoa) or order one from Very Vera in Augusta, Ga. (see Resources).

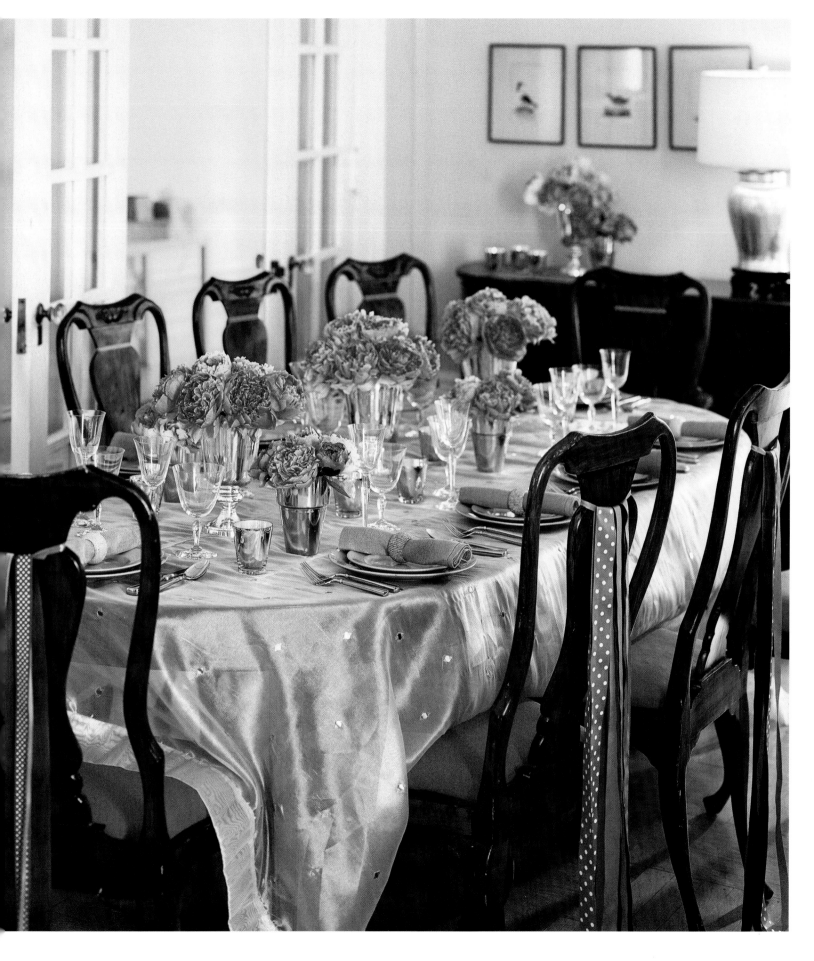

what to pour

Pink halo (serves 10): Pour 2 bottles (750 ml each) of champagne or sparkling wine and 1 cup raspberry-flavored vodka into large pitcher. Add a splash or 2 of grenadine to give the drinks a pinkish hue. Chill until cold. To serve, pour into champagne glasses and garnish with a skewer of raspberries. Since you're mixing the bubbles with a flavored spirit, don't bother with the expensive stuff. Pick affordable options such as Mionetto prosecco Doc or Domaine St. Michelle cuvée brut.

Wine Picks: With dinner offer an Italian pinot grigio from Silvio Jermann or Kriss, or a slightly sweet Spatlese riesling from Germany from Dr. Loosen or Reichsgraf von Kesselstatt.

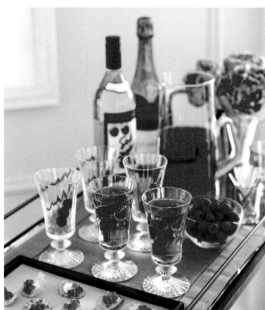

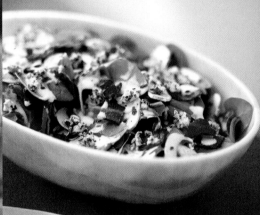

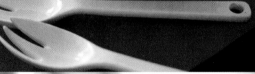

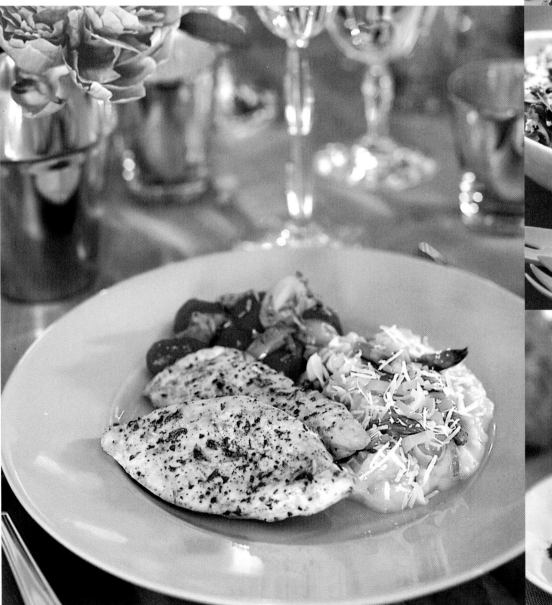

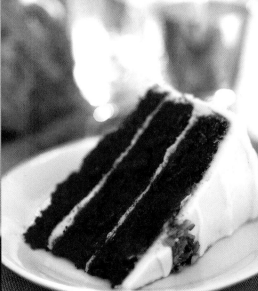

recipes

Potato Chips with Crème Fraîche and Salmon Caviar
(Serves 10)
8 oz. crème fraîche or sour cream
1 pkg. (5 oz.) salt-and-pepper potato chips or regular gourmet chips
1 tbsp cracked pepper
1 jar (2 oz.) salmon caviar

Spread crème fraîche over chips. Sprinkle with cracked pepper. Top with small dollop of caviar.

Green Crudités with Creamy Horseradish Dip
(Serves 10)
½ cup sour cream
½ cup mayonnaise
1 clove garlic, minced
2 tbsp prepared drained horseradish
1 tbsp plus 1 tsp minced fresh chives, divided
1½ tsp chopped fresh tarragon
½ tsp paprika
Salt and pepper to taste
8 cups assorted vegetables (sugar snap peas, asparagus, broccoli, celery, etc.), cleaned, trimmed and peeled

In medium bowl combine sour cream, mayonnaise, garlic, horseradish, 1 tbsp chives, tarragon and paprika. Season with salt and pepper. Cover with plastic wrap and refrigerate. Bring to room temperature 1 hr. before serving. Sprinkle remaining chives over dip. Arrange vegetables on platter; serve with dip.

Spinach Salad
(Serves 10)
10 cups cleaned baby spinach
10 slices cooked bacon, crumbled
1 pkg. (8 oz.) white mushrooms, sliced
1 tbsp minced fresh herbs (such as thyme, basil and parsley)
1 clove garlic, minced
12 oz. homemade or bottled blue cheese dressing

In large bowl toss together first 5 ingredients. Serve with blue cheese dressing.

Spring Vegetable Risotto
(Serves 10)
4 tbsp olive oil, divided
¾ lb. asparagus, trimmed and cut in 1" pieces
Salt and pepper to taste
6 cups chicken broth
2 medium leeks, thinly sliced
2 cloves garlic, minced
2 cups arborio rice
1½ cups freshly grated Parmesan
1 cup frozen peas, thawed

Heat 1 tbsp oil in medium skillet over medium-high heat. Add asparagus; sprinkle with salt and pepper. Sauté until asparagus begins to soften, about 2 min. Set aside. Bring broth to simmer in medium saucepan over low heat. Cover; keep warm. Heat remaining 3 tbsp olive oil in large heavy pot over medium-high heat. Add leeks and garlic. Sauté until leeks begin to soften, 3–4 min. Add rice; stir until rice is translucent, about 3 min. Reduce heat to medium. Add ½ cup broth; stir until liquid is absorbed. Add broth, 1 cup at a time, stirring constantly until each addition is absorbed before adding the next cup, until there is only 1 cup broth remaining. Add cheese, peas and remaining broth. Simmer until vegetables are just tender and risotto is creamy. Season with salt and pepper.

Roasted Cherry Tomatoes
(Serves 10)
2½ lb. red and/or yellow cherry or grape tomatoes, halved
2 tbsp olive oil
½ tsp salt
¼ tsp pepper
¼ cup chopped fresh basil

Heat oven to 400ºF. In large bowl toss tomatoes with olive oil, salt and pepper. Place on baking sheet in a single layer. Roast 30–35 min., or until skins begin to wrinkle. Toss with basil. Season with additional salt and pepper, if desired.

Serve warm or at room temperature.

Garlic Chicken Piccata
(Serves 10)
¼ cup olive oil
6 cloves garlic, minced
2 tbsp chopped fresh thyme
2 tsp chopped fresh tarragon
2 tbsp fresh lemon juice
1 tsp salt
½ tsp pepper
3½ lb. boneless, skinless chicken breasts or tenders, thinly sliced,
½ cup reduced-sodium chicken broth

Heat oven to 400ºF. In small bowl combine all ingredients except chicken and broth. Place chicken in large baking dish in single layer; spoon herb mixture on top and pour broth over. Bake 3–4 min. on each side, or until cooked through. To serve, arrange chicken on platter and pour pan juices over it.

Red Velvet Cake
(Serves 10)
½ cup shortening
1½ cups sugar
2 eggs
2 tbsp cocoa
1½ oz. red food coloring
1 tsp salt
2½ cups flour
1 tsp vanilla
1 cup buttermilk
1 tsp soda
1 tbsp vinegar

Cream shortening; gradually beat in sugar. Add eggs 1 at a time and beat well. Make paste of cocoa and food coloring; add to creamed mixture. Add salt, flour, vanilla and buttermilk, beating well. Sprinkle soda over vinegar; pour vinegar over batter. Stir until thoroughly mixed. Bake in 2 9" pans for 30 min. at 350ºF. Let cool; frost with homemade or store-bought cream cheese icing. Destem and cluster 4 blown open peonies (in varying shades of pink and white) in center of cake. Insert long thin red candles.

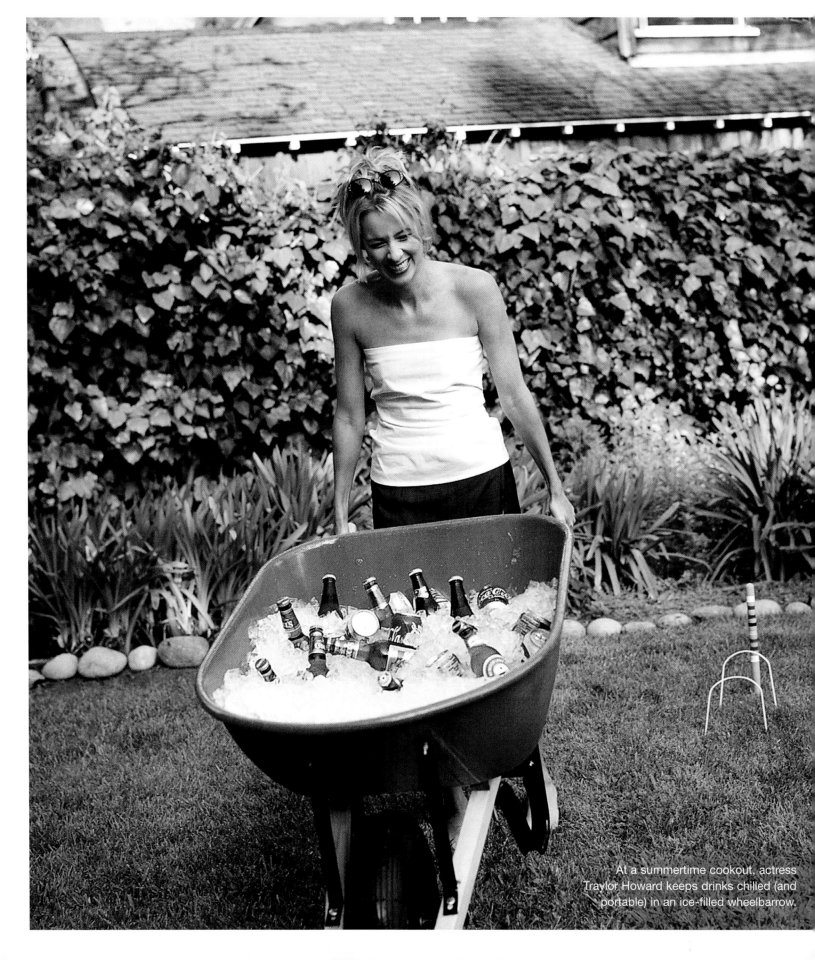

At a summertime cookout, actress Traylor Howard keeps drinks chilled (and portable) in an ice-filled wheelbarrow.

summer parties

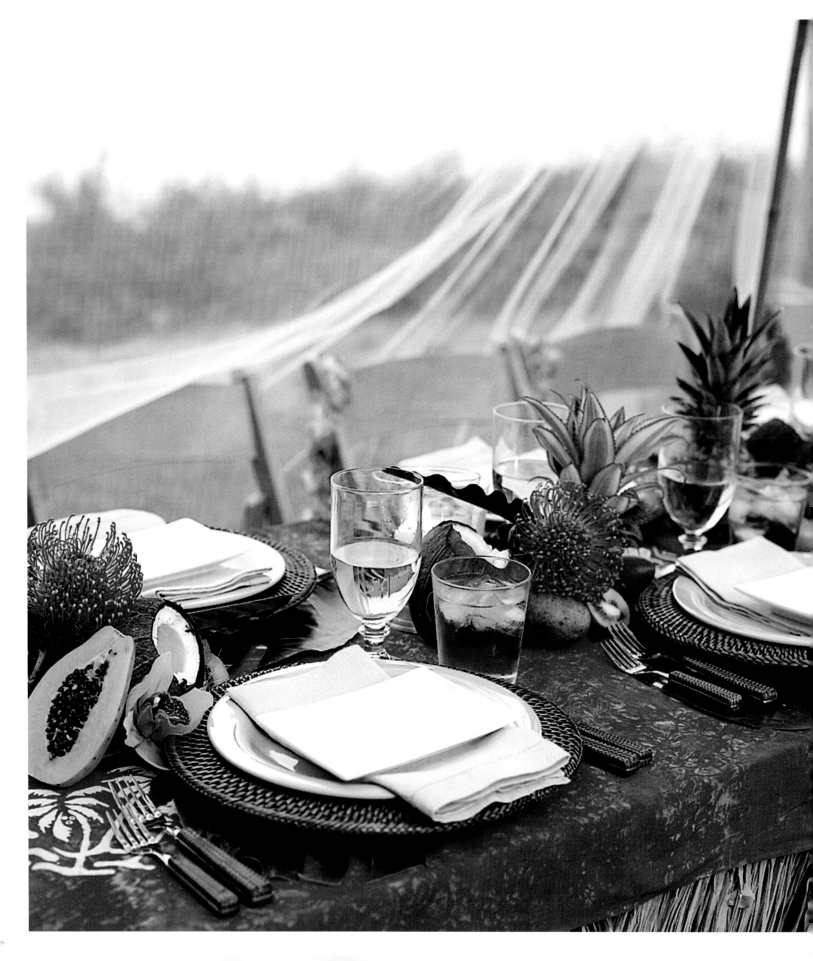

backyard luau

Break out the paper parasols and crank up the theme from *Hawaii Five-O*: Long summer evenings cry out for a luau. But rest assured that "tiki" doesn't have to mean "tacky." Event guru Colin Cowie believes that when giving a theme party the key to success is tasteful restraint, which is why he keeps this **Polynesian dinner** for 12 warm, fun and casual (and not over the top: There are no flame-throwers and roasted pigs at this bash). Friends ease into the evening with mai tais. A **pan-Asian menu** is served under a canopied structure lit by Chinese lanterns and surrounded by tiki torches. And Hawaiian tunes lull guests into a tropical reverie, giving new meaning to the term "Maui wowie."

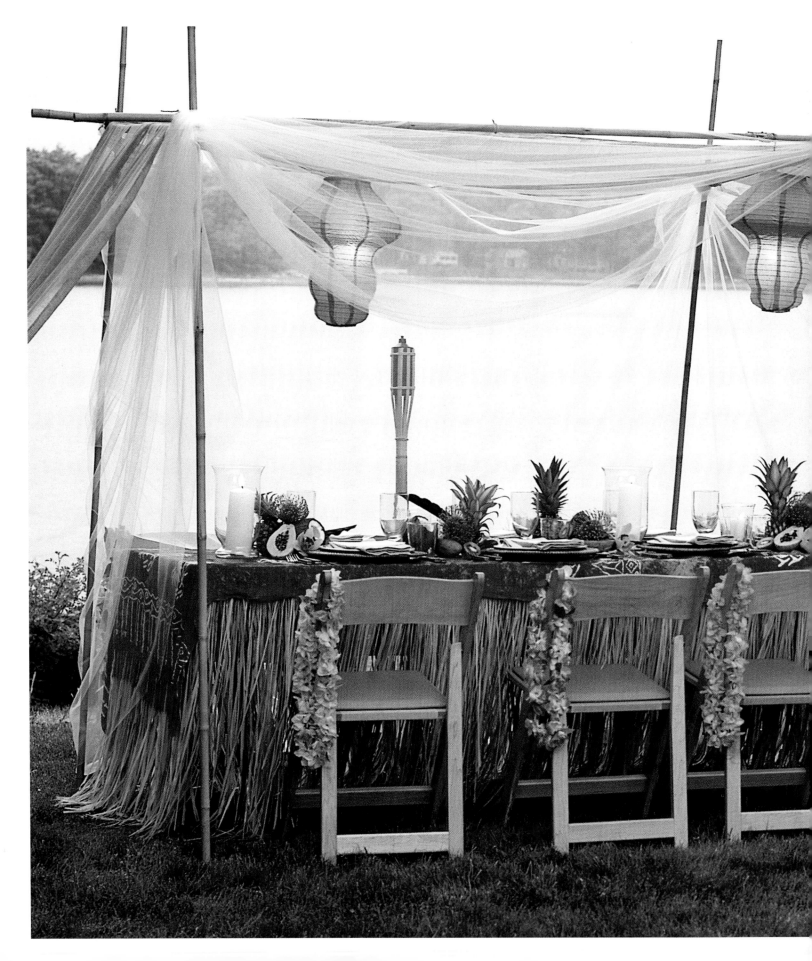

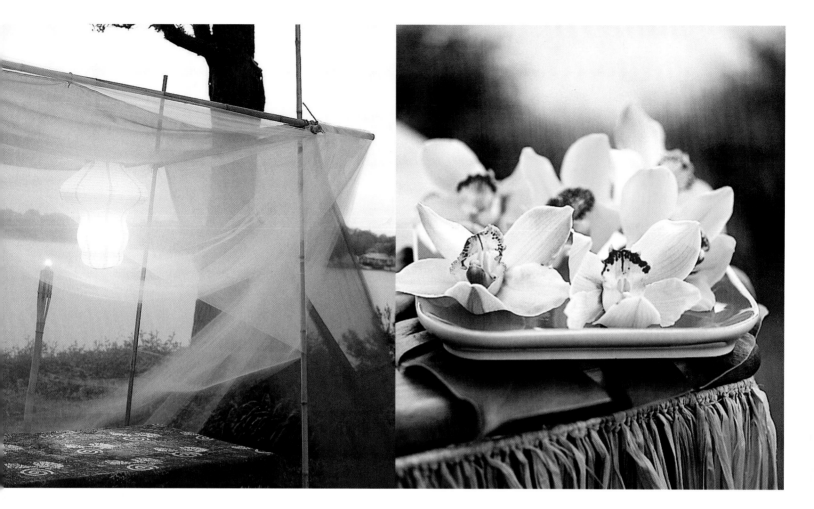

the menu

Signature drink: Mai tai
Hors d'oeuvres: Shrimp-and-pineapple skewers, spicy chicken skewers, potstickers, crab salad on Chinese soup spoons (available at Pearl River Mart; see Resources).
Appetizer: Mixed greens and tropical fruit with sake vinaigrette
Main course: Parchment-wrapped mahimahi with mushrooms and savory rice
Dessert: Ice cream or sorbet with vanilla-spiked pineapple

setting the scene

The invitation: Pick invitations with a tropical theme: Look for some printed with palm trees, hibiscus flowers or pineapples. Get guests into a tropical mood with a suggested dress code: pareos for the women and Hawaiian shirts for the guys.

The tabletop: Cover the sides of a rectangular table with grass skirting (available at Oriental Trading Co.; see Resources); use pareos (available at Zunimaya, see Resources) as a tablecloth. Hang fabric leis on chairs (they're available at party supply stores or from Hilo Hattie; see Resources). Use large tropical leaves such as monstera as place mats (about $2 per leaf; at florists). Down the length of the table, alternate hurricane lamps with mounds of whole and halved tropical fruits: coconuts, pineapples, papayas, mangoes, passion fruit and kiwis, all studded with tropical flowers.

The music: Authentic Hawaiian greatest hits collections from Don Ho and Arthur Lyman make for fun cocktail music, as does Martin Denny's *The Exotic Sounds of Martin Denny.* For something cool and contemporary try surfer turned singer Jack Johnson's *On and On.* After dinner up the tempo with classic pop from the Beach Boys or surf-inspired rock: *Wipe Out! The Best of the Surfaris* or Jan & Dean's *The Sunshine Collection.*

countdown

Four weeks: Order leis, grass skirting and pareos.
Three weeks: Mail invitations.
Two weeks: Buy outdoor lights, citronella torches and canopy materials, if desired.
One week: Order flowers and fish. Buy nonperishable ingredients, music, wine and bar supplies.
Two days: Shop for remaining groceries.
One day: Pick up fish, flowers and take-out potstickers from a Chinese or Thai restaurant. Cook shrimp; make sauces.
Morning of: Build canopy. Set table except for the fruit centerpieces. Chill wine. Arrange flowers.
Seven hours: Make salad, rice and roasted pineapple.
Five hours: Prep fish packets and skewers (cook later).
Two hours: Make centerpieces. Mix mai tais.
One hour: Cook chicken skewers; reheat potstickers in oven and assemble crab appetizer. Light torches.
Party time: Light candles. Start music. Toss salad for first course.
During first course: Bake fish; reheat rice and pineapple.

even easier

Instead of buying themed invitations, make handwritten ones with bright orange and hot pink cards and envelopes.
If you need to rent a long table and chairs, look under Party Supplies in the Yellow Pages. Have them delivered the evening before, or morning of, the luau.
Rather than building a canopy, set up your table underneath a large tree limb. Wind strings of lights around the limb or hang Chinese lanterns from the branches.
Omit the crab salad and shrimp skewers from the menu and increase amount of chicken skewers and take-out potstickers. Order extra dipping sauces so you don't run out.

creating a canopy

For an intimate, pretty dinner, create a romantic, exotic mood by setting up a bamboo canopy. (If you prefer to rent a canopy, look under Tents in the yellow pages.)

A 16' x 8' x 7½' structure that will cover a rectangular table for 12 requires 13 8' bamboo poles (about $5 each at garden centers and lumberyards).
Stake six poles, three on each long side (use metal tent stakes to make the holes). Use three of the poles for the crossbars on the top, or roof of the structure; set up the other 4 poles lengthwise. Tie poles together with heavy twine.
Make a roof running lengthwise (see photo on previous page) using colored cotton muslin (available at fabric stores; you'll need about 40' of a 72½"-wide roll) and stake the ends into the ground. Hang lengths of tulle or mosquito netting (also from fabric stores) on the sides of the canopy, tying at each crossbar, and allow the fabric to drape down the sides.
Inside, hang Chinese lanterns using a drop socket (a cord with a bulb socket; ask for it at a hardware store).
To repel bugs, set up a perimeter of citronella torches about 10' from the tent.

bar under the stars

Set up a small table to serve as a bar and hors d'oeuvres station; position it close to the house so guests reach it before the dining tent. Cover the sides with a grass skirt to match the dining table and top it with pareos.
Decorate the table and serving trays with tropical foliage and flowers. Set out an iced pitcher of mai tais and fill a flat-bottom bowl with crushed ice to hold wine bottles. Place tropical flowers or stemmed miniature pineapples (order them from a florist) into the ice for a festive touch. Use wood and rattan serving pieces to hold appetizers.
To cut down on kitchen runs, stash extra supplies in baskets under the table: Include carafes of mai tais, bottles of wine, extra ice and dipping sauces, along with towels to mop up spills.

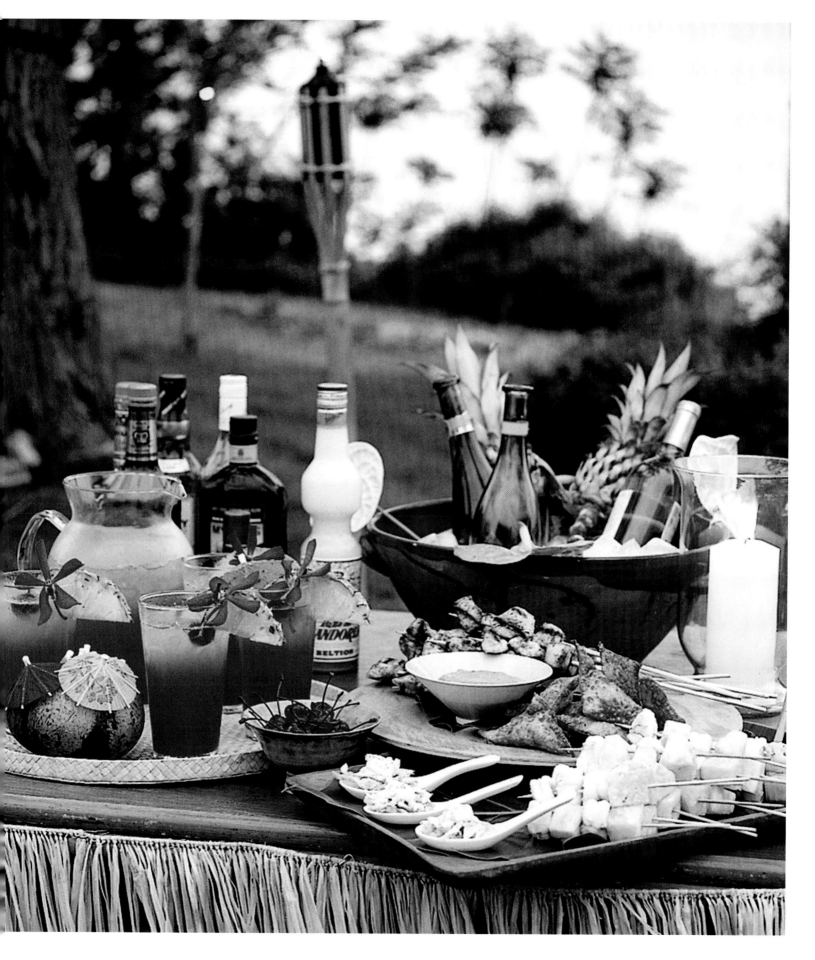

what to pour

Mai tai (serves 12): Combine 3 cups light rum, 1½ cups orange-flavored liqueur, ¾ cup fresh lime juice, ½ cup almond-flavored syrup, ½ cup grenadine and 2 tbsp confectioners' sugar in bowl; in batches mix in a shaker filled with ice. Strain into glasses half-filled with crushed ice. Garnish with a pineapple slice, cherry and orchid blossom (paper parasol optional). For small, affordable orchids, buy dendrobium branches, which are filled with the small blooms that are used in Hawaiian leis, and make sure they're pesticide-free.

Wine pick: A Kabinett riesling from Germany, such as Gunderlach, Fritz Haag or J.J. Prüm, will be the best match for this Asian fusion menu.

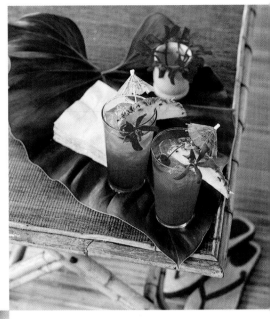

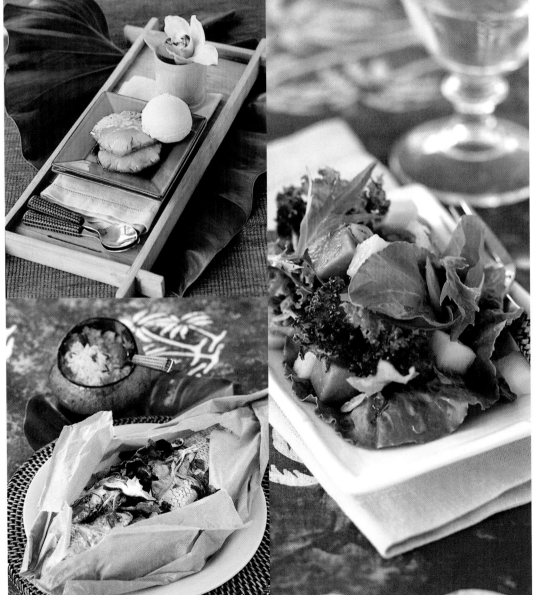

recipes

Shrimp-and-Pineapple Skewers
(Makes 36)
1 cup orange juice
½ cup low-sodium soy sauce
2 tbsp sesame oil
Pepper to taste
36 super-colossal shrimp, peeled, deveined and cooked
2 pineapples, peeled, cored, cut in 1" cubes

In small bowl combine first 4 ingredients for sauce. Cut each shrimp into 3 pieces. On bamboo skewer alternately thread shrimp and pineapple. Arrange on platter and drizzle with sauce; serve remaining sauce on side.

Spicy Chicken Skewers
(Makes 36)
1 large onion, grated
1¼ cups coconut milk, divided
3 tbsp grated ginger
3 tbsp sugar, divided
3 tbsp soy sauce, divided
3 tsp ground coriander, divided
1 tsp plus 2 tbsp chili paste, divided
½ tsp salt
2 lb. boneless chicken breast, cut in strips
2 cups raw peanuts, toasted
¼ cup peanut oil
1 tsp minced lemongrass

Soak bamboo skewers in water for 30 min. In large bowl combine onion, ¼ cup coconut milk, ginger, 1 tbsp sugar, 1 tbsp soy sauce, 2 tsp coriander, 1 tsp chili paste and salt. Add chicken; toss well. Cover; refrigerate 1 hr. Grind peanuts in food processor until fine. Add remaining cup coconut milk, 2 tbsp sugar, 2 tbsp soy sauce, 1 tsp coriander, 2 tbsp chili paste, peanut oil, lemongrass and ½ cup water. Process until smooth. Bring peanut sauce to boil in medium saucepan; reduce heat and simmer 5 min. Heat broiler. Remove chicken from marinade; thread onto skewers. Place on rack and broil 6–7 min., turning once. Serve with peanut sauce.

Crab Salad on Soup Spoons
(Makes 36)
½ cup mayonnaise
2 tbsp heavy cream
2 tbsp chili sauce
1 tbsp chopped fresh flat-leaf parsley
1 tbsp grated onion
4 cups shredded iceberg lettuce
1 lb. lump crabmeat, picked through
Ground cayenne pepper for garnish

In small bowl combine first 5 ingredients for dressing. Place small amount of lettuce on spoons; top with crab. Drizzle dressing over crab and sprinkle lightly with cayenne pepper.

Mixed Greens and Tropical Fruit with Sake Vinaigrette
(Serves 12)
¼ cup sake
2 tbsp mirin (sweet sake; at Asian markets)
2 tbsp balsamic vinegar
1 tbsp minced shallot
1 tsp sugar
½ tsp pepper
¼ tsp salt
1 cup vegetable oil
12 cups assorted greens
3 scallions, sliced
1 large ripe mango, peeled, pitted, diced
1 ripe papaya, peeled, seeded, diced

In medium bowl combine first 7 ingredients; whisk in oil. In large bowl toss together greens, scallions, mango and papaya. Add desired amount of dressing. Toss well.

Parchment-Wrapped Mahimahi with Mushrooms
(Serves 12)
⅓ cup ginger paste (at Asian markets)
12 mahimahi fillets, divided (about 6 oz. each)
12 cups assorted fresh mushrooms, (such as shiitake, oyster or enoki) very thinly sliced
1 bunch scallions, julienned
½ cup chopped cilantro
¾ cup mirin
¾ cup black bean sauce (at Asian markets)
1 egg white
1 tsp salt

Spread about 1 tsp ginger paste on 1 side of each fillet. Cover with plastic wrap; refrigerate 1 hr. In large bowl combine mushrooms, scallions and cilantro. In medium bowl mix mirin and black bean sauce. Cut 12 pieces of parchment into 12" squares. Place ½ cup mushroom mixture in center. Top with fillet, another ½ cup mushroom mixture and 2 tbsp mirin mixture. In small bowl beat together egg white and salt; brush on 1" of outside edge of parchment and fold sides over, pressing against the egg white to adhere. Brush again to seal. Heat oven to 350°F. Continue assembling packets. Place on baking sheet. Bake in oven until packets puff, about 10 min. per 1" of thickness. Place packets on serving plate and carefully cut open with scissors.

Savory Rice
(Serves 12)
3 cups basmati rice
2 tbsp butter
2 cloves garlic, chopped
1 medium onion, chopped

1 red pepper, seeded and cubed
1 yellow pepper, seeded and cubed
½ tsp ground turmeric
1 cup chicken broth
1 cinnamon stick
1 tsp salt

Soak rice in cold water to cover for 30 min. In large skillet melt butter over medium-high heat. Add garlic, onion, peppers and turmeric; cook until vegetables have softened, 6–8 min. Drain rice and rinse it well. Add rice, 3 cups water, chicken broth, cinnamon stick and salt to deep skillet. Bring to boil; reduce heat to low, cover and cook 20 min., or until liquid has been absorbed. Remove from heat; let sit 5 min. Discard cinnamon stick. Serve hot.

Vanilla-Spiked Pineapple
(Serves 12)
3 vanilla beans, split
3 ripe pineapples, peeled, cored and halved
3 cups sugar
¾ cup dark rum

Cut vanilla beans into 2" lengths. Pierce pineapple flesh with a skewer and insert vanilla bean pieces in holes. Place pineapples in stockpot. In medium bowl combine sugar, 3 cups water and rum; pour over pineapples. Bring to boil. Reduce heat; simmer 1 hr. Remove pan from heat and let pineapples cool in syrup. Cut into 1" slices. Serve with mango sorbet or vanilla ice cream.

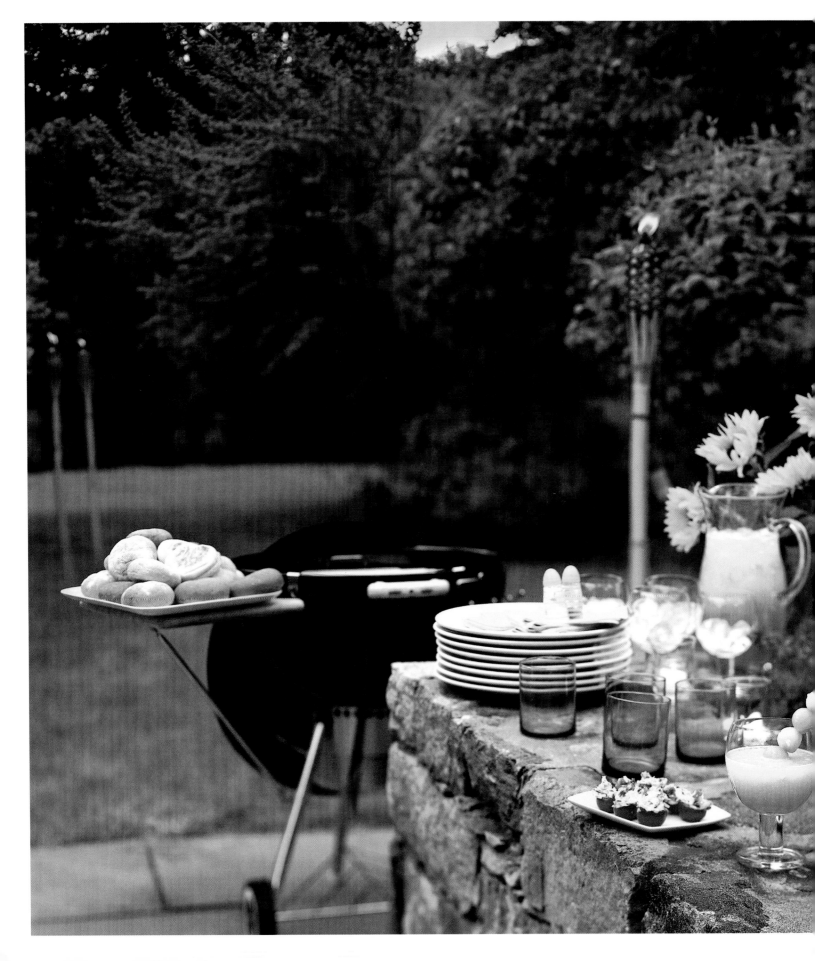

backyard
barbecue

For laid-back, no-fuss entertaining, it's hard to beat a backyard barbecue. New York City and Long Island event planner Christopher Robbins, who has staged outdoor fêtes for Jerry and Jessica Seinfeld, offers a refreshing, flavor-packed take on the traditional menu of burgers and salads. At this 10-person gathering, greet guests with summer melon coolers and serve food family-style on a sunny, paint-splattered cloth scattered with fresh flowers. It won't be long before your friends are just as fired up as the grill.

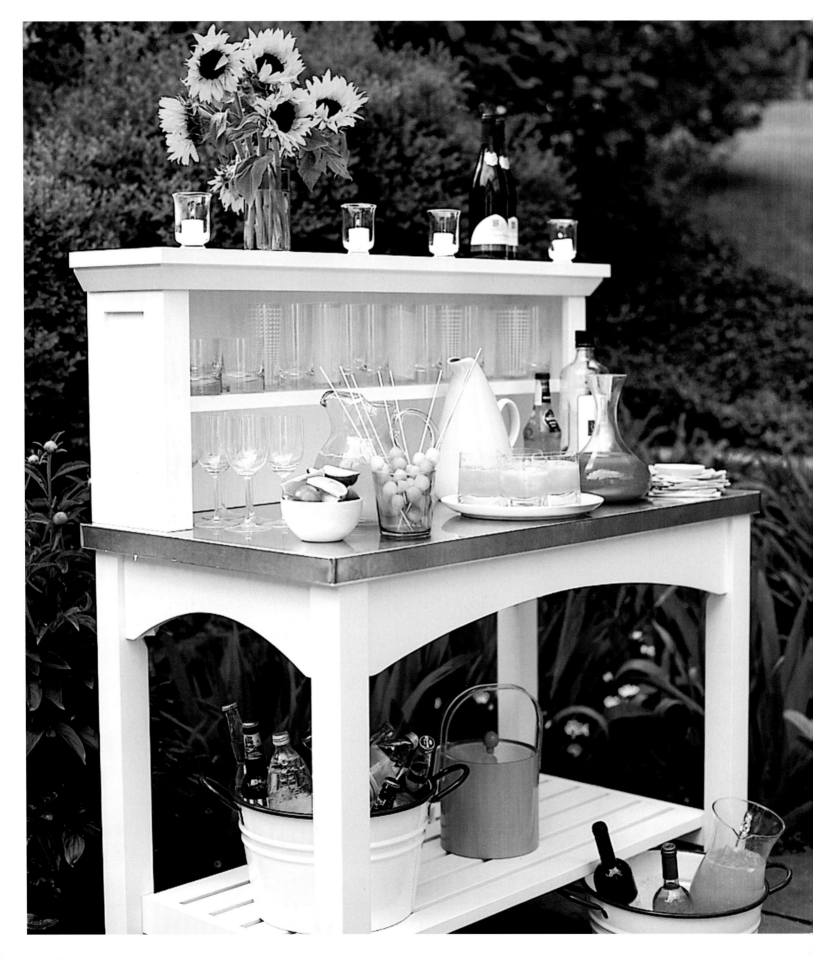

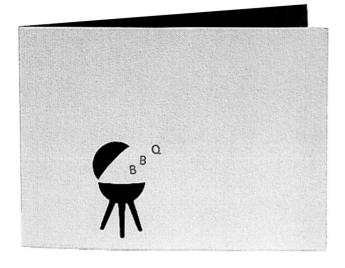

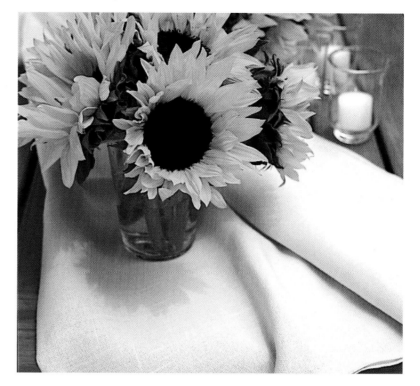

menu

Signature drink: Summer melon cooler
Hors d'oeuvres: BLT cherry tomatoes and egg-salad bites
Main course: Lamb and tuna burgers, black-and-white bean salad, dilled broccoli slaw, tomato salad with summer herbs
Dessert: Brownie s'mores

setting the scene

The tabletop. A palette of lime-green, sunny yellow and cream sets a fresh, energetic tone. Add to the fun by splattering different shades of yellow paint on a cotton drop cloth (available at hardware stores), starting with the darkest hue first. Cluster small hurricane lamps with white candles in the center of the table and scatter sunflowers cut off just below the bloom (yellow zinnias and gerbera daisies also work).

The setup. Place the dining table in the middle of the yard, with the bar closer to the house. Position the grill so smoke blows away from guests, but keep it close enough to the cocktail area or dining table that the chef doesn't feel excluded from the party. Place eight to 10 bamboo torches filled with citronella oil around the perimeter of the party area to add light and ward off insects. For additional bug protection, spray the air, ground and shrubbery with Raid Yard Guard outdoor fogger three hours before guests arrive.

The kiddie crowd. If you invite children, make an extra spatter-paint drop cloth to use as a picnic blanket. Serve carrot and celery sticks, grilled mini hamburgers on soft Parker House rolls, and fried chicken fingers with barbecue sauce. For dessert add a smear of peanut butter to the brownie s'mores. Keep kids busy with hula hoops and catch sets with Velcro mitts.

The music. During cocktails (or the beer blast, as the case may be), get guests to unwind with reggae music—you can't go wrong with *Legend: The Best of Bob Marley.* But if you prefer a sexy Rio-worthy vibe, then try Antonio Carlos Jobim's *Bossa Nova Brazil,* which also features Astrud Gliberto, or for a more contemporary twist, Gilberto Gil's The Pure Brazil series—*Caipirinha* and *Samba Soul Groove.* Or else download a summery selection of songs: The Cure's "Hot Hot Hot," Bananarama"s "Cruel Summer," Blondie's "The Tide is High," Donna Summer's "Hot Stuff," The Rolling Stone's "Hot Stuff," Nick Gilder and Time Machine's "Hot Child in the City," Bob Dylan's "Summer Days," Chet Baker's "Indian Summer," The Isley Brothers' "Summer Breeze," Miles Davis's "Summer Night," Yo La Tengo's "The Summer," Don Henley's "The Boys of Summer" and Abba's "Summer Nights"—performed by John Travolta and Olivia Newton-John—from the *Grease* soundtrack. Wind down the night with sophisticated songbirds like Sade and Everything But The Girl's Tracey Thorn.

countdown

Three weeks: Call invitees or send invitations.
Two weeks: Purchase music, tabletop items, drop cloth and paints.
One week: Order tuna and lamb.
Two days: Shop for groceries. Make brownies. Hard-boil eggs.
Day before: Buy flowers to scatter across table. Set up table and bar. Purée honeydew for cocktails.
Six hours: Prep tuna or lamb burgers and make broccoli slaw. Hollow out cherry tomatoes and make filling for BLT hors d'oeuvres.
Three hours: Spray yard with insect spray. Make bean salad. Make chocolate sauce for brownie s'mores.
One hour: Set table. Mix cocktails; chill.
30 minutes: Assemble egg-salad bites and cherry tomatoes; arrange on platters.
10 minutes: Sprinkle cut flowers on table. Light candles and torches. Start music.
After guests arrive: Light grill. After the main course, reheat chocolate sauce and crush graham crackers for brownie s'mores.

even easier

Skip the splatter painting and use a yellow or pale green tablecloth. Instead of arranging cut blooms, fill clear or green glass tumblers with flowers.
Bypass the summer melon cooler in favor of easy spiked pink lemonade: Fill a half-gallon pitcher with ⅓ vodka and ⅓ lemonade, then fill to top with equal parts cranberry juice and club soda.
For faster hors d'oeuvres, serve cherry tomatoes or radishes with lemon-seasoned salt or a dip of half mayonnaise and half sour cream with any combination of chopped shallots, capers, garlic and green olives blended in.

Serve beef, turkey and veggie burgers instead of lamb and tuna. For extra spice, top beef burgers with pepper ketchup (mix equal parts ketchup and puréed homemade or bottled roasted red peppers; season with freshly cracked pepper). Add chopped shallots and fresh sage and thyme to ground turkey meat and serve them on brioche rolls with mayo spiked with fresh lemon juice. Enliven bland veggie burgers with sun-dried-tomato purée or pesto mayo.

grill basics

A gas grill is a big investment ($200 for a decent model; $450 and up for a high-end one) but pays off in convenience because it preheats in 10–15 min. Many grilling enthusiasts swear by charcoal grills, which cost less (good ones start at $100) but can be messy and slower to heat (20 min. or more).
Portable charcoal grills are a great option for the beach or park and can serve as a supplementary grill at home when entertaining.
To keep food from sticking, brush it with olive or vegetable oil before placing it on the grill (for extra protection, brush the grill with a vegetable oil or coat with a nonstick spray before heating. Do not use aerosol cans near flames). Grill with the top closed to retain heat and decrease cooking time). Use tongs to turn meat—a fork pokes holes and lets out juices.
Before serving, always let meat rest so juices can be absorbed; burgers should rest 2–5 min.

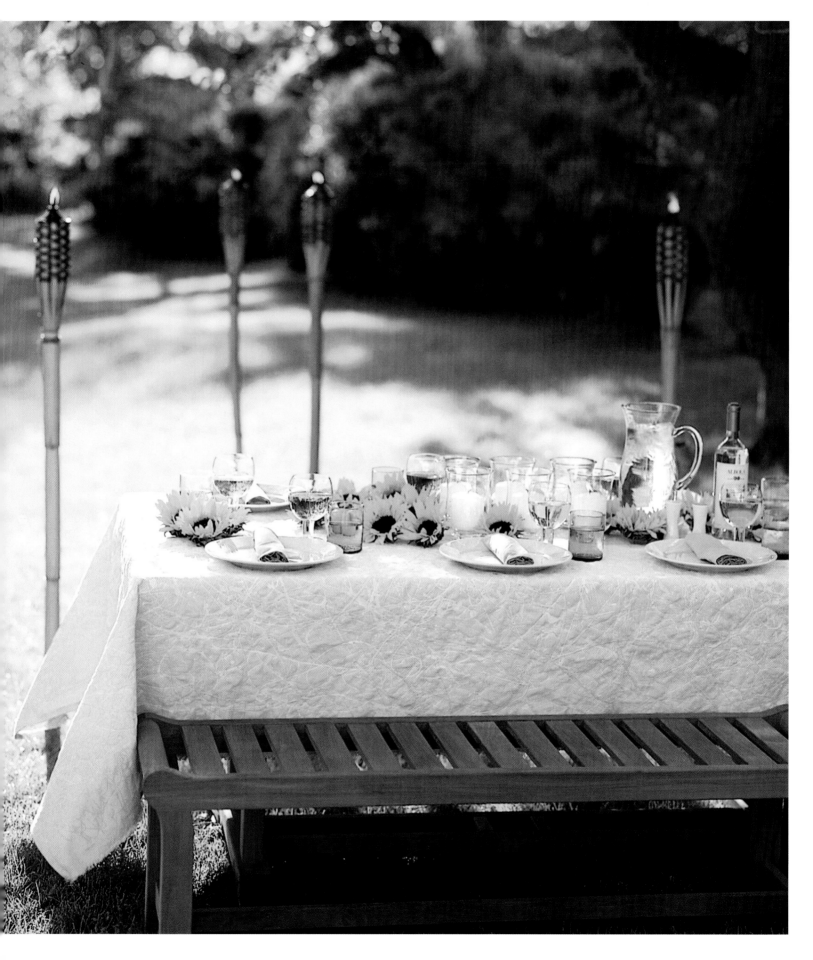

what to pour

Summer melon cooler (serves 12): Fill ½ gal. pitcher ⅓ full of vodka. Stir in purée of 1 honeydew melon (about 3 cups), 2 cups each Midori liqueur and Sprite, and 1 cup club soda. Serve over ice and garnish with skewered melon balls. Offer a nonalcoholic spritzer as well: Mix equal parts orange juice, cranberry juice and sparkling water.

Wine picks: For white, pour a California chardonnay such as Marimar Torres, Landmark or Chalone. For red, serve a Côtes du Rhône from Guigal or Vieille Ferme.

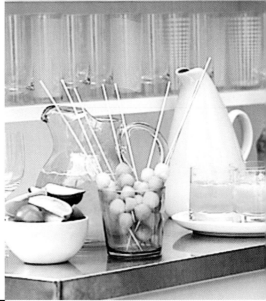

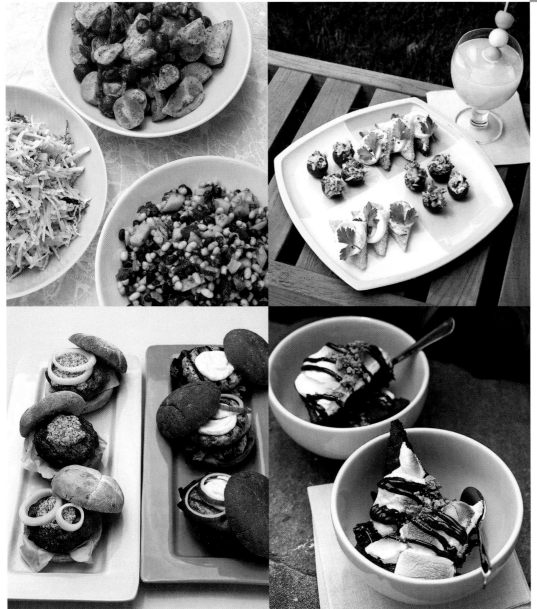

recipes

BLT Cherry Tomatoes
(Makes 36)

36 red and/or yellow cherry tomatoes, stems removed
2 cups chopped butter lettuce
½ cup chopped cooked bacon (about 8 slices)
3–4 tbsp mayonnaise
Salt and pepper to taste

Barely slice tops from cherry tomatoes and scrape out and discard pulp and seeds. Then slice just enough off the bottom of each tomato to form a flat base so the tomato will sit up. Place tomatoes upside down on paper towels to drain. In small bowl combine lettuce, bacon and just enough mayonnaise to hold stuffing together. Season with salt and pepper. Fill tomato shells with lettuce-and-bacon stuffing and arrange on platter.

Egg-Salad Bites
(Makes 36)

1 cup mayonnaise
2 tbsp capers, drained and chopped
2 tbsp Dijon mustard
9 slices firm white bread, crusts removed, then toasted
6 hard-boiled eggs, shelled and sliced ¼" thick
Fresh flat-leaf parsley for garnish

In small bowl combine mayonnaise, capers and mustard. Cut each slice of toasted bread to form 4 triangles. Spread each with ½ tsp mayonnaise-and-caper mixture. Top with 1 slice of hard-boiled egg (use only flat center slices of eggs). Spread an additional ½ tsp mayonnaise on top of egg. Remove crusts. Arrange egg-salad bites on platter and garnish with chopped parsley or whole leaves.

Dilled Broccoli Slaw

(Serves 12)

1½ cups plain yogurt
½ cup chopped fresh dill
¾ cup chopped onion
3 large heads broccoli
1 small head cabbage, cored, shredded
Salt and pepper to taste

In medium bowl mix yogurt, dill and onion. Cut florets from broccoli and reserve for another use. Peel broccoli stems, and shred using a box grater or food processor. In large bowl combine broccoli and cabbage with yogurt mixture. Season with salt and pepper; refrigerate 30 min. Mix well and check seasoning.

Black-and-White Bean Salad with Mango and Cilantro

(Serves 12)

3 sun-dried tomatoes in oil, chopped
2 medium tomatoes, seeded and chopped
¼ cup chopped cilantro
1 shallot, minced
2 tbsp white wine vinegar
½ cup olive oil
Salt and pepper to taste
2 cans (15½ oz. each) black beans, rinsed and drained
2 cans (15½ oz. each) navy beans, rinsed and drained
1 ripe mango, peeled and diced
1 medium cucumber, peeled, seeded and diced

In medium bowl combine tomatoes, cilantro and shallot. Stir in vinegar, then gradually whisk in olive oil until emulsified. Season with salt and pepper. In large serving bowl combine beans, mango and cucumber. Pour dressing over bean mixture and toss well. Set aside, unrefrigerated, for 30 min. Serve at room temperature.

Lamb Burgers with Mint-Pesto Mayonnaise

(Makes 12 burgers)

2 cups tightly packed fresh mint leaves
½ cup chopped red onion
¼ cup grated Pecorino Romano cheese
¼ cup olive oil
¼ cup mayonnaise
Salt and pepper to taste
Vegetable oil or nonstick cooking spray
3 lb. ground lamb
1 onion, chopped (about 1 cup)
½ cup chopped fresh flat-leaf parsley
1 tsp salt
½ tsp pepper
12 English muffins or buns, toasted

Purée mint, red onion and grated cheese in food processor. With machine running, slowly add oil through feed tube. Place mixture in small bowl; stir in mayonnaise. Season with salt and pepper, cover with plastic wrap and set aside. Heat gas grill to medium-high, or heat broiler. Lightly broil rack. In large bowl combine lamb, onion, parsley, salt and pepper. With moistened hands, form mixture into 12 patties. Grill or broil burgers 3–4" from heat source for 4–5 min. per side, or until desired degree of doneness. Serve on toasted English muffins or buns with mint pesto.

Tuna Burgers with Wasabi-Mustard Sauce

(Makes 12 burgers)

1 tbsp wasabi powder
8 oz. sour cream
2 tsp Dijon mustard
2 tsp sugar
¼ cup vegetable oil, plus extra for coating grill
6 tuna steaks (about 3 lb. total)
2 egg whites, lightly beaten
2 tbsp soy sauce
1 tbsp black sesame seeds
12 brioche rolls or buns

In small bowl mix 1 tbsp water with wasabi powder to form paste, then stir in sour cream, mustard and sugar. Cover with plastic wrap and set aside. Prepare charcoal grill, heat gas grill to medium-high, or heat broiler. Lightly brush grill rack with vegetable oil or coat broiler pan rack with nonstick cooking spray. Cut tuna into large chunks, place in food processor, and pulse just until coarsely ground. Transfer tuna to large bowl and stir in egg whites, soy sauce and sesame seeds. With moistened hands, form mixture into 12 patties. Brush both sides of each burger with vegetable oil. Grill or broil burgers 3–4" from heat source for 2–3 min. on each side, or until desired degree of doneness. Serve on brioche rolls or buns with wasabi-mustard sauce.

Brownie S'mores

(Serves 16)

2 boxes brownie mix or homemade recipe
6 squares (1 oz. each) semisweet chocolate, chopped
1 cup heavy cream
1 package (1 lb.) large marshmallows, halved
1 cup crushed graham crackers

Use homemade or store-bought brownie mix to bake brownies. To bake: Line baking pans with enough foil to hang over sides. Lightly coat foil with non-stick cooking spray. While brownies are baking, melt chocolate in top of double boiler over simmering water. Remove from heat. Pour cream into chocolate, stirring until smooth; set aside. When brownies are done switch oven to broil setting. Arrange marshmallows, cut side down, on top of brownies. Broil 1–2 min., until marshmallows are golden brown (watch carefully—marshmallows can burn quickly). Use overhanging foil to lift brownies out of pans and place on rack; let cool slightly. Cut each brownie slab into 16 2" squares. To serve, place 2 brownie squares on a dessert plate, drizzle with chocolate sauce, and sprinkle crushed graham crackers over top.

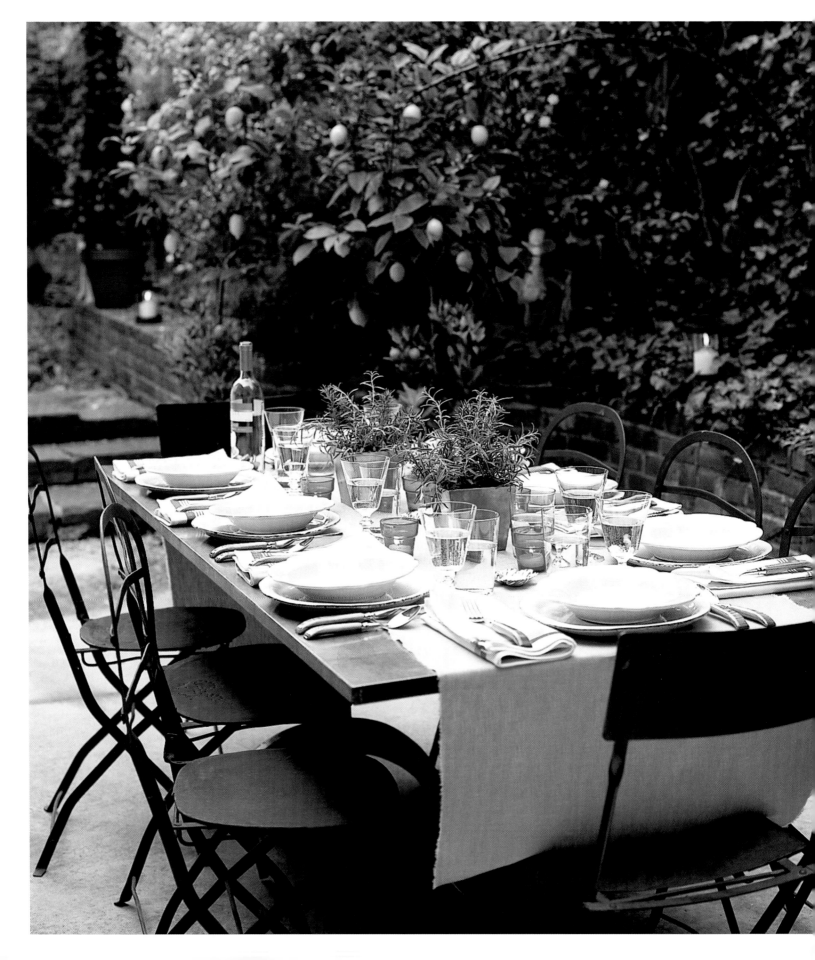

tuscan dinner

It's lovely to dine alfresco on a balmy evening. For an elegant twist, head to Italy (in spirit, that is) and serve a lush—and luscious—Tuscan feast for eight guests. The menu for this dinner, created by British culinary expert and author Nigella Lawson, begins with refreshing Tuscan spritzers and savory Italian snacks. After drinks, serve a family-style meal of pasta with clam sauce and grilled steak with Parmesan shards and chopped greens. Add a selection of vibrant wines and some fragrant rosemary centerpieces, and you'll easily transport friends to the Tuscan countryside.

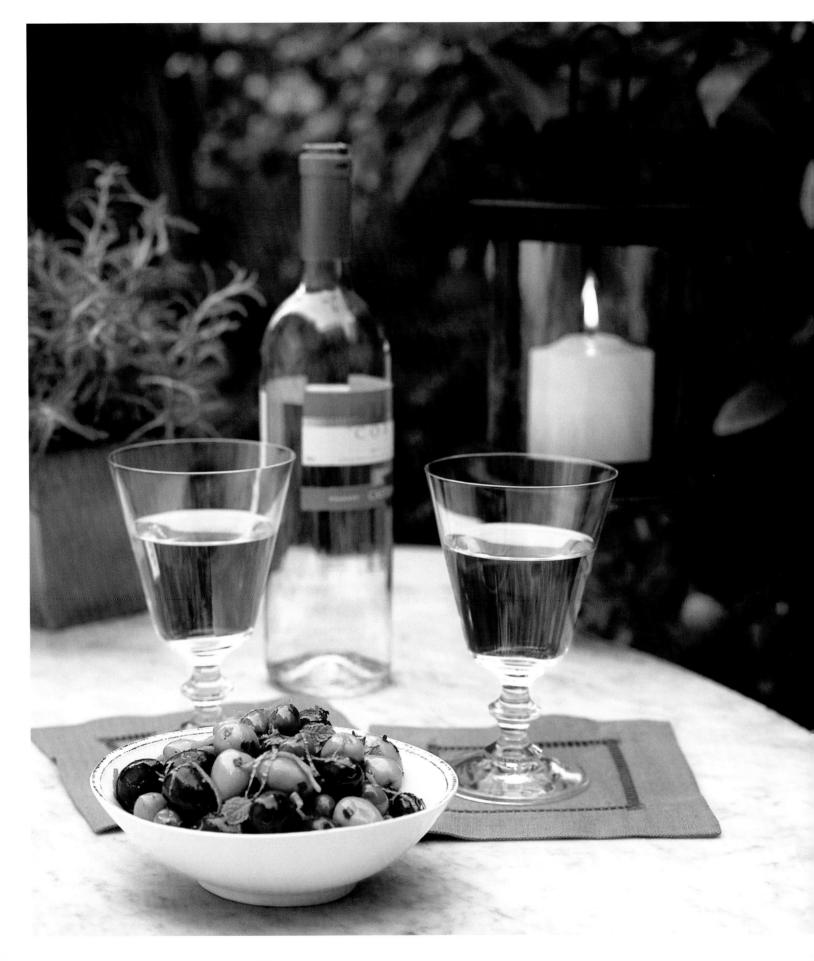

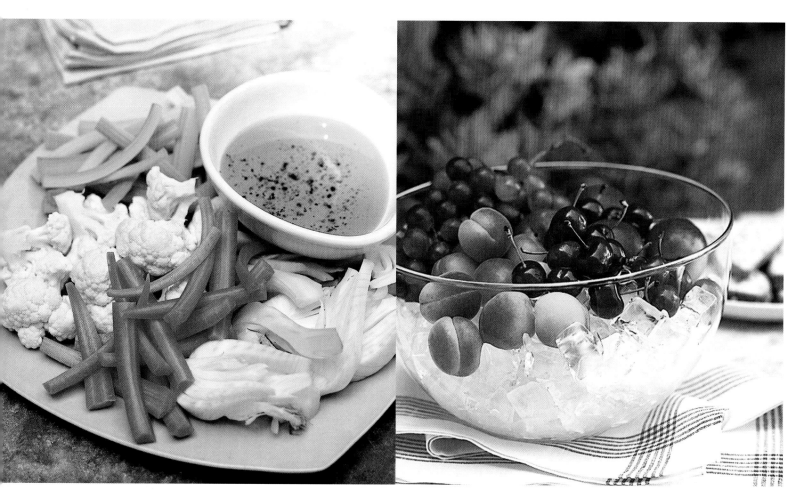

the menu

Signature drink: Tuscan spritzer
Hors d'oeuvres: Pinziminio (crudités with olive oil), marinated olives, warm salted almonds, sliced salami
First course: Spaghetti with white clam sauce
Second course: Sliced steak with radicchio and Parmesan on arugula, Tuscan white beans, zucchini fritters
Dessert: Affogato (vanilla ice cream in hot espresso), biscotti with vin santo

setting the scene

The décor: In a shaded area, set up a bar with bottles of wine and sparkling water and glasses. For extra atmosphere, place a few lanterns, with candles inside, around your patio. Scatter little bowls of olives and almonds and plates of salami, and set out a platter of pinziminio, which is a very simple Italian hors d'oeuvre of raw vegetables (like carrots, celery, cauliflower and fennel) served with a dip of good olive oil sprinkled with sea salt and freshly ground pepper. Keep the dinner table pared down and pretty, so it blends into the outdoor setting and doesn't look out of place. Cover it with a pale-blue or biscuit-colored tablecloth or leave it uncovered. Sprinkle the surface with lots of tea lights in sky-blue votive holders, and place two or three small rosemary plants in pots down the center. Use casual flatware and earthenware plates along with thick linen napkins. Set out pepper mills, small bowls of good-quality sea salt, and a basket of breads with high-quality olive oil in a spouted serving bottle.

The meal: Serve dinner family-style. Begin with spaghetti with clam sauce, followed by the steak on a bed of arugula with accompanying serving dishes of white beans and zucchini fritters. Finish with biscotti and glasses of vin santo (Italian dessert wine) and/or affogato—vanilla ice cream or gelato topped with piping hot espresso, which must be served quickly, before it melts.

The music: For a refined crowd, stick to classic Italian opera music such as *La Traviata* and *Tosca;* or for a more wild affair, create a Fellini-esque ambience with Nino Rota's *La Dolce Vita* soundtrack, Daniele Luppi's *An Italian Story* and Mina's *Viva La Diva.* For added Italian flavor, throw in Dean Martin's *Italian Love Song*s and download his version of "Mambo Italiano" from *Dino: The Essential Dean Martin.* End the party on an upbeat note with fun Italian house music that's more cheesy than a plate of mozzarella: *Strike It Up: The Best of Black Box.*

countdown

Three weeks: Send invitations.
One week: Buy wine and music.
Two days: Buy groceries and herbs for table.
Day before: Soak white beans.
Morning of: Chill white wine and sparkling water. Arrange flowers.
Five hours: Set up bar and dinner table.
Three hours: Prep radicchio, Parmesan and arugula salad for the steak. Chop garlic and parsley for the clam sauce. Make beans.
Two hours: Make zucchini fritters; let cool. Scrub clams. Stock bar.
One hour: Prep and set out pinziminio, olives and salami.
30 minutes: Take steak out of the refrigerator. Put a pot of water (for pasta) on stove, but don't turn the burner on.
20 minutes: Light candles. Start music.
As guests arrive: Toast and serve almonds. Boil water for pasta; keep it simmering until you're ready to cook.
Right before dinner: Light barbecue if grilling outdoors. Make spaghetti with clam sauce; reheat zucchini fritters in the oven.
During party: Grill steak.
After dinner: Make espresso; pour over ice cream or gelato and serve with biscotti and vin santo.

even easier

Simplify the centerpieces. If you don't have time to buy rosemary plants, scatter rosemary branches, which you can buy at the grocery store, down the center of the table. An even easier centerpiece is a big bowl of lemons.
Save time on side dishes. Instead of dried cannellini beans, use canned. Just rinse and drain them well before adding the olive oil, lemon juice and parsley. Rather than making zucchini fritters, do a quick sauté of shredded or sliced zucchini with chopped scallions and fresh basil.
Skip the affogato dessert. Along with the biscotti serve a bowl of fresh fruit, such as grapes, plums, peaches and cherries, on ice (a clear bowl best shows off the ice and the vivid colors of the fruit). If you like, also set out plates and knives, along with a few wedges of cheese.

the perfect steak

Don't feel obligated to spend a lot of money on steak. If you have limited grilling experience, all that cash could go right up in flames. It makes more sense to marinate a cheaper, more forgiving cut than sirloin, such as flank. If you do want a pricier cut that doesn't require marinating, sirloin is a flavorful choice. Look for meat that is slightly marbled with fat, for extra flavor.
Always bring meat to room temperature before you cook it. Take it out of the refrigerator an hour before the grill is ready. Chefs test steak for doneness by pressing on the meat. If it's soft, like raw meat, it's very rare. If it's got a little bounce, it's medium-rare. The more resistance you feel when you press on it, the more cooked it is. For surefire results, use an instant-read thermometer: 130°F is rare, 135°F–140°F is medium-rare, 145°F–150°F is medium and 155°F–160°F is well done. (Note: USDA guidelines are 10°F higher.) Or simply make a small cut in the meat to check doneness. Keep in mind that steak continues to cook after it's removed from the fire, so take it off when it's less cooked than you like.
Once it's done, loosely wrap steaks in aluminum foil and keep them in a warm area to rest for 30 min. before slicing.

tuscan traditions

Olive oil is made all over Tuscany. Tuscan oil is known for its strong, peppery character and is often set on the table to drizzle over salads and meats.
In Italy pasta is usually served as a first course—and in smaller portions, to leave room for a main course.
Tuscans eat lots of beef and game. One of the most famous steak preparations is bistecca alla Fiorentina, a T-bone that is grilled plain, sprinkled with salt and pepper, sliced at the table, and served with olive oil and a simple arugula salad. The steak in this menu is a slight variation on that dish. Lemon wedges are traditionally served with steaks; a squeeze of juice cuts the richness of the meat.
Tuscans are also known for cooking and serving meat with herbs. A popular dish is grilled steak topped with olive oil mixed with a paste of lemon juice, parsley, finely chopped rosemary, garlic, lemon zest, salt and pepper.
White wine—pinot grigio, pinot blanco, sauvignon blanc—is commonly served with a light pasta or fish course. Red wine, often a chianti, goes well with meats and pastas with red sauces.
Italians rarely serve elaborate desserts. At the end of a meal, it's common to serve a bottle of vin santo dessert wine, which has a musty, honey flavor, and cantucini (hard almond biscotti), which guests dunk into the wine to soften before eating.

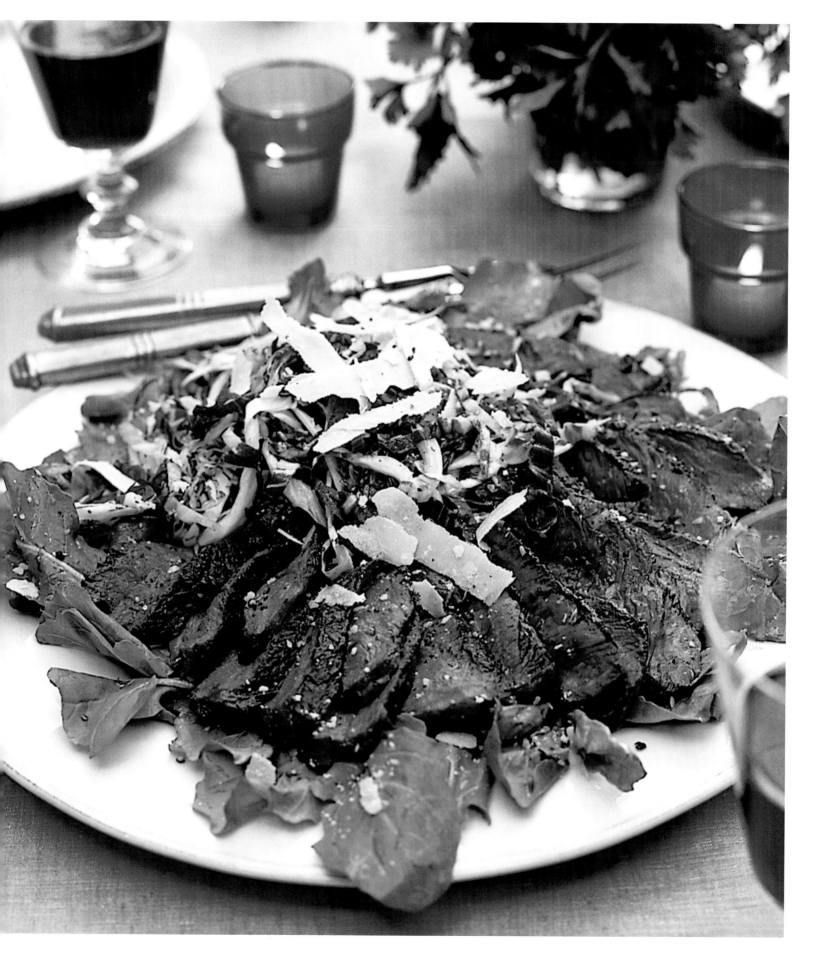

what to pour

Tuscan spritzer (serves 8): Pour chilled pinot grigio (try Pighin 2003 or Ecco Domani 2003) into glasses; top with a splash of sparkling water. Garnish with a twist of lemon zest.

Wine picks: Take a tour of Italy: With the spaghetti, serve a pinot grigio from Lageder or Kriss (from Alto Adige) or a soave from Pieropan or Gini (from the Venito). Serve a chianti classico (from Antinori, Felsina or Fontodi) with the steak. With dessert, splurge on a Tuscan vin santo from Felsina or substitute a refreshing moscato d'asti (from the Piedmont) by Paulo Saracco, La Spinetta or Viette.

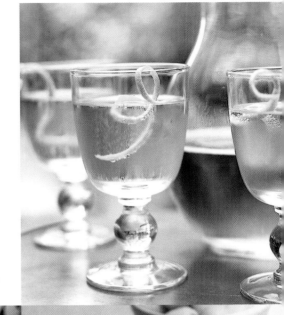

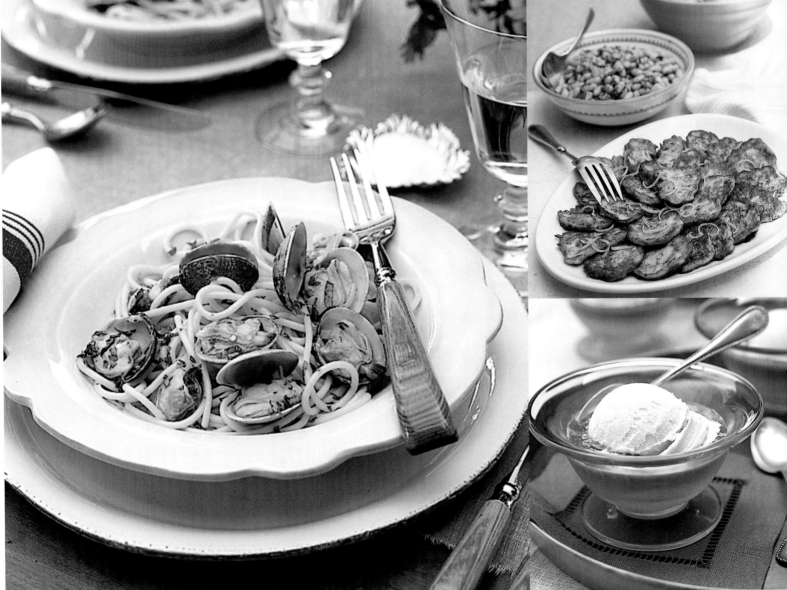

recipes

Marinated Olives

(Makes 3 cups)

3 cups olives (kalamata, niçoise, Spanish)
3 tbsp orange juice
2 tbsp orange zest
2 tbsp chopped fresh mint or parsley
¼–½ tsp crushed red pepper flakes

Toss all ingredients in medium bowl. Cover with plastic wrap until served.

Warm Salted Almonds

(Makes 2½ cups)
¾ lb. (about 2½ cups) blanched almonds
Salt to taste

Toast nuts in hot pan or on baking sheet in 400°F oven until they begin to brown (3–4 min.). Sprinkle with sea salt while warm; serve.

Spaghetti with White Clam Sauce

(Serves 8)
⅔ cup olive oil
6 large cloves garlic, minced
6 dozen Manila clams, scrubbed
1½ cups dry white wine
⅓ cup chopped fresh flat-leaf parsley
½ tsp crushed red pepper flakes
1 tsp salt
1½ lb. spaghetti

In large saucepan cook oil and garlic over medium heat until garlic begins to sizzle. Stir in clams, wine, parsley, red pepper flakes and salt. Cover; bring to boil over high heat. Cook, shaking pan occasionally, until clams begin to open, about 3 min. Remove open clams to large bowl; continue to cook, removing clams as they open (discard any that do not open). Meanwhile cook pasta in boiling, salted water until al dente; drain. Return clams to pan; add pasta and simmer 2 min., or until heated through.

Sliced Steak with Radicchio and Parmesan on Arugula

(Serves 8)
2 sirloin steaks (1½ lb. each)
Salt and pepper
⅓ cup olive oil
2–3 tbsp fresh lemon juice
8 cups arugula, cleaned and stemmed
3 cups chopped radicchio
½ lb. Parmesan, shaved

Season both sides of steaks with salt and pepper. If not grilling outdoors, heat a cast-iron skillet over high heat. Add steaks; cook until done (5–6 min. per side for medium-rare). Remove; let stand as much as 30 min. before slicing. Meanwhile whisk oil, lemon juice, and salt and pepper to taste. Toss with arugula; place on platter. Arrange sliced steak on arugula; top with radicchio and Parmesan.

Tuscan White Beans

(Serves 8)
1 package (1 lb.) dried cannellini beans
3 cloves garlic
1 onion, quartered
2 bay leaves
⅓ cup olive oil
2 tbsp fresh lemon juice
½ cup chopped fresh flat-leaf parsley
Salt and pepper to taste

Soak beans overnight in cold water to cover. Drain; place in Dutch oven with garlic, onion, bay leaves and water to cover by 2". Bring to boil; reduce heat. Simmer covered 30–45 min., or until tender. Drain; discard garlic, onion and bay leaves. Toss with olive oil, lemon juice, parsley, salt and pepper. Serve at room temperature.

Zucchini Fritters

(Makes 32)
¾ cup ricotta
½ cup chopped scallions
2 tbsp chopped fresh basil
2 tbsp chopped fresh flat-leaf parsley
1 cup all-purpose flour
3 eggs, lightly beaten
3 cups shredded zucchini
½ cup shredded Parmesan
1 tsp salt
¼ tsp pepper
4 tbsp olive oil, divided
Lemon zest for garnish

In large bowl combine first 4 ingredients. Stir in flour. Add eggs; stir well. Stir in zucchini, Parmesan, salt and pepper. Heat 2 tbsp oil in large nonstick skillet over medium heat. Drop batter by tablespoonfuls into skillet. Cook 3–4 min., turning once, until golden. Remove fritters to baking sheet lined with paper towels. Repeat, using remaining oil as needed. Arrange on platter; garnish.

the resources

It's one thing to look at pictures of a colorful and original party in a book and be inspired to recreate it, but it's quite another to actually make it happen. Even the most gifted and energetic host can lose steam when faced with a long list of decorations and ingredients. What's the fun of giving a tropical-theme cocktail party when you have to spend weeks hunting down coral branches for centerpieces? Or roaming from store to store in search of an imported Thai spice? Or breaking the budget on floral-print pareos? Well, here's a huge shortcut. To make entertaining in your home as effortless as possible, just refer to this insider's list of some of the most delicious food and chicest décor sources from across the country. Everything here is available online or, in a few instances, via phone order, and, best of all, *In Style*'s editors have done the legwork, testing the goods for quality, flavor and consistency. These reputable companies offer everything from charming invitations to sleek tableware to gourmet hors d'oeuvres and desserts, as well as hard-to-find ingredients and whimsical items for parties with specific themes. Just search by category, stock up on supplies, and let the fun begin.

invitations

Artbeads.com
www.artbeads.com
253-857-3433
For a special touch, add these reasonably priced charms and beads to invitations or wineglasses.

Crane & Co.
www.crane.com
800-268-2281
This classic stationery source offers stylish invitations as well as ones that can be filled in online (just go to the site's Print Center, choose a font, and type the information) and printed from any computer.

Kate's Paperie
www.katespaperie.com
800-809-9880
Reliably tasteful (and often whimsical) invitations for celebrations as specific as wine and champagne tastings, birthday parties and housewarming parties, plus dozens of top-quality stationery lines.

Paper Source
www.paper-source.com
888-727-3711
The company's do-it-yourself digital invitation kits come with all the ingredients for a lovely invitation: paper for printing information, colorful backings, patterned paper sashes and envelopes.

Petite Alma
www.petitealma.com
713-942-7792
Petite Alma's selection of birth announcements and baby shower may be small, but the simple designs are irresistibly sweet.

Smythson of Bond Street
www.smythson.com
877-769-8476
The invitations and blank note cards from this British stationery company come in crisp, fashionable colors (red, cornflower blue, hot pink) and convey understated glamour.

Soolip
www.soolip.com
310-360-0545
Known for its handcrafted, organic aesthetic, Soolip offers invitations in materials such as handmade paper and silk tissue. One collection features sheer glassine paper affixed to heavy card stock with sealing wax.

Sugar Paper
www.sugarpaper.com
310-277-7804
This Los Angeles company specializes in customized invitations with a hip, energetic vibe and also sells paper goods from other adorable companies like Egg Press.

Twinklecards
www.twinklecards.com
Stationery at its craftiest: These invitations are fashioned from handmade Japanese paper and embellished with glass beads, crystals, rhinestones, pearls and balsa wood.

the bar

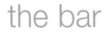

Crate & Barrel
www.crateandbarrel.com
800-967-6696
This Web site is an easy source for all-purpose glassware, including two best-of-class offerings: the elegant Balaton martini glass, $10 each, and the Nora white wine glass, $8 each, an excellent universal wineglass.

Fishs Eddy
www.fishseddy.com
877-347-4733
Affordable glasses and bar accessories with a retro feel (much of the inventory consists of vintage pieces from old restaurants across the country), and good-looking, basic serving pieces include simple white olive boats for bar snacks.

Ikea
www.ikea.com
800-434-4532
Ikea has a wide selection of cocktail glasses and napkins. In addition, the great-looking wine glasses are so inexpensive ($4 each) you can buy them in bulk.

Mixology's
www.mixologys.com
888-345-6497
Shop here for the best wine and bar accessories—from stemware to shakers to swizzle sticks.

Plum Party
www.plumparty.com
800-227-0314
Crystal-encrusted swizzle sticks, colorful mini cocktail shakers and coasters of every kind (from gold lacquer to Pucci-like prints to discs printed with art, music and sports trivia).

the pantry

American Spoon
www.spoon.com
800-222-5886
Try artisanal preserves in flavors like blueberry lime, strawberry rhubarb and black raspberry, and fruit butters infused with crab apple, pumpkin and mango. Cherry-pepper jelly and sweet tomato and red pepper relishes add oomph to burgers.

A Southern Season
www.southernseason.com
800-253-3663
Bestsellers from this Chapel Hill, N.C., store include spicy North Carolina cocktail pecans, mini cheddar biscuits (which come vacuum-packed) and Appalachian trail mix—a blend of almonds, cashews, sesame sticks and cheddar chips.

Chile Today Hot Tamale
www.chiletoday.com
Kettle chips in fiery flavors such as ancho toasted onion, chipotle-and-Romano, and habañero Cajun, plus gourmet salsa mixes.

Convito Italiano
www.convitoitaliano.com
847-251-3654
Olive oils from Italy, Greece and Spain, and 22 authentic Italian pasta sauces like matriciana (tomato and bacon), puttanesca (tomatoes, anchovies and olives) and salsa bianca con piselli (cream, Parmesan and peas).

El Paso Chile Co.
www.elpasochile.com
888-472-5727
Hot sauces and salsa with extra Texan heat: Try the hot pepper–peach preserves or the jalapeño-laced Cowboy Catsup.

June Taylor Co.
www.junetaylorjams.com
510-548-2236
Exotic, intensely flavored marmalades (made from blood orange, bergamot and meyer lemon), butters (blended with quince, plums and white nectarines) and syrups (to mix with champagne) made from organic fruits.

Kernel Season's
www.nomorenakedpopcorn.com
773-292-4567
Ten gourmet popcorn flavorings including ranch, jalepeño and barbecue—just sprinkle, toss and serve.

Peanut Shop of Williamsburg
www.thepeanutshop.com
800-637-3268
Stock up on fresh, crunchy savories such as Indian cashews, Marcona almonds and wasabi peanuts. For dessert, bring out the light-as-air peanut brittle.

Stonewall Kitchen
www.stonewallkitchen.com
800-207-5267
Drizzle the company's chocolate peanut butter or coffee caramel sauces over ice cream; pour its popular wild Maine blueberry or raspberry syrup onto pancakes.

Trader Vic's
www.tradervics.com
877-762-4824
Their famous hot-buttered-rum batter makes a decadent, old-fashioned cold-weather drink.

Unique Pretzel Bakery
www.uniquesplits.com
888-477-5487
Keep these classic Pennsylvania hard pretzels on hand for impromptu parties. The company's most popular item, the six-pound variety pack, comes with jars of mustard and peanut butter for dipping.

Zapp's Potato Chips
www.zapps.com
800-468-2447
These chips come in 11 Louisiana-inspired flavors, including Hotter 'n Hot jalapeño, cajun dill and sour cream-and-creole onion.

hors d'oeuvres

Black Tie Hors d'Oeuvres
www.blacktiehorsdoeuvres.com
877-304-2626
Fancy, high-quality frozen hors d'oeuvres such as mini quiches, crab cakes and crostini (and many, many more).

Dufour Pastry Kitchen
212-929-2800
For gourmet bites, fill your freezer with these handmade, ready-to-bake appetizers, including wild mushroom phyllo triangles and Roquefort mascarpone puffs.

Good Wives
www.goodwives.com
800-521-8160
Delectable heat-and-serve spring rolls, empanadas, seafood thermidor puff pastries and mini bries en croute.

Mackenzie Limited

www.mackenzieltd.com
800-858-7100
This British food purveyor offers lobster spread, olives in puff pastry and two kinds of rich, flaky brie en croute: mushroom garlic and apple pecan.

cheese

Artisanal Cheese Center

www.artisanalcheese.com
877-797-1200
The Web site lets you search over 100 artisanal cheeses by milk type, country of origin or type of cheese. The company also ships carefully selected cheese platters and cheese courses.

Formaggio Kitchen

www.formaggiokitchen.com
888-212-3224
This Boston company specializes in rare cheeses from small farms around the world. Order its cheese samplers (Artisan Mountain, French, Italian), and they'll hand-pick an unusual selection for you.

iGourmet

www.igourmet.com
877-446-8763
This site sells hundreds of cheeses from around the world and offers in-depth descriptions of each: its history, flavor, texture and ideal accompanying foods.

Murray's Cheese

www.murrayscheese.com
888-692-4339
Browse more than 250 domestic and imported cheeses, and click on the site's Beverage Pairing option to match cheeses to different kinds of wines, beers and spirits.

Zingerman's

www.zingermans.com
888-636-8162
The well-edited selection includes Zingerman's own handmade fresh cheeses as well as delicious, undiscovered artisan varieties made all over North America.

fresh and prepared meats

Chef Shop

www.chefshop.com
877-337-2491
This gourmet site is known for its incredibly moist, organic smoked whole turkeys, which are totally free of chemicals and artificial plumpers. Just warm in the oven and serve.

Ham I Am

www.hamiam.com
800-742-6426
These flavorful, not-too-salty hams (available with or without a pepper coating) have been smoked for 22 hours with real hickory wood. One ham serves 20 to 25 people—just right for an easy main course.

Jamison Farm

www.jamisonfarm.com
800-237-5262
The lamb meat from this Appalachian foothills farm is free of hormones, antibiotics, herbicides and pesticides, and the meat is tender, flavorful and very low in fat.

King's Restaurant

www.kingsbbq.com
800-332-6465
This company specializes in Eastern North Carolina, vinegar-based chopped pork barbecue (no heavy, gooey sauces), which it ships frozen. Order hush puppies and collard greens on the side.

Lobel's of New York

www.lobels.com
877-783-4512
Famous for its vast selection of hand-cut, never-frozen dry-aged beef, all-natural lamb and veal, and rich, juicy, marbled Kurobuta pork (produced on small Midwestern farms).

Niman Ranch

www.nimanranch.com
866-808-0340
In addition to selling the beef from its ranch in Marin County, Calif., the company works with more than 300 independent farmers who produce beef, pork and lamb from humanely raised animals.

Nodine's Smokehouse

www.nodinesmokehouse.com
800-222-2059
A reliable source for flavorful bacons, hams and beef jerkies, but most famous for its ready-to-eat apple-smoked pork loin.

Nueske's

www.nueskes.com
800-392-2266
The applewood-smoked ham is lean, meaty and not too salty, and the homemade sausages (spicy chicken and cheddar bratwurst are just two varieties) are perfect to throw on the grill.

The Salt Lick Barbecue Restaurant

www.saltlickbbq.com
888-725-8542
Slow-cooked pork ribs, beef brisket, sausage and smoked turkey breast shipped straight from the Hill Country of Texas.

Salumi

www.salumicuredmeats.com
877-223-0813
Armandino Batali (father of chef Mario) uses old-fashioned Italian curing techniques to produce authentic salamis

like spicy paprika and hot sopressata, and cured meats (coppa and lamb "prosciutto").

Smithfield Hams

www.smithfieldhams.com
800-926-8448
Home of the famously salty and pungent Smithfield ham, which is dry-salt-cured, slowly hickory smoked, and aged for six months to one year. For a traditional Southern treat, slice it paper thin and serve on biscuits.

Snake River Farms

www.snakeriverfarms.com
800-657-6305
Buttery, tender American-style Kobe beef, available in tenderloin, ribeye and strip loin cuts, as well as boneless short ribs and luxe hamburgers.

Sticky Fingers

www.shopstickyfingers.com
800-784-2597
Pick a combination of Memphis-style ribs, pulled pork and wings, then choose from six famous sauces, which come in flavors like Tennessee Whiskey and Carolina Classic.

The Texacan Beef & Pork Co.

www.texacan.com
877-877-8766
The state-of-the-art oven at the Ashburn, Va., company smokes more than 3,000 pounds of pulled pork and ribs over Georgia pecan wood a day. The result: meat that is tender and tangy but not too sweet.

Willie Bird

www.williebird.com
877-494-5592
This operation has been producing its famous fresh and smoked free-range organic turkeys for more than 40 years.

seafood

Chef John Folse & Co

www.jfolse.com
225-644-6000
This Louisiana company ships fresh, seasonal seafood (crawfish tails, lump crab) but is best known for its tasty regional soups like Bourbon Street seafood gumbo and Creole corn-and-shrimp soup.

Fenwick Crab House

www.crabcakeexpress.com
888-539-6559
These crab cakes are made from sweet blue crabs, contain no bread crumbs or other fillers, and have never been cooked or frozen.

The Fresh Lobster Co.

www.thefreshlobstercompany.com
508-451-2467
Live lobsters, Rockport lobster bisque, and clambake gift baskets with the works: lobsters, clams, corn on the cob, lemon, butter, lobster crackers, bibs and wet naps.

Harbour House Crabs

www.ilovecrabs.com
888-458-8272
This company ships succulent Maryland blue crabs, live, or steamed and coated in secret seasoning overnight. Order by the dozen, half bushel (three dozen) or bushel (six dozen).

Joe's Stone Crab

www.joesstonecrab.com
800-780-2722
Shipped overnight, this Miami restaurant's huge stone crab claws arrive cooked, chilled and ready to be cracked open. Dip them in the company's signature creamy mustard sauce.

Kelley's Katch

www.kelleyskatch.com
888-681-8565
For more than 20 years, this Tennessee company has harvested plump, briny, fresh (unpasteurized) domestic paddlefish caviar.

Russ & Daughters

www.russanddaughters.com
800-787-7229
Ten varieties of impeccably smoked and cured salmon and eight kinds of premier imported and domestic caviar.

Stolt Sea Farm California

www.sterlingcaviar.com
800-525-0333
This farm produces American sturgeon caviar that's as firm and flavorful as imported caviar.

specialty foods

Corn Maiden Foods

www.cornmaidenfoods.com
310-338-3383
Chef Bobby Flay loves the handmade, lard-free tamales from this California company, which come in vegan, cheese, seafood, poultry and meat varieties.

Diamond Organics

www.diamondorganics.com
888-674-2642
The site features an excellent selection of organic fresh produce, herbs, salts and spices, all produced on the California coast.

Earthy Delights

www.earthy.com
800-367-4709
Exotic wild mushrooms (shiitake, wood-ear, enoki), dried mushrooms (morel, chanterelle, porcini) and truffles delivered overnight.

Ethnic Grocer
www.ethnicgrocer.com
630-860-1733
Hundreds of hard-to-find ingredients from around the world, including bottarga di tonno (tuna in extra-virgin olive oil) from Italy, pure saffron from Spain, and bulgogi barbecue sauce from Korea.

Hot Damn, Tamales!
www.hotdamntamales.com
888-385-0125
Gourmet tamales (varieties include tomatillo chicken, ancho pork, and black bean and Oaxaca cheese for vegetarians) made with 100% vegetable shortening.

Johnny's Fine Foods
www.johnnysfinefoods.com
800-962-1462
Seasoning salt and salad dressings are this company's claim to fame, but the site also bursts with condiments, snacks and sweets from around the world.

Kalustyan's
www.kalustyans.com
800-352-3451
This New York City specialty food store sells 100-plus flavors of chutney, including coconut, mango, ginger and chili lime.

Mustapha's Fine Foods of Morocco
www.mustaphas.com
206-382-1706
Here are gourmet products imported from Morocco, including green olives in cinnamon, preserved lemons and beautiful jars of harissa.

Penzeys Spices
www.penzeys.com
800-741-7787
The site sells more than 250 herbs, spices and seasonings from around the world—scan the index for detailed descriptions and recipe suggestions for each.

desserts

Anna's Puff
www.yummypuff.com
708-386-4780
These buttery, organic palmiers, which come in unexpected flavors like green tea, French cocoa and lemon tarragon, as well as lavender, chamomile and honey, are almost too beautiful to eat.

Bittersweet Pastries
www.bittersweetpastries.com
800-537-7791
This bakery's tarts come in 18 varieties and look like small works of art; its famous flourless chocolate truffle cakes are rich but not too sweet.

Blue Bell Creameries
www.bluebell.com
979-836-7977
Texas ice cream famous for its fresh, homemade flavor—the company packs it in dry ice in a Styrofoam cooler and ships it overnight anywhere in the continental U.S.

Capogiro Gelato Artisans
www.capogirogelato.com
215-351-0900
The site sells 250 rotating flavors produced every morning in small batches using only local, seasonal or organic ingredients. A recent sampling: Champagne mango, salted bitter almond and bananas Foster.

Di Camillo Bakery
www.dicamillobakery.com
800-634-4363
This 85-year-old company makes the best mail-order biscotti available (in eight signature varieties), and a bevy of other traditional Italian cookies and confections.

Divine Delights
www.divinedelights.com

800-443-2836
These beautiful iced petits fours and the addictive cranberry orange tea cake are perfect for any kind of shower or afternoon tea.

Graeter's Ice Cream
www.graeters.com
This Ohio-based ice cream company, in business since 1870, is known for the huge chocolate chips in its signature "chip" flavors (black raspberry is most popular). Orders arrive in six- or 12-pint coolers.

Haydel's Bakery
www.haydelbakery.com
800-442-1342
Look no farther for an authentic Mardi Gras king cake: This confection of braided dough, flavored with cinnamon and sugar, and decorated with fondant icing and purple, green and gold sugar, serves 30-plus people.

Heritage Pie Co.
www.texaspie.com
866-489-9400
Sometimes quality and quantity go hand in hand: 10 to 12 apples go into each of this company's flaky, buttery, preservative-free apple pies.

Il Laboratorio del Gelato
www.laboratoriodelgelato.com
212-343-9922
More than 75 gourmet flavors of gelato (name a fruit or nut, and it's on the menu) with a firm, ice cream–like texture.

Little Pie Co.
www.littlepiecompany.com
877-872-7437
This New York City bakery makes old-fashioned apple, cherry and key lime pies, plus over-the-top treats like New York cheesecake with graham cracker crust, and sour-cream apple-walnut pie.

Miles of Chocolate

www.milesofchocolate.com
512-323-5900
These dense, fudgy brownies are as buttery and smooth as dark chocolate truffles and come in pre-baked frozen blocks.

Payard Pâtisserie

www.payard.com
212-717-5252
The Parisian-style, pastel-colored macaroons, made from ground almonds, sugar and egg whites, are crunchy on the outside and soft in the center and come in four flavors: vanilla, chocolate, strawberry and coffee.

Peninsula Grill

www.peninsulagrill.com
843-723-0700
This luxurious Charleston, S.C., inn is renowned for its ultimate coconut cake, which weighs in at a dense, decadent 12 pounds.

Pfeil and Holing

www.cakedecostore.com
800-247-7955
Almost 300 kinds of delicate icing flowers (from roses to orchids to lilies to holly leaves) to instantly upgrade any cake.

Solomon's Gourmet Cookies

www.solomonscookies.com
773-384-8575
Chocolate mint brownies, jam-filled butter cookies and Caramelitas (oatmeal, chocolate and caramel bars) are all certified kosher.

St. Clair Ice Cream

www.stclairicecream.com
203-853-4774
These elegant, hand-molded ice cream and sorbet desserts—shaped into flowers, fruit, shells and more—are an eye-catching touch for any event.

Tennessee Ritzy Cakes

www.1800rumcake.com
Serve the buttery, boozy Ritzy rum cake, loaded with roasted nuts and warm spices, with afternoon coffee or for dessert after a holiday meal.

Tiny Trapeze

www.tinytrapeze.com
617-364-3200
These Boston artisanal confectioners specialize in melt-in-your-mouth, hand-cut marshmallows flavored with chocolate, vanilla and lemon.

Very Vera

www.veryvera.com
800-500-8372
Incredible homemade pound cakes (try buttered rum, amaretto or brandied peach) and layer cakes, including strawberry, lemon and authentic coconut cream.

confections

Alexis Estate Bonbons

www.alexisbonbons.com
707-967-3500
These Napa Valley truffles, infused with dark chocolate and red wine, are the result of a collaboration between Swanson Vineyards and Vosges Haut-Chocolat.

Candy's Confections

www.candysconfections.com
253-848-5640
Willy Wonka would approve of this company's huge selection of old-fashioned gummy candies, licorices, bubblegums and retro favorites.

Dylan's Candy Bar

www.dylanscandybar.com
646-735-0078
All the classic and novelty confections you can imagine, including football candies for your superbowl party, as well

as M&Ms and Jelly Bellies (in dozens of colors) sold in bulk.

Economycandy.com

www.economycandy.com
800-352-4544
An old-fashioned penny-candy store online, complete with gumballs, Good and Plenty's, Jaw Breakers and Jolly Ranchers.

Elk Candy Co.

www.elkcandy.com
212-650-1177
This New York City shop, which has been in business since 1933, offers an endless array of marzipan and chocolates, made on the premises.

Garrison Confections

www.garrisonconfections.com
401-490-2740
These artisanal chocolate bonbons and bars are spiked with crystallized fruit, nuts and toffee. Bestsellers include peanut butter patties, carmelized hazelnuts and the Ultimate nougat bar.

Hometown Favorites

www.hometownfavorites.com
This company sells so many obscure, retro candy brands that the Web site organizes them by decade. Start with the 1950s (chocolate cigarettes and Necco Wafers) and work your way to the present.

Knudsen's

888-388-1970
Pure, simple and totally delicious, these creamy, chewy buttery homemade caramels are made from a Minnesota grandmother's recipe.

Recchiuti Confections

www.recchiuticonfections.com
800-500-3396, ext. 201
The couture confections from this San Francisco company include fleur de sel

caramels, pâtes de fruits and gorgeously imprinted chocolates.

Woodhouse Chocolate
www.woodhousechocolate.com
800-966-3468
Gorgeous chocolates filled with exotic ingredients (Thai ginger, fresh mint, nutmeg, cloves), packaged in pretty pale-blue round boxes.

coffee, tea and cocoa

In Pursuit of Tea
www.inpursuitoftea.com
866-878-3832
Many of the loose-leaf teas on this site come from small farms and collectives around the world and contain no added flavors, perfumes or sweeteners.

La Colombe
www.lacolombe.com
800-563-0860
Some of the country's pickiest chefs serve the five coffee blends from this company (including a rich, full-bodied decaf) in their restaurants.

Marie Belle
www.mariebelle.com
866-925-8800
Stock up on the best-selling Aztec Original hot chocolate, made from highly concentrated Venezuelan cocoa. Just add hot water or milk and stir.

Remy Sol Coffee
www.remysol.com
805-878-5005
The beans that go into this rich, smoky coffee are fresh-roasted and hand-packed on a farm in Costa Rica.

Rishi Tea
www.rishi-tea.com
A well-edited selection of black, green, white, oolong, chai and yerba maté teas, as well as almost 30 caffeine-free botanical blends (including chrysanthemum, jasmine and hibiscus).

Scharffen Berger Chocolate Maker
www.scharffenberger.com
510-981-4050
The decadent Drinking Chocolate, made from dark chocolate shavings, is so richly flavored that you might want to serve it in espresso cups.

Upton Tea Imports
www.uptontea.com
800-234-8327
Connoisseurs can scan the Web site for detailed flavor descriptions, then choose from more than 300 varieties of loose tea.

the tabletop

Crate & Barrel
www.crateandbarrel.com
800-967-6696
An easy-access source for inexpensive, modern-looking serving platters, vases, candles and linens (in summer, look for sleek, brightly colored plastic and acrylic pieces for outdoor parties).

Foster's
www.shopfosters.com
800-734-8511
Woven linen place mats and runners by Chilewich, ultra versatile white bistroware from Rhubarb and color-saturated ceramic plates from Waechtersbach.

Paris Hotel Boutique
www.parishotelboutique.com
Unique heavy silver-plated pieces (platters, trays, tureens, pitchers, serving bowls and tea pots) from places like the

Waldorf-Astoria hotel in New York and the Hotel Fontainebleau in Miami.

Pearl River Mart
www.pearlriver.com
800-989-2446
This Manhattan store offers a variety of colorful Chinese tableware, including bowls, soup spoons and other items.

the décor

Anvente Enterprises
www.silkflowersandmore.com
866-588-7455
Browse the enormous selection of totally natural-looking silk flowers (every species seems to be represented). Even the silk rose petals come in nine different shades.

Delaware River Trading Co.
www.delawarerivertrading.com
800-732-4791
This site specializes in home and garden furnishings. Stock up on silver-plated mint julep cups, which are the perfect vessels for small, classic bouquets.

GM Floral
www.gmfloral.com
213-489-7050
A great resource for fresh flower orders or floral supplies (including the elegant square vases featured in many of the parties in this book).

Lindsay Olives
www.lindsayolives.com
800-252-3557
For a lovely twist on traditional holiday greens, order its elegant, square-shaped fresh olive-branch wreath—all proceeds to go the hunger-relief organization America's Second Harvest.

The Monogram Shop
www.themonogramshop.com

631-329-3379
Have your name, initials or address printed (with crisp, preppy flair) on colorful matchbooks, cocktail napkins and hand towels.

Pearl River Mart
www.pearlriver.com
800-989-2446
The Chinese-American department store also stocks more than 50 paper lantern styles in a variety of colors, shapes and patterns, as well as strings of mini lanterns with tiny lighbulbs inside.

Ribbonshop.com
www.ribbonshop.com
877-742-5142
Miles of high-quality ribbons (both plain and wire-edge) in every color and pattern (stripes, checks, polka dots) imaginable.

Smith & Hawken
www.smithandhawken.com
800-776-3336
Make your garden or backyard twinkle for an outdoor party with lanterns, mini torches and whimsical light strings from this site.

theme elements

Abracadabra
www.abracadabrasuperstore.com
212-627-7523
Halloween has never been easier: This store sells rubber spiders, snakes and bugs and a huge selection of costumes.

Big Island Candies
www.bigislandcandies.com
800-935-5510
Hawaiian specialties such as crisp, buttery macadamia shortbread cookies, chocolate-covered macadamia nuts and bite-size Kona coffee cookies.

Broadway Panhandler
www.broadwaypanhandler.com
866-266-5927
A great source for all of your kitchen needs, including the playing-card cookie cutters featured in the Game Night party.

FPC
www.fpcfilm.com
800-814-1333
Order the five and one-quarter-inch diameter shiny film cannisters ($2 each) to make extra special Oscar Party invitations.

Game Daze
www.gamedaze.com
480-317-9181
Order extra dice, dominos and checkers pieces to use as decorations on game night.

Hilo Hattie
www.hilohattie.com
Hawaiian-theme party goods: fresh and silk flower leis, pineapple-shaped platters, tropical-print gift bags.

Kaskey Kids
www.kaskeykids.com
866-527-5437
Arrange the miniature plastic football players and goalposts in a patch of wheatgrass for a Super Bowl party centerpiece.

La Mariposa
www.lamariposaimports.com
877-826-0069
Celebrate Cinco de Mayo with colorful Mexican accents: pretty piñatas, sombreros and fluffy paper flowers.

Latin Works Co.
www.latinworksco.com
A wonderful selection of Mexican folk art objects: piñatas, maracas, mini mariachi hats, handpainted tequila shot glasses and *cascarones* (colorful, confetti-filled eggshells).

Seashell City
www.seashellcity.com
888-743-5524
Shop here for an instant ocean theme. The site offers decorative coral pieces, sand dollars, starfish and seashells in all sizes and varieties.

Wincraft Sports
800-533-8006
Decorate your home for a Super Bowl bash with miniature football pennants from this sports emporium.

Zunimaya
www.zunimaya.com
800-769-9638
Pretty, affordable pareos for a tropical party: Drape them over tables and bars or ask guests to put them on when they walk in the door.

general party supplies

These comprehensive party sites are the places to go for cocktail umbrellas, Mardi Gras beads, smoke and bubble machines, mirrored disco balls, faux gold trophies, costumes and anything else you can dream up.

Oriental Trading Co.
www.orientaltrading.com
800-228-2269

Plum Party
www.plumparty.com
800-227-0314

U.S. Toy
www.ustoy.com
800-832-0572

About the Party Planners

Colin Cowie, Colin Cowie Lifestyle
New Year's Eve Supper, Backyard Luau
Colin Cowie Lifestyle is an event-planning, interior-design, and lifestyle-consulting company with offices in New York and Los Angeles. Cowie is the author of five books on style and entertaining and appears regularly on the CBS *Early Show* and on *The Oprah Winfrey Show* as a lifestyle correspondent covering food, fashion, travel, entertaining and interior design. His celebrity clientele includes Oprah Winfrey, Jerry Seinfeld, Tom Cruise, Nicole Kidman, Jennifer Aniston, Bruce Willis, Demi Moore, Jenny McCarthy and Sela Ward, among others.

Ann David and Nicky Reinhard, David Reinhard Events
Baby Shower
Ann David and Nicky Reinhard founded David Reinhard Events in the fall of 2000, and its planning services range from creating an intimate dinner party for 15 to a wedding party for 400. Although based in New York City, David Reinhard has planned events in California, Georgia, Florida and Italy. Its services and weddings have been featured in *In Style Weddings, New York Weddings, Redbook, W, Vogue* and *Vanity Fair,* among others.

Jo Gartin, Love Luck and Angels
Holiday Cocktail Party
Jo Gartin offers her clients an à la carte menu when planning an event. Her custom invitations and exquisite floral designs have drawn a client list that includes Courteney Cox, Brooke Shields, Molly Shannon and Taye Diggs. Gartin's floral designs have graced the covers of *In Style Weddings* issues and they frequently appear inside *In Style* magazine as well. *Vogue* featured Gartin in its "Working Women" article in September 2003 and listed her as its No. 1 recommended wedding coordinator in the February 2004 issue. Her first book for brides will be released in 2006.

Nigella Lawson
Mediterranean Dinner, Tuscan Dinner
Nigella Lawson is the British bestselling author of *Forever Summer, Nigella Bites, How to Be a Domestic Goddess* and *How to Eat.* She contributes a bi-monthly food column for *The New York Times* section "Dining In, Dining Out" and has written for a variety of magazines and newspapers, including the *Sunday Times* and *Evening Standard* in England, and in the U.S. for *Gourmet* and *Bon Appétit. Nigella Bites* received the WH Smith Book Awards 2002 lifestyle book of the year, with the cooking series based on the book winning the Gold Ladle for best television food show from the World Food Media Awards in 2001.

Paula LeDuc, Paula LeDuc Fine Catering
Early Autumn Supper
Paula LeDuc Fine Catering, established in 1980, has become the industry leader in Northern California providing catering and event-planning services to high-end corporate, social and private clients, including Bill Clinton, Al Gore, President George W. Bush and Prince Phillip. Her company has been featured in *In Style, Martha Stewart Living, Town and Country Weddings, Bon Appétit, Fine Cooking* and *House Beautiful* and has partnered with celebrity chefs, including Alice Waters, Daniel Boulud, Emeril Lagasse and Thomas Keller.

Robyn Leuthe and Tom Byrne
Oscar Party
In 1988, after working at Glorious Food in New York, Tom Byrne started La Cuisine Catering Co. in Los Angeles. Soon after, Byrne was joined by Robyn Leuthe, who had previously coordinated events for Party Planners West. La Cuisine quickly established itself as one of the premier caterers in the Los Angeles area, serving such notables as Barry Diller, Elizabeth Taylor, Nancy and Ronald Reagan, and Courtney Cox Arquette, as well as large premiére parties, fashion-related events and Academy Awards celebrations.

Christopher Robbins, Robbins Wolfe Eventeurs
Backyard Barbecue
Christopher Robbins is the vice president of Robbins Wolfe Eventeurs, a leading upscale catering and event-planning firm located in New York City, and on Long Island in the Hamptons and Locust Valley. The company boasts a significant, high-profile celebrity, social and corporate client list, including Jennifer Lopez and Marc Anthony, Jessica and Jerry Seinfeld, Steven Spielberg's SHOAH Foundation, and Ellen Barkin and Ronald Perelman. Robbins has appeared on television on Bravo's "Queer Eye for the Straight Guy," the Discovery Channel's "Party Planner with David Tutera," and the Food Network's "Behind the Bash."

Alyse Sobel and Marianne Weiman-Nelson, Special Occasions
Super Bowl Party (Marianne Weiman-Nelson) and Game Night (Alyse Sobel and Marianne Weiman-Nelson)
Special Occasions is a worldwide event-production company that focuses on and specializes in entertainment, private, destination, corporate and social events along with weddings. The company has produced events for Lisa Rinna and Harry Hamlin, Janet Jackson, Teri Hatcher, Jennie Garth, Rick Fox, LeAnn Rimes, and Stacey and Henry Winkler.

Alexis Ufland, SPARTY!
Afternoon Spa Party
Ufland is the founder and owner of Lexi Design, the spa consultancy firm that has developed premier day spas, resort spas and medical spas across Europe, Asia, South America and the United States. The brains behind some of New York's top spas, Alexis developed spas for renowned dermatologist Laurie Polis's Mezzanine Spa and for Deepak Chopra's the Chopra Center: a Spa, Yoga and Wellness Center located at Vikram Chatwal's Dream Hotel.

Diann Valentine, D.R. Valentine & Associates
Birthday Dinner Party
Diann Valentine is the owner of D.R. Valentine & Associates, a Pasadena, California–based wedding, events and interior design firm. Celebrity clients include Toni Braxton, Lela Rochon, Mike Tyson and Shawn Stockman, neo-soul singer Kelis, as well as corporate clients such as Nike, Fedex and Schieffelin & Somerset. Diann's events have received exposure in national print and broadcast media. Her book *Weddings Valentine Style* will be released in 2006.

Bronson van Wyck
Halloween Cocktail Buffet
Raised on a family farm in Arkansas, 29-year-old event designer Bronson van Wyck went on to Yale and then the set design department of Star Trek. He and his mother, Mary Lynn, and sister, Mimi, have decorated events for President and Mrs. George W. Bush, Sean Combs, Madonna and Bill and Hillary Clintons.

Mindy Weiss, Mindy Weiss Party Consultants
Spring Dinner
Based in Beverly Hills, Mindy Weiss is the owner and principle planner/designer of Mindy Weiss Party Consultants. The company provides professional event-planning services for weddings, parties, corporate events and bar/bat mitzvahs and offers a line of lifestyle products for brides and grooms, wedding guests, wedding parties and newlywed couples. She has created weddings and events for Trista and Ryan of "The Bachelorette"; Christian Slater; Shaquille O'Neal; Jessica Simpson and Nick Lachey; Brooke Shields; Gwen Stefani and Gavin Rossdale; Adam Sandler; Kimberly Williams and Brad Paisley; and Kate Beckinsale. She has been featured on a variety of television shows, including "Entertainment Tonight," various morning shows, and a special segment on "The Learning Channel."

Acknowledgments

Special thanks to all the party planners who have generously contributed to this book.

Thanks also to Bozena Bannett, Bronwyn Barnes, Alexandra Bliss, Alessandra Bocco, Glenn Buonocore, David Brown, Bernadette Corbie, Heidi Ernst, Maureen Griffin, Robert Marasco, Kathryn McCarver, Brooke McGuire, Jonathan Polsky, Holly Rothman, Ilene Schreider, Lindsey Stanberry, Shoshana Thaler, Adriana Tierno and Megan Worman.

Photo credits

Page 10: Alex Berliner
Page 13: Peter Wintersteller
Page 14: Ray Kachatorian
Page 24: Ray Kachatorian
Page 30: Todd Plitt
Page 36: Paul Costello
Page 40: Eric Boman/H&K/CPi
Page 44: Lisa Romerein
Pages 46–52: Lisa Hubbard
Pages 54–61: Quentin Bacon
Pages 62–68: Maura McEvoy
Page 70: Maura McEvoy
Pages 72–78: Christopher Hirsheimer
Pages 80–86: William Meppem

Pages 88–94: Quentin Bacon
Pages 96–102: Maura McEvoy
Page 104: © Corbis Outline
Pages 106–112: Lisa Hubbard
Pages 122–128: Lisa Hubbard
Pages 130–136: Maura McEvoy
Pages 138–144: Ann Stratton
Pages 146–152: Maura McEvoy
Page 154: Catherine Ledner
Pages 156–162: Ellen Silverman
Pages 164–170: Lisa Hubbard
Pages 173–178: Ann Stratton

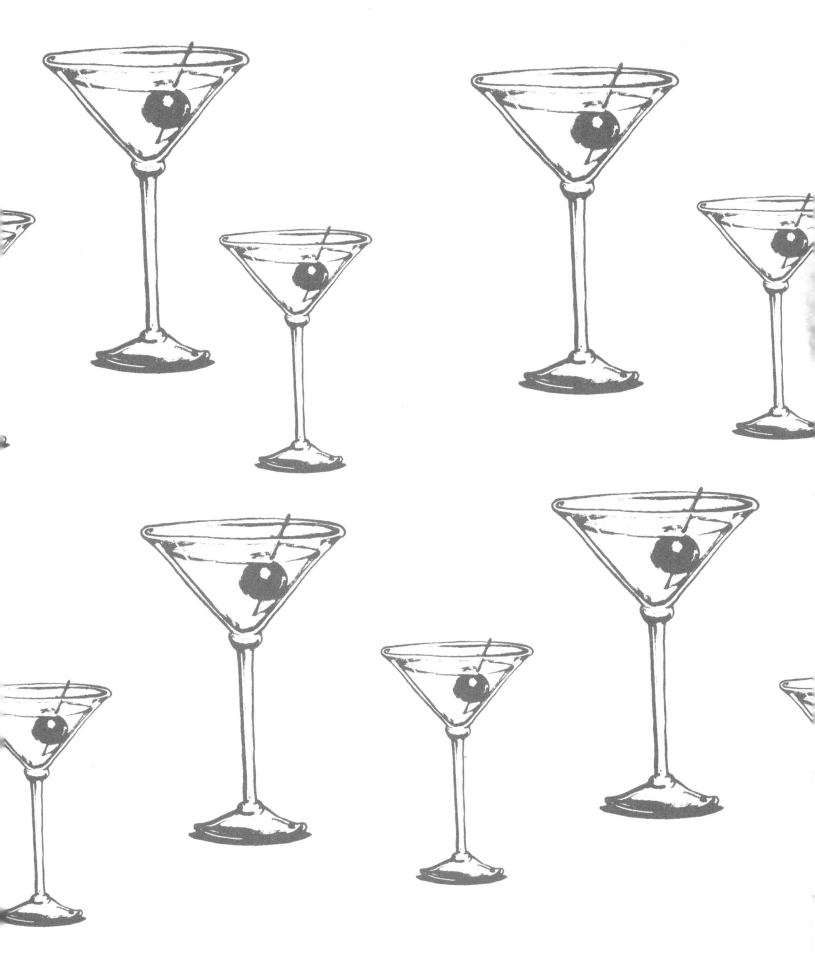